Praise for

THE DEVIANT'S ADVANTAGE

"*The Deviant's Advantage* is a seminal work. As time goes by, I believe it will come to be viewed on a par with McLuhan."
—LEE MORIN, M.D., PH.D., 412th human in space

"Ryan and Watts have crafted a fascinating read. They clearly understand the dynamics of change in the world of business today and challenge the reader to think about how to create, anticipate, or respond to change effectively. Those deviants!"
—DAN C. SWANDER, president and COO,
International Multifoods Corporation (Multifoods)

"Once again Ryan Mathews and Watts Wacker have given us an enlightened vision which allows us to see future marketing opportunities through a tuned-in view of the present. Mathews and Wacker ask us to do more than just embrace change—we must embrace the 'devox' to successfully meet the two biggest challenges faced by marketers today—innovation and relevance. *The Deviant's Advantage* offers provocative insights for business leaders determined to seize competitive advantage and stay ahead of the pace of change. It's a great read."
—CAROLYN CATER, president, Grey Global Group
Europe, Middle East, and Africa

"Where do breakthrough ideas come from? Where do you look to find the next great business concept, the next box-office bonanza, the next Broadway smash, the next social revolution? As this fun, insightful, and brilliant book makes clear, if you want to be ahead of the curve of change, you've got to spend time on the fringes of society. The spot-on lesson: Don't be afraid of deviants—embrace them! They are creating the future before it arrives for the rest of us."
—ALAN M. WEBBER, founding editor, *Fast Company*

"Leave it to Wacker and Mathews to bring much-deserved honor to deviant thinking and to insert it into the business world. They not only question several fundamental business norms but they pretty much condemn them to that vast purgatory that exists in between breakaway success and spectacular failure—which is precisely where conservative, non-deviant businesses usually end up."

—SCOTT BEDBURY, author of *A Brand New World: Eight Principles for Achieving Brand Leadership in the 21st Century* and CEO, Brandstream

"In *The Deviant's Advantage,* Watts Wacker and Ryan Mathews offer insights and ideas that are truly 'out of the box.' But make no mistake—their unorthodox theories connecting the concept of deviance with innovation and creativity ring true for many businesses."

—O. BURTCH DRAKE, president-CEO, American Association of Advertising Agencies

"*The Deviant's Advantage* is the best book ever written about how companies can benefit from strange new ideas and the oddballs and misfits who dream them up. Mathews and Wacker write so well that, although I should have been doing other things, I kept turning the pages. They provide compelling stories and arguments about how and why companies can benefit from fringe ideas and people, but at the same time, warn both companies and people of the hazards of embracing deviance."

—ROBERT I. SUTTON, professor, Stanford University, codirector of the Center for Work, Technology and Organization, and author of *Weird Ideas That Work*

"Ryan Mathews and Watts Wacker will challenge both the right and left sides of your brain. The opportunity to harness genius is all around you but requires dramatic stretching of peripheral vision to bring the fringe into focus. If you haven't yet made the observation that everything, including time itself, is accelerating, you most certainly will after reading *The Deviant's Advantage.* But you'll also be challenged to examine new dimensions of your potential for personal development by coming to understand that business doesn't exist in isolation. It's part of our overall culture. A new breed of leaders is embracing the apparent contradictions of our society and harnessing what seem like emerging aberrant concepts to shape the future."

—RANDY J. ROSE, president, Energizer Battery, Inc.

ALSO BY RYAN MATHEWS

The Myth of Excellence

ALSO BY WATTS WACKER

The Visionary's Handbook

The 500-Year Delta

THE
DEVIANT'S
ADVANTAGE

How Fringe Ideas Create Mass Markets

RYAN MATHEWS and
WATTS WACKER

CROWN
BUSINESS
NEW YORK

Published by Crown Business, New York, New York.
Member of the Crown Publishing Group, a division of Random House, Inc.
www.randomhouse.com

CROWN BUSINESS is a trademark and the Rising Sun colophon is a registered trademark of Random House, Inc.

Printed in the United States of America

Design by Helene Berinsky

Library of Congress Cataloging-in-Publication Data

Mathews, Ryan.
The deviant's advantage : how fringe ideas create mass markets / Ryan Mathews and Watts Wacker.—1st ed.
Includes bibliographical references.
1. New products—Marketing. 2. Business forecasting. 3. Originality—Economic aspects. 4. Marketing. 5. Technological innovations—Economic aspects.
I. Wacker, Watts. II. Title.
HF5415.I536 2002
658—dc21   2002004806

ISBN 0-609-60958-0

10 9 8 7 6 5 4 3 2 1

First Edition

To Sierra, who reminds me every day that life is good,
and Priscilla, who proves she is right.

—Ryan Mathews

To my favorite kind of deviant:
the Fanatic and the most deviant person I've ever met,
my late mother, Jane Clarke Sewell.

—Watts Wacker

ACKNOWLEDGMENTS

Ryan and Watts would both like to thank the deviant publishing team that helped make this book possible. We'd like to begin with John Mahaney, the godfather of Crown Business, who took a risk on an unusual idea and nursed it lovingly until it was a real book. We'd also like to thank John's right-hand deviant, Shana Wingert; Will Weisser; and the rest of the Crown Business team. A special word of thanks to Ruth Mills, who first believed, and to Rafe Sagalyn of The Sagalyn Agency for once again making the sale.

A special note of thanks to Priscilla Donegan, who triumphed over jet lag and sleep deprivation just long enough to correct errors of both grammar and judgment. We would also like to thank Steve Barnett and Howard Means, who agreed to review the manuscript before it had been whipped into syntactical submission. A special note of thanks to Alan Webber of *Fast Company* magazine, who defied the fates to further this project.

We'd also like to acknowledge the help and support of the First-Matter team: Mary DeVito, the Queen of Our Universe and perpetual cat herder, who keeps us focused and the business running; Darrell Stewart, who once again delivered research support above and beyond the call of duty; and Michael Strother, who continues to suffer (primarily) in silence at our collective ineptitude with technology.

On a personal note, I would like to acknowledge that this book might never have happened without the patience, love, and support of Sierra Maria Mathews. No daughter has ever done a better job of watching over a father. This book literally would not have been possible without her understanding and grace. An encore thanks to Priscilla Donegan for making this, and everything else positive, possible. And, while this book is dedicated to the women in my life, I would be remiss if I didn't thank the three young men who make it so interesting, beginning with my son, Gabriel, who continues to delight me as he fashions his vision of the world, and Adam and Zack Fischer, who have tolerated my presence better than most people do.

Also a quick acknowledgment to the Motor City posse, who have supported me and my family over the course of this book, beginning with the Oben family—Mary Jo, Stephanie, Marlee, Sarah, and Gabby—for the extraordinary kindness they have selflessly demonstrated to me and most especially to Sierra. Thanks also to the Yung family of Shogun—Gary, Maggie, Barry, Ann, and Diane—for great sushi, great friendship, and shelter against the storm. And continuing thanks to my chosen Motor City family: Rob Abate, who's shared the music since we were twelve; Rick and Sheila Kelpin, who have taught me so much about courage and loyalty; "Maximum Bob" and Rose Leahey, who have proved it's possible to go on no matter what happens; Mike Himes and the gang at Record Time; Simon Bennett and the tribe at Nami and Ronin; Gerry and Kate Dunn for a friendship and love so deep it's passed to another generation; "Mr. Pete" Traskal, Tara Olynyk for the smiles and support; Mark Dikowski of Ariel's Enchanted Garden, Detroit's best florist; and Rick Jackson, still the friendliest soul in the Detroit Airport. And, of course, that special wink and a nod to WTB and PTH because the world needs a little magic more than ever.

Also a note of thanks to the extended family outside Detroit: Fred and Chris Crawford, Mike and Mary Ann Maurer, Mark and Cathy Baum, Patrick and Marilyn Kiernan, Frank and Linda Babel, John and Jean Gray, Joe and Pat Finegan, Steve Barnett and JoAnn Magdoff, Tom and Mary Ann Zatina, and all the rest of you.

A very special acknowledgment goes out to the late Samantha Marie Leahey, whose life ended tragically and senselessly as this book was being written, with the understanding that memories and love never die.

—Ryan Mathews

Beyond those who help me with every project (and who have been publicly acknowledged in each book . . . my family), I'd like to acknowledge my deviant content providers: Anita Hall, Tom Heintz, and Mary Ellen.

—Watts Wacker

CONTENTS

PART THREE
DEVIANCE AND BUSINESS

INTRODUCTION

But then they danced down the street like dingledodies, and I
shambled after as I've been doing all my life after people who interest
me, because the only people for me are the mad ones, the ones who
are mad to live, mad to talk, mad to be saved, desirous of everything
at the same time, the ones who never yawn or say a commonplace
thing, but burn, burn, burn like fabulous yellow Roman candles
exploding like spiders across the stars and in the middle you see the
blue centerlight pop and everybody goes "Awww!"

—JACK KEROUAC

The barbarians aren't just at the gate; they've kicked it in. In fact,
they're running the castle. What happened? Our simple answer is that
deviance happened, and our simple bet is that the barbarians haven't
even begun to party.

Beneath their reassuring veneers of solidity and strength, the bedrocks
of both social convention and established business practice float uneasily
on a churning ocean of deviance. The tides of that deviant ocean are an
uncompromising force, battering away at the line that separates all we've
come to know from that we've yet, or dare not, to imagine. They relent-
lessly pound the shores of our conventional wisdom; distort all we've
been taught; assault our shared sense of order; and challenge and undermine the established landscape of our collective understanding.

Don't let the words *deviant* and *deviance* scare you. They're being
used in their purest definition—something or someone operating in a

defined measure away from the norm. This book champions the deviant impulse but is not championing all forms of deviant behavior. By definition, everything that is different is deviant. Of course, there is positive and negative deviance—the former a force for transformation, the latter a source of unspeakable evil. We're concerned here with positive deviance, the kind of transformational change that takes fringe ideas and morphs them into mass markets.

Deviance transforms traditional markets and washes them away. Apply any measurement you want and you'll see that the tides of deviance are clearly gaining in their attack against the beaches of social convention. As Jim Morrison of the Doors sang in what seems cultural eons ago, "Strange days have found us/Strange days have tracked us down."

By the same token, the well of deviance also irrigates the imagination; offers an inexhaustible font of new ideas, products, and services; and, in the end, is the source of all innovation, new-market creation, and, for business, ultimately represents the basis of all incremental profit. Deviance equals innovation and innovation equals opportunity. Opportunity creates markets that in turn are destroyed by deviance.

Without deviance there would be no art, no scientific breakthroughs, no technological advances, not even any physical evolution. Without deviance, in other words, there would be no biological mutation and therefore no life, at least as we know it. Without deviance there would certainly be no commerce. You wouldn't be in business and, odds are, you wouldn't even be a sentient life-form.

Of course, there would also be no war, no terrorism, no crime, and no hatred. At its base, deviance is nothing more than a measurable distance from the norm. Whether that distance spans good or evil often depends on the judgment of history.

In *The Deviant's Advantage* we'll demonstrate how the intensity of the tidal motion of deviance has increased to the point that the beach of normalcy—and anyone standing on that beach—doesn't have a chance of emerging untouched. Everything is changing, faster than we can imagine and in ways we can't.

We recognize that every author brings his or her own biases to a book, and we are certainly no different. The first assumption has already been stated—that deviation is the ultimate source of growth and innovation. Our next assumption is that changes in society drive changes in business, and that as society becomes more and more deviant, businesses in turn have to become more deviant to prosper, or even survive. We also assume that deviance follows a linear pattern from the time it leaves the fervid mind of its creator until the day it becomes established social practice.

We describe this pattern as the movement from the Fringe, to the Edge, to the Realm of the Cool, to the Next Big Thing, and, finally, to Social Convention. From there we believe deviance can follow several roads leading to stages we call Cliché, Icon, Archetype, and Oblivion. Of course, not every idea that starts on the Fringe ends up as Social Convention, but our premise is that all Social Convention began as Fringe thinking.

We've coined a neologism for *The Deviant's Advantage*—the *devox*—to describe the voice, spirit, or incarnation of deviant ideas, products, and individuals. We use the devox as a metaphor to illustrate the point that things have changed—and continue to change—at such a rate that conventional language is no longer an effective tool for describing what's going on around us.

The products, markets, and ideas emerging in the wake of the devox are sometimes positive and sometimes negative. The popularization of jazz, mainstream acceptance of the value of a holistic approach to medicine, and even personal computing are all examples of positive deviation at work.

We'll use a touch of poetic license here to describe another example of positive deviation—the emergence and evolution of born-again Christianity. Imagine it's summertime in the adolescence of the Psychedelic Era, say 1967. Somewhere a longhaired, bearded, tie-dyed young hippie is adjusting the volume of a Grateful Dead album on the stereo, lighting his favorite all-day candles, breathing in the patchouli-incense-drenched air, and settling down for his hundredth acid trip. We'll call him Joshua. The drugs kick in and his mind seems to take on a life of its own. He hears a voice. He begins to shiver against the warmth of the day. Soon Joshua finds himself in what he believes to be the presence of Jesus. The experience stays with him long after the drugs wear off. He becomes convinced that Christ wants him to renew his mission among the young pleasure seekers who surround him.

Joshua drops out of school and cuts his ties with his family, his lover, and his friends. He quits working to devote more and more time to studying the Bible for clues about what he should do next. He loses his apartment and gives away his car and all his worldly possessions with the exception of one change of clothes and his Bible. He moves to skid row to be closer to the poor. He sleeps in alleys and eats out of Dumpsters. He devotes all his attention to witnessing. He is frequently seen standing in a public park, not so much trying to convert people to his cause, but verbalizing a private conversation with God.

A year passes and slowly Joshua begins to build a small audience, young people whose lives couldn't bridge from what they hoped really would be the Summer of Love to what they clearly recognize as the Winter of Their Discontent. They are tired from too many drugs, too much sex, too much change. They have found all the "new" answers bankrupt and are ready to reexamine older approaches, albeit on their own terms. They listen to Joshua and become convinced that drug-damaged as he appears, he may have stumbled onto the truth. They return to their college dorm and begin spending their evenings studying the Bible together. At first they invite Joshua to join them, but they soon find his presence and his nonstop bantering exhausting. He drifts back to skid row, but his seed has been sown.

Slowly, the Bible-study groups begin to build momentum. The small circle keeps expanding until eventually it needs to break into first two, then three, then four and more groups. As the world plunges deeper and deeper into civil unrest and protest, as Vietnam drags out in horrific detail, and as more and more young people have negative personal experiences tied to sex, drugs, and a philosophy of "if it feels good, do it," Joshua's simple message of faith, made somewhat more acceptable by Bible-study groups, becomes more and more attractive to more and more people. Soon the new converts opt to take their message across the country, one campus at a time. They join groups like the Campus Crusade for Christ and others, some well established, some of which emerge from the ashes of the failed promises of the sixties. The media of the day has a name for these young people: Jesus freaks.

The Jesus freaks attract more and more media attention. They are now a major force among young people. Politicians, especially Republican politicians, begin to see these young people as potential allies. Their values perfectly dovetail with classic Republican rhetoric. The young people aren't stupid. They are after all representatives of the best-educated, most-aware, and most-indulged generation America has ever produced. They know the value of power when they see it. And so they organize themselves into not-for-profit organizations and institutes. They learn how to modify their witnessing and evangelism and therefore how to be even more acceptable to the Republican establishment. They are referred to less often as Jesus freaks and more often as the Moral Majority or the extreme right wing of the Republican party. Joshua's vision is just about ready for prime time.

Beginning in the late 1970s and through today it becomes impossible for the Republican presidential candidate to stand for election on a platform that does not incorporate planks supplied directly by Joshua's intellectual descendants. So mainstream have those ideas become that in many cases even the Democrats are forced to include them in their platforms.

In this example Joshua was a creature of the Fringe. The initial Bible-study groups represent the Edge. The Jesus freaks existed in the Realm of the Cool, and the Moral Majority occupied space in the Next Big Thing. Finally, the inclusion of Christian principles into political campaigning shows that this particular version of the devox has arrived at the heart of Social Convention. Now let's look at another example of the devox in action that resulted in a Social Convention that is either positive or negative, depending on your point of view. It starts with the stuff of legend.

Here's how the legend has it: It's 1945. World War II is beginning its slow, measured march into memory. About seven miles from the center of downtown Las Vegas, on a piece of sun-baked ground that hadn't seen water since the Ice Age, a handsome, murderous sociopath named Benny "Bugsy" Siegel kicks the dirt in a symbolic groundbreaking for a vision he has—a luxury gambling oasis emerging out of the desert.

If Siegel's eyes had been focused on reality instead of his dream, he would have seen Las Vegas for what it was—little more than a couple of low-rent dude ranches and "resorts." In 1945 Vegas was a crossroads in the middle of a desert, so hot in the summer that the tires often melted on the few cars trying to make the two-hour drive to Los Angeles. Gambling was legal there, but the only ones who cared were the locals—servicemen from nearby gunnery and pilot schools and a cast of characters coughed up from the last act of the Wild West.

Bugsy picked an interesting time to decide to open a sinner's paradise. America was tired of war and the parents of the baby boomers were trying to restore a sense of normalcy to their lives. This was, after all, "the greatest generation"—straight arrows, dedicated to family, hard work, and fundamental American values that didn't happen to include roulette wheels, slot machines, public drunkenness, prostitution, and an insatiable appetite for all forms of hedonistic pursuits.

Siegel was a deviant's deviant. A gangster almost from birth, the Brooklyn-born Benjamin Siegelbaum had been an extortionist as a child and had grown into a full-service criminal—killer, white slaver, gambler, and labor racketeer. Siegel was so deviant, in fact, that his fellow deviants—men like Lucky Luciano, Meyer Lansky, Frank Costello, and Vito Genovese—had passed him over for head of Murder, Inc., because they thought he was, if you can believe it, too dangerous for the job. His personal deviance may have put him in better touch with the rumblings of the devox.

The country was full of men—and women—who had come of age in war, people who had had a steady diet of peak experience and adrenaline rushes for four years. Sure, they were working hard to pay off that suburban bungalow, but every once in a while they had that itch for action—and scratching that itch was one of Bugsy's core competencies. Vegas was an escapist sinner's "field of dreams." If he built it, he knew they would come. The deviant was building a mousetrap and baiting it with the repressed appetite for deviance that he intuitively knew existed. Like any good predator, he knew where the next kill was coming from even if nobody else could see it.

So, the legend has it, Siegel took a pile of organized crime money and built his vision: the Flamingo Hotel, which opened on December 26, 1946. Plagued by dozens of problems, all ultimately tied to Siegel, the Flamingo closed on February 1, 1947, reopening exactly a month later. The complex—which Siegel had promised would cost the mob $1 million and produce instant profits—had actually cost closer to $6 million and was still operating in the red on June 20, 1947, when a person or persons still unknown put a pair of bullets in Siegel's skull. The deviant was dead, but his dream lives on.

The Flamingo lost its direct mob connection in 1967 when Kirk Kerkorian bought it, selling it later to the Hilton Corporation. Throughout the 1960s and 1970s the onetime deviant's dream became a neon-lit and sequined parody of life on the edge—gambling, boozing, and loose morals all served up with cheap buffets and charter room rates on what seemed every year to be an exponentially grander and more garish scale. As Siegel imagined, Vegas became the place where respectable people could get their itch scratched, entertain business associates in ways they'd never dream of at home, and leave with their conventional facades intact. In fact, they probably believed it was good that Las Vegas existed. After all, containing organized sin in Nevada might keep it from spreading to their communities.

But the devox has a way of changing the rules. What was shocking in 1947 was pretty shopworn two decades later. The children of the men who snuck out to Vegas were now doing things in public their parents didn't even think about in private. Sin took on more and more extreme forms, and Vegas began to look tame. A decade later state governments were in the legalized gambling business, and Vegas suddenly found itself competing with respectable society for gaming revenue.

Today, Vegas has transformed itself from a white, male, middle-class version of Fantasy Island into a gigantic family-oriented theme park, albeit one with slots and roulette wheels. It has become a vacation destination for the entire family, not just a place Dad and his business buddies sneak off to so they can be bad boys. In the year 2000, gambling revenues for the state of Nevada totaled $9.6 billion, half coming from the Las Vegas Strip. Poor Bugsy would have loved the action; but with all those kids around, he'd hardly recognize the place.

A little over a year after Bugsy bought his one-way ticket into American folk mythology, the National Wrestling Alliance (the forerunner of World Championship Wrestling) was founded. The NWA began as an umbrella association housing a number of regional promoters. In the 1960s a tighter consolidation strategy was launched by a promoter named Vince McMahon Sr. McMahon called his organization the World Wrestling Federation (WWF).

In McMahon's day the audience for professional wrestling was made up of a motley assortment of hardworking proletarians—from farmers on the great Canadian prairies to first- and second-generation blue-collar industrial workers. Television had extended that reach a bit, causing the sport to morph from its provenance in the arenas of physical culture and brute strength to mini passion plays among characters whose personas were developing in direct proportion to their larger-than-life torsos. By the early 1960s a series of increasingly deviant wrestlers that included Dick the Bruiser, the proto-androgynous Gorgeous George, the enormous Haystack Calhoun, the evil Sheik, and the ever-popular BoBo Brazil battled weekly in an endless tug-of-war between the forces of good and evil and began to build a younger and younger audience.

But it wasn't until McMahon's son, Vince Jr., took over the family business in the 1980s, transforming professional wrestling into sports entertainment, that the former Fringe sport really moved onto center stage. Initially expanding his franchise literally on the backs of telegenic WWF superstars such as Hulk Hogan, Randy Savage, Jake "the Snake" Roberts, and various and sundry members of the Canadian Hart family wrestling dynasty, McMahon turned wrestling into a mainstream entertainment genre. He parlayed cable television, Pay-Per-View, and shrewd licensing agreements into a media empire. Soon the out-of-the-ring drama began to overshadow the activities in the ring, spurring spin-offs, magazines, and more licensing.

All this didn't escape the attention of Ted Turner, who promoted World Championship Wrestling. Wrestlers began defecting to the Turner camp. Eventually even McMahon's main star, Hulk Hogan, left the WWF. In an attempt to shore up ratings and keep headliners, the plots, in and out of the ring, became more and more extreme and the characters more violent, crude, deviant, and bizarre. The former family entertainment venue now regularly features crude language, sexual innuendo, and plots so arcane and twisted they would have put the Borgias to shame.

So what's the market cap of mayhem? Well, wrestlers like Mick Foley have gone on to dominate *The New York Times* bestseller list. Hogan and more recently The Rock have attempted to move from the "squared circle" to the big screen. In 2001 World Wrestling Federation Entertainment, Inc., enjoyed revenues of $456 million, a P/E of 69.6 (against 33.0 for the industry), a market cap of $863 million, and a net worth of more than $2 billion. It doesn't stop there. Wrestling's real deviants have their own group—Extreme Championship Wrestling—which adds gallons of blood to the McMahon formula and boasts its own cast of superstars, including such notables as Balls Mahoney, Big Dick Dudley, Justin Credible, Mikey Whipwreck, and the Blue Meanie.

There are also more conventional examples of how deviance builds markets. Take Richard Branson, the poster boy for the deviant capitalist. Branson has built an empire on breaking rules and thumbing his nose at the social and business establishment. We're not sure how many other self-made billionaires made their money on ganja-smoking Rastafarians and punk rockers; made exotic vacations accessible to pub keepers and taxi drivers; used their money to finance innumerable daring hot-air trips; spit in the face of some of the largest brand builders in the world; and celebrated new business ventures by appearing in drag (actually a bridal dress); but we think it's a pretty short list. Branson has made (and lost) small fortunes doing things his own, highly unorthodox way. Everything about the way he runs his business—from his R&D process (listen when somebody brings you an interesting idea and then put that person in charge of developing it) to his choice of venues in which to compete (like American telephony)—smacks of the unconventional.

But we don't think these things make Branson deviant. The deviant idea that sleeps at the core of the Virgin empire is Branson's notion that people of ordinary means should have access to lifestyles and markets that would normally be closed to them. Consider the fruits of his labor. Branson's Virgin brand began in the 1970s as a small independent record label with acts like the Sex Pistols that sent "respectable folk" running in the opposite direction. Thanks to Branson, Johnny Rotten and Sid Vicious found their way into the homes of the establishment via their children. Today the Virgin Group supervises the activities of more than two hundred entertainment, media, telecommunications, bridal wear, food, and travel companies, with sales in excess of $5 billion. Take a look at the next photo you see of Branson. Odds are, he's smiling in it. The unrepentant deviant is having the last laugh.

If Branson is the poster boy for the deviant capitalist, then our vote for the deviant anticapitalist has to go to Linus Torvalds. Torvalds, as we'll see later, developed a superproduct and then simply gave it away. The product was Linux, and any number of companies have transformed the deviant idea of freeware into significant businesses. Torvalds is a true deviant, driven to succeed like a Bill Gates but with the ethical standards of a Robin Hood.

Torvalds developed Linux while living at home with Mom and has refused to take a penny directly from his invention. So how do you support yourself when you've deliberately refused billions of dollars? Well, like most working stiffs, Torvalds has a job and draws a paycheck. If Torvalds's model of personal finance is still out there on the Fringe, Linux itself has moved front and center.

Red Hat, for example, which sells software on which Linux runs, went public in 1999 with a capitalization of $6.5 billion and in 2000 enjoyed net sales of $103.4 million. Silicon Valley history is replete with stories of dropouts, misfits, and dreamers who parlayed their deviant visions into successful businesses. Torvalds, however, is a deviant's deviant who made a conscious decision to stay true to the Fringe visions of freeware even if it cost him billions. And, like Branson, he seems to smile a good deal.

The devox destroys, or abolishes, one context and then creates another that it later destroys. What we're observing today is a marked acceleration in the speed of this pattern and an unprecedented intensification in the degree of change. None of us are fully ready for what's happening around us, let alone what's lurking ahead in the shadows of the future. There's no turning back and there's no escape.

Historically, it's been the job of society in general, and business in particular, to either tame the deviant and harvest the fruits of his or her idiosyncratic labors or—better still—eliminate the deviant and co-opt his or her vision into a commercial offering. In *The Deviant's Advantage* we'll show that the genie of devox is out of the bottle and why, now that it's liberated, it will persistently and successfully resist recapture. We provide a blueprint for identifying the essence of deviance, whether it's manifest in an individual, an idea, a product, a service, or an offering that blends all of these elements, and using that essence (which we call the devox, or voice of deviance) to effect positive change in your company and even in your life.

To understand deviance you have to embrace it on its own terms. As a result, throughout this book we'll provide peeks behind the curtains of the fragile patina of order that separates the world we like to believe we live in from the world we actually inhabit. We'll draw on ideas and people haunting the fringes of sex and science and the edges of art and language. We'll visit the world of the cool hunters and the self-proclaimed high priests of hip. And we'll look inside business—from macro looks at the environment down to microanalyses of human resources and leadership practices.

We want you to begin thinking in a completely different way. The world you knew yesterday is gone. The world you will see tomorrow will differ in exciting and sometimes disturbing and even alarming ways from the one you woke up to today. And, as we'll show you, everything about this new world—its art, science, communication protocols, and faith system—is evolving at exponential rates. Some of the examples are meant to be provocative; some may even be shocking. But all of them illustrate the point that like Las Vegas and evangelical Christianity, what's out there on the Fringe today may, unlikely as it seems, be mainstream tomorrow.

Remember that everything you read about in this book doesn't exist on the Fringe or even the Edge; it's either arrived dead center or it's on its way. The real trick is to learn how to start managing the Edge, not the center. The real deal is out there somewhere—raw, messy, and untamed. By the time the devox reaches the center it's almost always a mere shadow of its deviant self, stripped of its power, its authenticity, and its impact. Managing the Edge requires a constant exposure to ideas and people that are foreign, uncomfortable, and, more often than not, downright hostile and threatening.

Markets of increasing size and profitability arise at every step of this journey; authenticity diminishes with every step toward broad-line Social Convention and may increase with every step past it. We also believe most trend watchers have it wrong, that they wait until the devox has been sanitized and diminished before they even become aware of its existence. Finally, we believe that it's possible to take what we say in this book and translate it into specific actions and a specific mind-set that can move your business forward.

A quick note on organization: We've divided this book into three parts, each containing several chapters. Part One (Chapters 1 through 4) offers a process map, describes the stages we've touched on here in much greater depth, and shows how this pattern applies to business. Part Two (Chapters 5 through 9) addresses our hypothesis on the relationship between social change and business change. Our intent in this section is twofold. First, we want to examine how the devox manifests itself in a variety of areas from sex to government to demonstrate how different the context of these activities is becoming. Next, we want to explore what this change of context means for business. Again, our hypothesis is that changes in business follow changes in society, making an understanding of social change a prerequisite to understanding what lies ahead for commerce.

In Part Three (Chapters 10 through 17) we'll look at what all this means for business and how you can capture some positive deviance in your organization and your career. This section also looks at the deviant's toolbox and how to use these tools in whatever future you find yourself. It is our observation that successful businesses share an important core competency. They are superb cultural stalking-horses, routinely popping out from behind the blind of existing business practice to bag opportunities created by social change. Part Two maps some of the social and cultural changes deviance is creating. The traditional business book reader may want to move directly from Part One, which outlines the evolution of deviance, to Part Three, which tracks its immediate and tangible impact on business. If that's the approach you choose, we can only hope you then go back and read Part Two, which we believe delivers the cultural fuel needed to power the engine of business change.

All we ask of you is an open mind. Beyond all the wildness and weirdness are multimillion- and even multibillion-dollar business opportunities. If you're not interested in looking at them, don't worry. We're sure at least one of your potential competitors is.

PART ONE

DEVIANT EVOLUTION

Our first four chapters map the progress of the devox from the Fringe to Social Convention and beyond. Think of these chapters as a template that can be applied to any and all innovation.

The underlying assumptions behind our model are outlined in Chapter 1. They include the belief that innovation is a cyclical activity—that change is the only certainty and that the path of change is predictable and exploitable. We also believe that the distance from what we call the Fringe, the *prima materia* of deviance, to the heart of social acceptance has compressed at the same time as the speed by which we cover that distance has increased. Further, we assume that while Social Convention used to retain the right to marginalize ideas, trends, products, and people, increasingly what's going on at the Fringe of society defines what will happen at the center of society.

Chapter 2 traces the specific steps of this process from Fringe, to Edge, to the Realm of the Cool, to the Next Big Thing, and finally to Social Convention. We'll examine each of these stages in depth. It's important to remember that as the devox moves from Fringe to Social Convention it builds markets in its wake. The closer it moves to the center, the larger the market potential becomes. Again, keep in mind that we are not saying every deviant idea follows this progression but rather that everything we see around us, everything we buy and sell, did.

Chapter 3 follows the devox as it leaves Social Convention in a nonlinear progression to stages we call Cliché, Icon, Archetype, and Oblivion. In the same way that the devox makes markets on its way to Social Convention, it creates markets after it has fallen out of favor. As we'll see, sometimes the devox's real market potential isn't realized until it has moved away from mass adoption.

Finally, in Chapter 4 we'll introduce a concept called the Abolition of Context. Context is an important part of framing market offerings or gaining personal bearings. We believe that the accelerating pace of the devox's progress has essentially abolished traditional context, creating and re-creating contexts that could be exploited if they could only be understood. Businesses would be better served understanding that their customers are essentially living through a series of serial realities and adjust their offerings accordingly. And so, without further introduction, let's meet the devox.

1

Greetings, Fellow Deviants

Mad has become mainstream. Either that or society has sunk to our level.

—JOHN FICARRA, coeditor, *Mad* magazine

*M*ad isn't the only deviant to find its way to the center of Social Convention. Turn on your television and you can witness corporate America's commercial embrace of the dark side in living color and Dolby surround sound. A clip from *Easy Rider*—the 1960s paean to outlaw biking, the counterculture, casual sex, and selling cocaine—is being used to hawk Diners Club and Diet Pepsi. "I Put a Spell on You," a 1954 song by Screamin' Jay Hawkins—the singer once rumored to be a cannibal who, wearing a bone through his nose to complement the ones in his necklace, began his act by rising out of a coffin—is now a jingle pushing Pringles, the most sanitized, processed, standardized incarnation of a potato in history. Push away from the edge a bit further and commercial life starts getting really weird. Former presidential candidate Bob Dole appears in Pepsi ads talking about his "little blue friend," parodying his role as a spokesman for Viagra. If the idea of a senior statesman marketing himself as the poster boy for erectile dysfunction doesn't strike you as quite odd enough, go online (cajohns.com) and you can find CaJohn Fiery Foods of Cleveland, Ohio, a fire extinguisher firm that also markets Vicious Viper, a laboratory-enhanced "hot" sauce that is actually too hot for most people to eat. The weirdness is out there—alive and well—and lots of people are finding ways to make money off it.

Despite the increasingly surly growls of bear marketers, we still live in one of the most economically prosperous periods in history. And the truth—whether we like to admit it or not—is that we owe everything we know, have, and think to the long line of deviants who have come before us.

Most of you reading this book no doubt work for companies founded by a deviant, even (or perhaps especially) if you're self-employed. Some are born to deviance, but everyone can profit from studying how deviance is transforming society and creating market opportunities. Deviance is the backbeat of commerce, the rhythm of innovation that drives wealth creation and defines attitudes and values. Socially, we shun the deviant while remaining addicted to the fruits of their sometimes misguided labors. By their very nature deviants define the essence of social and commercial change, creating new products and markets in their wake. This might explain why today there's such a big market for deviants (we should know, we're part of it), as long as they're not full-time employees.

The Fringe has arrived center stage in everything from extreme sports (skateboarding, snowboarding, mountain biking, and even the ill-fated XFL), to extreme foods (both the title and theme of a popular Food Network cable show), to even, yes, something called extreme pornography (which seems to involve midgets, simultaneous multiple couplings, and the creative use of large lengths of surgical tubing). Extreme media has moved beyond the trailer-trash confines of rampant Jerry Springerism to embrace "reality television" in all its forms, from the media-famous, depixilated naked Richard Hatch of the original *Survivor* series; to the sex, drugs, and rock 'n' roll of MTV's *Road Rules* and *Real World;* to the sleaziness of *Temptation Island,* where people compete for the right to debase themselves and others in front of a national audience; to the star-crossed millionaire marriage of Darva

Conger and Rick Rockwell. If you're not seeing a pattern here just wait for our next military engagement, complete with bombs whose warheads have been modified to hold cameras so that CNN viewers across the planet can be guaranteed the best seat in the house.

It isn't just society or the media that's a bit out of kilter; mainstream business culture has been equally infected by the deviance bug. We've seen what in a kinder, gentler time might have seemed like strange corporate bedfellows—the short union of Coca-Cola and Procter & Gamble, two branding giants unused to seeking alliances; Federal Express and the United States Postal Service, in effect direct competitors; and Boeing and the U.S. Department of Defense, public and private sector—happily rolling together under the covers of capitalism. We've seen McDonald's pick up the mantle of animal rights activists with a vengeance by setting the global standards for laying-hen cages, and Madonna furthering her commercial empire by producing "What It Feels Like for a Girl," a video so violent it was banned as "entertainment" by both MTV and VH1—although both stations and a host of other broadcast media did air it (on a heavily marketed onetime basis) as "news." And let's not forget that once upon a time sports fans saw commercials as necessary evils, while today's post–Super Bowl analysis is more often than not about which ad—not which team—scored a touchdown.

ODD MAN OUT IS IN

Historically, most deviants have been content to express their deviance and go home. They still make their presence known on their own time and in their own voice, but they increasingly refuse to gracefully fade into the cultural wallpaper. We're writing this book at a time when Microsoft, one of America's most prominent corporations, is led by a college dropout (albeit a Harvard dropout); the last U.S. president of the twentieth century opted for hormones over an honored place in history; and music furthering negative racial and sexual stereotyping is all the rage. Business magazines like *Fast Company, Business 2.0,* and even

Entrepreneur fill their pages with stories not of executives who just played the game well, but of those men and women who play the game differently or don't play at all. Instead of breaking the rules they make their own rules. Bill Gates did not see himself as the lucky guy chosen to be IBM's vendor for the operating system when IBM entered the PC market more than twenty years ago. Instead *he* used IBM as the springboard for building his own empire.

Something is happening in the corporate world and in the world at large that is changing both the timetable of change and every aspect of personal, social, and commercial engagement. Businesses are increasingly being challenged to rethink, redefine, and renew—often along fairly radical lines—or fail. This poses a significant challenge to most CEOs, who, having made their bones dealing with established markets, are being asked to produce constantly improving results in markets that simply don't respond to traditional approaches. The rules have changed while the conventional players are still on the field. In a world seemingly turned topsy-turvy, the odd man out is increasingly calling the shots—not a problem if you can translate the language of deviancy, but one hell of a challenge if you're mired in the quicksand of convention. It's painfully clear that there's more than a touch of madness in most successful methods, but it remains to be seen whether there's much method left in our collective madness. We believe not only that there is, but also that individuals and companies can learn to understand, control, and exploit the principles and lessons deviance has to offer.

Before we refine our hypothesis, we want to take some time to clarify language, beginning with the word *deviance,* which we suspect has a fairly negative connotation in your mind. As we use it, deviance is the conscious or unconscious, voluntary or involuntary following of any path other than the norm. In our lexicon deviance can have a positive impact, a negative impact, or an impact so marginal it appears to be nonexistent. Historically, deviance has been defined by "normal" people as the distance between themselves and the people, products, services, and ideas they find all but unthinkable. The intentions and/or consequences of deviance are not always obvious. Often deviance is an end in itself. Finally, and most importantly, deviance is the source of all true innovation, growth, and indeed our collective survival. Deviance is defined by time, place, and circumstances. Physical evolution is perhaps the perfect example of deviance in action. Without mutation—essentially deviance from an established DNA pattern—nature would remain static; mankind would still be scrambling about on all fours; and modern agriculture wouldn't exist.

Throughout history the deviant has been the often-unconscious exponent of deviance—the freak, the lunatic, the prophet without honor, the dreamer, the visionary well ahead of his or her time. They have been easily identified by their stark opposition to the standards of their time or their lack of favor with the establishment. Not all deviants are bad, especially in the clarifying light of history. Christ was a deviant, as were Galileo, Leonardo da Vinci, Pasteur, and Picasso. The first person to challenge the accepted order of things is deviant by definition. Henry Ford, Albert Einstein, John D. Rockefeller, Bill Gates, and Steve Jobs are all examples of successful twentieth- and twenty-first-century deviants.

Today, especially in the corporate environment, one can be deviant by choice. The label—formerly something to be avoided at all costs—is, at least in selected circumstances, something of a badge of honor. What used to be pejorative has, in certain circles, become almost laudatory. The Silicon Valley stereotype—sloppily dressed, sending Frisbees across the room, choosing their own hours, and ingesting questionable botanicals in pursuit of out-of-the-box solutions—provides a classic example. Of course, one could argue that the true deviant in Silicon Valley would report to work at exactly 9:00 A.M. in a three-piece Brooks Brothers suit and wing tips, carry a briefcase instead of a backpack, go out for a three-martini lunch exactly at noon, return at 2:45, and leave work at exactly 5:00 P.M.

Popular culture, especially popular language—historically a vehicle for marginalizing Edge players—has been used as a way to convey sta-

tus and to challenge the center. In the 1960s African American opponents of the war in Vietnam rallied under banners reading "No Viet-
namese ever called me nigger." Today young African Americans and
their white "wigger" counterparts pay up to $20 a CD to hear a range
of rappers and hip-hop artists (black and white) gratuitously use the
"N word" in song after song. Street entrepreneur extraordinaire Ice T
appears on VH1 with his young son on his lap putting forth proud
paternal proclamations like "Yeah, he's a player, a pimp, everything"
and shows up on HBO being honored as Pimp of the Year. Yesterday's
"cool" and "hip" have been usurped by today's "phat" and "sick."

Despite the meteoric rise (and apparently equally meteoric fall) of
computer capitalism, business has been slow to openly acknowledge the
power of dancing with deviance. At FirstMatter our professional business is futuring, but our real product is deviance. Businesses, not-for-
profits, and even government agencies hire us to behave in ways they
assiduously guard against when hiring. The entire coloring-outside-the-
lines industry—futuring, innovation, ideation, long-range strategic
planning, visioning, teaching creativity, or whatever you want to call
it—exists precisely because businesses understand what they lack and
need, and because they understand the danger of letting the deviant
sleep under the tent too long. Throughout this book we'll explore some
of the lessons we've learned along the way, as well as provide examples
of what we would do if—perish the thought—somebody actually asked
us how to reposition Microsoft, Eastman Kodak, or the Ford Motor
Company. But for now we want to share one observation with you:
Despite the fact that global businesses spend aggregate billions of dollars every year seeking out the Edge and Edge thinkers, very little of
what they find or what they are told ever gets accepted, disseminated,
or executed. And that's why Microsoft (when it was still a deviant company) beat IBM at its own game; why Xerox isn't the leader in global
computation; why the Swiss lost a huge share of the watch industry to
the Japanese; why Jesse Ventura won the Minnesota gubernatorial race;
why *Harry Potter* became a bestseller list almost all by itself; and why

a one-store Ben Franklin operator named Sam Walton took over global retailing armed only with a used pickup truck and a dog of questionable genetic origin.

Your father's Oldsmobile succumbed to deviant designs from the SUV to the PT Cruiser in the same way that the traditional view of deviance needs to succumb to a more creative interpretation. We believe—and we'll demonstrate—that changing your view of deviance can allow you to grow on a personal level; help build the success of both brands and corporations; significantly enhance competitive ability; allow companies to organically renew rather than disruptively reengineer; and, finally, provide a blueprint for internal reorganization that yields a host of benefits, from maximizing intellectual property to true knowledge management.

A NEW MODEL FOR EFFECTIVE COMPETITION

In a global economy the table stakes for business are high, whether we're in a bull market or a bear market. The organizations that hire us—and, more significantly, the organizations that would never think of hiring us—are often in desperate need of new analytics to address markets and customers who seemingly are driven by entropic madness. We believe that most, if not all, businesses could benefit from implementing a new framework for viewing and understanding changes in the commercial and socioeconomic processes and that a study of deviance provides a key to this new view and understanding. Along the way we'll also offer some new deviance-inspired language, tools, and metrics to help corporate neodeviants get up to speed; take a look at the development of the Post-Information Age; and give you a new model for effective competition. And we'll take a look at authenticity and how companies can tell faux-Fringe fads from the real-deal exploitable market opportunity. Authenticity is critical because people—deviant or not—hate dealing with phonies. Think of how disappointed those happy hippie Ben & Jerry's lickers must have been when the two biggest proponents of hip capitalism and antiestablishment corporate consciousness sold out to Unilever in April 2000 for $326 million. The paradox of the deviants growing fat at the table of global capitalism wasn't lost on anybody, least of all the company's namesakes. A Ben & Jerry's press release dated April 12, 2000, quoted company cofounders Ben Cohen and Jerry Greenfield saying:

> Neither of us could have anticipated, twenty years ago, that a major multinational would some day sign on, enthusiastically, to pursue and expand the social mission that continues to be an essential part of Ben & Jerry's and a driving force behind our many successes. But today Unilever has done just that. While we and others certainly would have preferred to pursue our mission as an independent enterprise, we hope that, as part of Unilever, Ben & Jerry's will continue to expand its role in society.

That same press release also quoted Richard Goldstein, then president of Unilever Foods North America, as saying, "Unilever believes the super premium segment of the ice cream market will continue to grow and that the Ben & Jerry's brand will lead that growth." Unilever chairmen Anthony Burgmans and Niall Fitzgerald also stressed category expansion over social values. The Unilever press release of April 12, 2000, quoted the chairmen echoing Goldstein's sentiments: "We are delighted to welcome Ben & Jerry's into the Unilever family. It takes us into the super premium category for the first time." Score: corporate capitalists 2, deviants 1.

As Buffalo Springfield put it in "For What It's Worth," "Something's happening here, what it is ain't exactly clear." Or is it? In the course of this book we'll develop ten major themes:

1. Innovations—from products, services, ideas, and even celebrity—move from the Fringe to the center of Social Convention.

2. The process of moving from the Fringe to the center is predictable and measurable.

3. The process of innovation is cyclical. Just as something is settling into comfortable acceptance, another, newer idea, good or bad, has begun its inexorable path toward the mainstream.

4. The distance from the Fringe of society to the center of Social Convention has been compressed at the same time that the pace of making the trip has accelerated.

5. As a result of this simultaneous acceleration and compression, which we've dubbed the "Abolition of Context," Social Convention has eroded to the point that it loses the authority to define reality for the society it theoretically describes.

6. Historically, the Fringe or deviant was largely defined by the mainstream. Today the Fringe is more and more often defining what the mainstream looks like.

7. At each step along the path of deviant acceptance, markets are created and unique and incremental opportunities exist for commercial exploitation. Those opportunities, like the process itself, can be mapped and calculated.

8. Most companies earnestly seeking the Edge of fashion, technology, consumer trends, or anything else for that matter are really picking up on deviance well after it's begun its socialization process.

9. The result of not picking up on the real Fringe is measured not just in missed opportunities but also in costs associated with jumping on the inauthentic or faux Fringe.

10. While most companies stop when an idea, product, service, or offering has finally reached the center (Social Convention), there is a secondary evolutionary cycle that describes what happens to products, services, ideas, brands, companies, and even celebrities as they fall out of favor with mainstream markets. At this stage, most companies are giving away their equity to others

smart enough to exploit the decline—and sometimes redemp-
tion—of deviance.

The devox is always there. All you have to do to move it from
Fringe concept to mass-market Social Convention is recognize it before
anyone else does. You don't have to look too far to see how downright
Fringe ideas quickly create mass markets. Just think about BOTOX,
currently all the rage among the forever-young set. Who do you suppose first got the idea of injecting botulism into rich people's faces so
they would be partially paralyzed and could therefore avoid wrinkling?
If that isn't a deviant idea, we've never heard one.

Now let's consider two standbys of every respectable college student's dorm room—the Frisbee and Post-it notes. Although Yale
attempts to claim credit for inventing the Frisbee, the truth is that the
fabulous flying disk began life as a modest disposable pie plate. The
Frisbie Baking Company of Bridgeport, Connecticut (1871–1950), supplied Yale and a number of other schools with what we would now call
foodservice baked goods. Somewhere along the line some deviant student decided to fling one of the empty plates at another student, uncon-
sciously discovering that the plates (when inverted) were fairly
aerodynamic. Soon lots of Edgy blue-blooded students were hurling
the tins at each other.

The Frisbee might have stayed out there on the Edge of eastern col-
leges if it hadn't been for Walter Frederick Morrison and his partner,
Warren Franscioni, who invented their own Frisbie Pie–like disk out of
plastic in 1948. Morrison split from Franscioni but he stuck with the
idea, which he relabeled the Pluto Platter to cash in on the UFO frenzy
of the early 1950s. Eventually Morrison sold the Pluto Platter to
Wham-O Toys, which launched its own version of the Pluto Platter in
1957. Shortly thereafter Wham-O renamed the Platter the Frisbee and
the rest is, as they say, history. Wham-O and later Mattel brought Frisbees from the Edge of the toy world where Morrison existed right
through to the center of Social Convention. In 1964 the first professional Frisbee was introduced and just four years later the U.S. Navy

spent almost $400,000 studying how Frisbees performed in wind tunnels. Can't get much more mainstream than the Department of Defense.

The Post-it note has a similarly twisted history. Way back in 1968 Dr. Spencer Silver, a 3M scientist, was working on a way to improve acrylate adhesives. Silver was looking for a stronger bonding agent. What he discovered was exactly the opposite—an adhesive that formed itself into tiny spheres with a diameter of a paper fiber. Silver's spheres would not dissolve, could not be melted, and were, individually, very sticky. However, since they were spheres they made only intermittent contact with other spheres and so didn't stick very strongly. Silver, a brilliant chemist, was the classic corporate Fringe character. He spent the next five years holding internal seminars and trying to convince anyone and everyone at the company that his adhesive had great practical application. Like all true Fringe players, Silver got nowhere fast. True, in 1973 he managed to move Post-its from the Fringe to the Edge by exciting Geoff Nicholson, 3M's Commercial Tape Division's new products development manager, about his product. But together they went nowhere with the idea.

Official 3M lore attributes the Post-it note not to Silver or Nicholson, but rather to Art Fry. Fry, a new product development researcher, had attended Silver's seminars. He knew all about the adhesive. He really wasn't as interested in moving the product from the Edge to the Realm of the Cool as he was in not losing his place when he sang in his church choir. Fry applied Silver's adhesive to paper bookmarks, thereby creating the world's first super bookmark. Fry began sticking notes on everything and managed to convince a growing audience inside 3M that Silver's idea had commercial application. Still, it was an uphill fight. The company's engineering and production people complained that the technology posed significant processing measurement and coating difficulties and would create huge waste. Fry overcame their objections, and in the late 1970s 3M dubbed Fry's bookmarks Post-it and began commercial trial. A 1977 test market all but failed and the idea might have died if Nicholson hadn't convinced Joe Ramey, the vice president of the Commercial Tape Division, to make cold calls with him in Richmond, Virginia. It worked, and Post-its moved to the Realm of the Cool. In 1981, one year after they were introduced, Post-its became the Next Big Thing when they were named 3M's outstanding new product. Today Post-its exist at the center of Social Convention. More than four hundred Post-it products are currently sold in more than a hundred countries around the world. They come in twenty-seven sizes, fifty-six shapes, and fifty colors. Fry gets the credit, Silver the satisfaction, and the world has a stationery fixture that started as a mistake and—even with the help of powerful allies—almost stayed (loosely) stuck on the drawing board.

So what can we conclude from our examples? What lessons do these deviant successes hold for us? Why do some incarnations of the devox create fortunes while others flounder? Here's our top-line assessment:

- More often than not the devox needs to escape the ownership (psychological, physical, and/or legal) of its creator. Fringe denizens just aren't, as a rule, the most effective champions.

- That said, the right champion needs to be found. Who's the right champion? Somebody who understands the system better than he or she even understands the product. Fringe minds are in love with what they create; Edge minds begin to see a broader application.

- More often than not the devox has to be significantly modified to move forward. This makes intuitive sense, since the Fringe is just a little too raw for most people's taste. An important part of this modification is the broadening of the application. It's hard to build a mass market around a very narrow concept. The devox needs to be democratized before it can move forward.

- It's also important to remember that the devox rarely breaks through on its first assault on convention. The lesson here is that ideas need to be revisited after they've been rejected, maybe several times.

- Finally, there's a certain element of luck or serendipity to the progress of the devox. Often this takes the form of being seen by the right person at the right time. This is another reason to not wait for the devox to come to you but rather to hunt it down where it first appears.

A quick note on methodology: It just wouldn't seem right to take a textbook approach to writing a book about deviance, especially for a couple of guys who market themselves as provocateurs, iconoclastic thinkers, and individuals generally incapable of coloring inside the lines. So rather than the traditional business book case studies, we'll offer anecdotes about our experiences, hypothetical models for incorporating positive uses of the deviant spirit into your company, direct input from some of today's leading deviants, and observations on great deviants of yesteryear. We're true believers in the power of storytelling, which may have been the original deviant art form, and in the ability of stories to convey images and messages.

Deviance is our business, so we take it pretty seriously. We believe it holds great potential even for those more comfortable a little farther away from the Edge. Insurgency, after all, may be the true cornerstone of profitability. In Chapters 2 and 3 we'll develop our deviancy map and show how ideas move from the Fringe to the center of Social Convention and beyond. But before we get there, there's one more thing: We hope you smile at least a little as you read this book. In a world that takes itself far too seriously, smiling may have become the ultimate act of positive deviation.

2

From Freak to Chic:
The Evolution of the Devox

At one time a young man zigzagging down the street, wriggling his hips and mumbling "bee boh, boh, boh, bee bee boh boh" or grimacing with gritted teeth and narrowed eyes, would have been mocked and so awakened. Today he encounters no opposition or criticism; everybody recognizes and understands the dream in which he is immersed, the dream made respectable by industry.

—ELÉMIRE ZOLLA, *The Eclipse of the Intellectual*

Much as most of us would hate to admit it, the truth is that deviance is the ultimate source of new ideas and products. Put another way, our entire society and, in fact, all societies, are the outgrowth of deviant thinking. The greatest inventions of all time, the most successful corporations in history, the greatest works of art and triumphs of science have their roots in the twisted mind of the deviant, the pariah, the social leper. Without the collective contribution of the deviant it's quite likely we'd all still be eating grubs and pounding each other with large sticks and sharp stones. Deviance is hardwired into our DNA and the master plan of the universe. Evolution itself is a deviant act, life breaking away from the established pattern, a sometimes mad journey into the uncharted waters or the endless emotional and intellectual dark night.

At some point, the fruits of deviance find their way to the public marketplace. There they are polished, trimmed, repositioned, and offered for sale—rarely, if ever, by the persons responsible for their creation. Deviation follows its own unique path of acceptance—linear and predictable at first and then wildly asymmetrical and, while still mappable, fundamentally beyond anticipation. We are not saying that every deviant idea, product, or individual completes this path of acceptance. As we will demonstrate, certain concepts and people are rejected long before they achieve the mainstream. We are saying that all the fruits of deviance—including deviants themselves—that make it to mainstream acceptance follow the same path.

As the devox, the voice of deviant ideas, evolves it gains in marketability and, by extension, commercial value. At each point along its journey from the outer Fringe of society to the heart of Social Convention, the devox becomes exponentially more commercially viable. Its market increases in both absolute numbers and breadth, building and building until it gains maximum attention and acceptance. And then, just as predictably as it arrived, the devox recedes from the collective consciousness, beginning—as we'll describe in the next chapter—an even more interesting journey to either functional cultural immortality or oblivion.

The chart on the next page is a reference tool for the discussion that follows. It traces the path of market formation and commercial potential, as well as demonstrates the shifting response of the society as a whole to the devox. At the Fringe the devox generally goes unnoticed unless something (usually something unpleasant) happens to the originating deviant. No one takes the devox seriously at this point either because it's not communicated or because it isn't communicated clearly enough. But from the Edge forward, the devox builds audience, commercial potential, and market size; it also garners increasingly favorable media coverage and, as a result, social acceptance.

So what does this have to do with business? Why should a high-technology firm, or an automobile manufacturer, or a media conglomerate, or anyone else for that matter care about admittedly deviant ideas? Because, to paraphrase Willy Sutton, the great deviant bank rob-

THE PATH OF THE DEVOX
FROM FRINGE TO SOCIAL CONVENTION

	Fringe	Edge	Realm of the Cool	Next Big Thing	Social Convention
Media Coverage	Mention of deviant's arrests and death	Oddity; freak	What you need to know	Where you need to be	What you need to own/do
Audience Size	One	Limited	Identifiable cohort	Multiple cohorts	Mass market
Who Benefits (Assuming a Benefit Exists)	Original deviant	Original deviant	Media; "cool watchers"; entrepreneurs	Marketers	Mass-market makers
Commercial Potential	0%	1–5%	10–25%	30–40%	70–100%
Role of Initiating Deviant	Originator	Object of veneration	More or less tolerated	Reference point	Needs to change or be eliminated
Authenticity Quotient	100%	85–90%	60–70%	30–40%	10%
Communication Vehicle	Originating deviant	Word of mouth	Events; feature stories	Mainstream news coverage	Advertising and marketing
Relationship to Conventional Society	Antagonistic	Hostile	Toleration; flirtation	Appreciation; cultivation	Acceptance

ber, "that's where the money is." Each year companies spend aggregate billions of dollars, yen, pounds, and now euros chasing the truly unique, the hip, the happening, the cool, and the new. They hire armies of consultants—from patient number-crunching market researchers to trend analysts, so-called cool watchers to, yes, people like us—to help them tune in to the latest trends, fads, and fashions. The results are more or less worth the investment. For every media company savvy enough to jump on hip-hop or club music when they were still primarily heard in clubs in neighborhoods in which most marketing executives and corporate leaders would be afraid to park their cars, there are dozens and dozens of companies that put their money on topless bathing suits,

Nehru jackets, and one-hit-wonder bands. For every rich cyber-pornographer there are a hundred failed dot-coms. And for every tattoo parlor and piercing studio jammed with young suburban kids seeking a more or less permanent reminder of youthful enthusiasm there are dozens of windmills and solar panels, WebTVs, and earth-friendly toilet papers.

Sure, we all know that trends begin "out there" somewhere and slowly work their way toward the mainstream, but why then is it so hard to predict which will hit and which will miss? And, just as importantly, how is a poor marketer or manufacturer supposed to predict the timing and duration of the devox's appearance?

Why are the three original *Star Wars* movies enduring classics whose licensed products appreciate with each listing on eBay while *The Phantom Menace* fell into syndication almost as fast as those Darth Maul licensed goods made their way to discount bins in toy stores and mass merchandisers from coast to coast? Why is a Furby more valuable than beluga caviar one minute and essentially valueless the next? What drives people to hoard wildly price-inflated Beanie Babies today only to liquidate them at substantial losses tomorrow? How does Harley-Davidson move from the transport of choice of outlaw bikers and other renegades to the weekend conveyance of dentists and accountants?

Even mass murderers can move from objects of ridicule and scorn to cleverly twisted commercial tie-ins. How can Charles Manson's image sell T-shirts associated with a (pardon the pun) squeaky-clean mass-market offering like the big-screen version of *Charlie's Angels*? And, speaking of Charlie, how is this guy—a 1960s media freak-show darling—still selling CDs in the third millennium? Don't believe it? Just check out your local music store.

Even apparent failure doesn't stop the devox. As indie singer-songwriter Mojo Nixon points out, "Elvis is everywhere." So how did a failing lounge act end up reincarnated on everything from postage stamps to precision parachuting teams, making more money dead than the King could ransom alive?

Why was "clear" good for spirits like vodka but bad when put into beer form by Zima? How has the tongue-in-cheek, boomer-friendly Fruitopia prospered while Gen-X-pitched O.K. Cola went down in test-market flames? And how did Barbie survive the sexual revolution and the women's movement only to devolve slowly in a pool of apathy at the dawn of the third millennium and then begin to make a comeback?

We think part of the answer lies in understanding how the devox moves from the Fringe to the center of society. The devox begins its journey on the Fringe—the real Fringe—a point located inside the mind of a deviant so removed from society that he or she passes all but unnoticed. At this point, the devox has almost no commercial marketability. One could make a case that French artist-turned-wine-merchant-turned-artist Jean Dubuffet (1901–1985) made a few bucks out of art brut (raw art) that essentially commercialized the work of mental patients. Or that Stephen, the young French shepherd from Cloyes, near Vendôme, who attempted to launch the first Children's Crusade in June 1212, picked up a bit of a following before being sent home by Philip II. But by and large the commercial value of the devox at the point of its inception on the Fringe is zero. Of course, at this stage the devox requires neither an audience nor even marginal acceptance. It burns bright in the heart of its creator but is unknown to the rest of us. The Fringe is the real, real deal, sustaining madness and great vision but few, if any, spectators. It's so authentic, in fact, that it repels us. Ideas and personalities at the Fringe exist outside judgment and just beyond collective awareness. The deviant's reward is the perpetuation of the devox, and that doesn't require a market—at least not yet.

A note here to soothe the silicon sensibilities of digerati and cyberians wherever they may be. Thanks to the Internet, there is a substantive change occurring at the margins of the Fringe. In pre-Net days the devox was generally confined by the deviant's often limited ability to communicate. The devox was heard in public spaces but generally didn't play to any but the most ephemeral audience. But now instead of trying to publish his manifesto in newspapers, the Unabomber could have his own (ironic in his case) website, which, if properly manipulated, could attract an audience far in excess of the aggregate audiences commanded by Fringe thinkers over time. Later we'll examine how the Internet and other factors are speeding the evolution of the devox, but for the moment we turn our attention to the territory we call the Edge.

THE EDGE: TEST-DRIVING THE DEVOX

The so-hip-it-hurts crowd generally first becomes aware of the devox as it exits the Fringe and enters a new stage—the Edge. During its sojourn across the Edge, the devox begins to build the embryonic trappings of a market; that is, supporters in the form of the congenitally early adopters. Often these are individuals only a half step removed from the Fringe themselves. The Edge is also the gathering spot for the trend spotters or cool watchers, many paid big bucks for heading the devox off at the pass. This is where the imaginers find wonder and ideationists of all descriptions earn their stripes. Our work has been described as "edgy" by individuals whose biggest personal risk is trying to decide whether to play a full eighteen holes before dinner or let it go at an exciting nine with a quick bar break. Why? Because the Edge is most interesting to the people who never go there, wouldn't think of going there (without a police escort), but who understand that today's street culture is tomorrow's suburban Social Convention.

There's a reason cool watchers troll the Edge with all the studied ardor and jaded passion of a bar full of Palm Springs multiple divorcées. Be the first on your block to find the latest, greatest color, beat, or fabric and you're halfway home to cornering the season. So the Edge plays host to two distinct communities: those who live there so they can define themselves by their proximity to the new and their opposition to convention, and the henchpersons of convention. The real Edge dwellers perform a valuable service for the rest of us: test-driving the devox into a vastly more communicable and inherently less threatening shadow of its former Fringe self. With that cultural honing comes the beginnings of rudimentary market formation. True avant-garde Edgers make markets even if they rarely harvest the fruits of their efforts. Edge

1960s bands like Detroit's MC5 and New York's Fugs built cult followings and paved the way for the punk sensibilities of the 1970s and the commercial success of bands ranging from Blondie to the Ramones. Early health-food devotees supported the odd nudist camp and health-food store, but it took the cool watchers to help the pharmaceutical industry understand that the difference between health and wellness is so large it can support a mountain of herbal additives and supplements in everything from teas to vitamins. The health-food store of the 1960s appealed only to a relative handful of people who believed that following an extreme diet was better for their health. The mass market for products like St. John's wort and ginseng didn't appear until the idea of wellness—defined as anything that helped improve quality of life, from herbal teas to aromatherapy—was marketed as a way to soothe the physical, mental, and spiritual aches and pains of aging baby boomers.

Edge dwellers are simultaneously attracted to and repelled by the devox—drawn to anything that appears to be against the established order and repelled by anything that seems to be too attractive to the mainstream. The irony of the Edge is that the more successful the Edge dwellers are at nurturing the devox, and therefore attracting others to it, the sooner they'll have to abandon it. Edge dwellers provide the original model for people who would refuse to join any club that would have them as a member.

There's no question that markets can be made on the Edge (or what most people mistakenly perceive as the Fringe). Our favorite examples include the Venice (California)–based Feral House, "the Publisher That Refuses to be Domesticated" (feralhouse.com), which publishes such weighty tomes as *Apocalypse Culture* (*I* and *II*), *Voluptuous Panic*, *Muerte!*, and *Snitch Culture;* and Amok Books, which bills itself as the "Sourcebook of the Extremes of Information in Print" and distributes such classics as *The Sniper's Handbook*, *The Color Atlas of Oral Cancers*, and the ever-popular *Physical Interrogation Techniques*. The Los Angeles–based Amok also organized a 1989 art exhibit of convicted serial killer John Wayne Gacy's Pogo the Clown paintings. One could easily dismiss all this as marginal activity until you realize there really is a growing market for the arcane, the bizarre, and what earlier, more genteel generations would have described as aberrant culture.

The lesson for businesses to remember is that the Edge is not the Fringe. At best (or, perhaps, at worst), it's the Fringe moved one critical iteration closer to civilization. Sometimes the real potential of a product (and here we're including people) or an idea is lost in the polishing process. We suspect that happens more than we know. In fact, if we knew about it, it couldn't—almost by definition—have happened. The fruits that the cool watchers harvest on the Edge aren't the truly disturbing, truly transformational ideas; they are the ideas tame enough to support an audience, no matter how ephemeral and/or radical they may seem. The original break-dancers and rap artists plied their art on street corners deemed too dangerous by the well-heeled crowds jamming themselves into the latest, hottest (and most secure) dance clubs in pursuit of an art that had lost the anger and passion of the streets.

There's also the problem of market scale as the Fringe moves to the Edge. Sure, Barnes & Noble and Borders and lots of other bookstores carry *Apocalypse Culture I* and *II*, compendiums of weird sexual and spiritual fetishism, political and personal insanities, and other homages to the outré. Sure, Jim Rose, operator of the Seattle-based Jim Rose Circus, and his associate Bébé the Circus Queen travel the world bringing solid citizens such acts as the straitjacket escape, face in glass, ladder of swords, bed of nails, and vacuum challenge (don't ask), along with freak acts and self-mutilation specialists, including female sumo wrestlers Katie "The Pile-Driver" and Judy "The Bull" Jenkins; Battery, the human electrical marvel; Dolly Parton, actually a man who suspends himself from nipple rings; and, of course, the obligatory wrestling Mexican transvestite. In case you can't wait to see them, Jim Rose and his friends were represented until this year by the William Morris Agency, apparently either true Edge devotees or at least savvy enough to make a buck on the Edge. Jim apparently has a good handle on his fans. If you want to call him, Jim is available at 206-726-2460, but beware of the admonition on his fan website (www.ambient.on.ca/jimrose/jimrose. html), which reads, "Please remember that Jim often has to call long distance to check his messages, so don't abuse this number." By the way, Jim apparently doesn't do e-mail. But one warning: Don't tell Jim or his crew that they're freaks. As the fan website explains, "The performers featured in these acts are self-made, unexploited, adult freaks capable of making decisions for themselves. If you have a problem with full-figured women with bare breasts, Mexican transvestite wrestling, pierced body parts, insectivores, penis contortions, and other such mature subjects, kindly go away." Makes you wonder what kind of account executives William Morris is hiring.

THE REALM OF THE COOL: WHERE BUZZ IS BUILT

Jim Rose and Feral House aside, real commercialization isn't possible until you enter the next stage of the devox's progress, a stage we've termed the Realm of the Cool. We're not saying that every deviant idea makes the full progression from the Fringe to Social Convention. But we are saying that all innovation is inherently deviant and follows this path. Lots of deviant ideas die on the Fringe or the Edge, most of them without fanfare or notice. The Realm of the Cool is the place where the devox really begins to scale itself into commercial viability. Media coverage of the Edge tends to treat various expressions of the devox as curiosities at best and extreme oddities at worst. At the Realm of the Cool, media coverage changes significantly. Yesterday's freak is almost miraculously transformed into tomorrow's fashion thanks to broadened acceptance and more favorable publicity. This is the point where hip-hop moved into the trendiest clubs; where the first crowds began to build behind the ropes at Studio 54; where the first extreme hairstyles and fashions are seen on trend makers at award shows. Often the Realm of the Cool is defined by a single individual like Madonna's pre–Material Girl incarnation, which sent thousands of pre- and postpubescent girls to thrift shops across America. There are plenty of casualties in the Realm of the Cool, but more often than not at least part of the devox survives. For example, on May 11, 2001, the day after the

World Wrestling Federation and NBC pulled the plug on the XFL (so-called extreme football), NBC Sports president Dick Ebersol was quoted in *USA Today* as suggesting that the idea of some incarnation of off-season football might succeed. In a separate story in the same issue, Ebersol was quoted as saying, "As strange as it may seem, this [XFL] was one of the most fun experiences of my life. . . . The first week showed us there was an appetite in football for the XFL." The critical element here is to remember that the devox morphs several times on its way to the center. We don't think we'll see Jesse Ventura broadcasting the Super Bowl, but Ebersol's comments suggest that in the future mainstream networks may find some value in an extreme version of traditional sports.

In fact, sports have proved fertile fodder for Realm of the Cool market formation, from real surfers launching demand for Hawaiian shirts and boogie boards in places where the choppiest water is found in a wave pool to legions of wanna-be climbers piling into the North Face after having seen *Everest,* David Breashears's IMAX documentary. Major marketers from British American Tobacco—which makes sure that the "right" dance clubs in Europe carry its brands (especially new products) to the exclusion, the company hopes, of its competition—to vodka marketers from Absolut to Grey Goose understand the value of getting their product into the hands of those who dwell in the Realm of the Cool. You could think of the Realm of the Cool as the place where buzz is built. It's still the domain of an elite, but it's a much broader elite than that found on the Edge. The Realm of the Cool is where the devox evolves from freak to chic. You find it on haute couture runways and—oddly enough—sometimes in the most conventional of places.

Fans of the 2001 preteensploitation movie marvel *Josie and the Pussycats* may remember Josie's horror at discovering that she'd been turned into a "trend pimp" by an evil cabal of music producers and bent FBI agents using banal teen music as a cover for an insidious subliminal marketing campaign. Anyone with even a cursory knowledge of the Realm of the Cool can understand poor Josie's shock. The Realm of the Cool is where the "hip whores" and "trend pimps" ply the world's second-oldest profession (marketing). Their job is to lure the innocent devox into the clutches of their corporate masters—a process characterized by a loss of innocence and authenticity and a gain in marketability. Buzz has always existed and has often been nurtured to commercial advantage, but today it's something that's artificially created and then implanted into the womb of the Realm of the Cool. Consider a story from *USA Today* titled "Freebies Take on Brash New Form: Marketers Dole Out Samples Like Never Before to Create Buzz," which detailed several examples of building a buzz for "cool" new items, including:

- How Kodak gave away cases of Kodak Advantix Preview cameras (retail value, $300) to audiences of the *Oprah* and *Rosie O'Donnell* shows.

- How SoBe introduced Adrenaline Rush by having models in clingy white nurses' uniforms driving around in high-tech ambulances giving samples to perceived trendsetters at extreme sporting events such as motocross and snowboarding competitions.

- How Nintendo pitched a new Nintendo 64 game to college students by erecting beachside gaming tents at favorite spring break locations and handing out various logo-laden items, from temporary tattoos to condoms.

Explaining the approach, SoBe marketing director Mike Joyce explained, "These guys [targeted trendsetters] are just too cool for themselves. There is no way [with traditional ads] you can tell them what to drink." Trend pimping even has its own esoteric language. Liquor companies, for example, use "leaners," also known as "influencers," who wander into too-trendy watering holes armed with a stash of cash and a script that is used to talk the hippest-looking customer into accepting a glass or bottle of "Brand X." There's also the "roach bait" technique. Here, an influencer merely sits in a prominent place at the bar talking up the brand he's been hired to hook for. All these tactics, by the way, fall under the meta-banner of "seeding." During the

1990s, Hennessy better than doubled its cognac sales during a five-year period when it employed people to walk into bars and order Hennessy martinis.

Building buzz in the Realm of the Cool is becoming a big business for companies ranging from traditional marketers like Procter & Gamble, whose ill-fated Tremor offering sought to establish a cyber-network of youth leaders who would serve as a test market for products and ideas, to entrepreneurs like Nico Golfar. A *Los Angeles* magazine article quotes Golfar, a London-born, L.A.-resident trend facilitator, as saying, "I'm referred to as a connector because I can put people from different worlds together." Connecting is Golfar's occupation. For a fee he'll connect products to his network of nine thousand close personal friends, a list that can presumably be customized for delivery to any ZIP code in the Realm of the Cool. Interested in building buzz among the indie music set, finding out what the latest underground fashion statement is, or trying to get a line on the newest in extreme sports? No problem; Golfar will set you up.

Of course, from the annual Burning Man festival in the Temporary Autonomous Zone (also known as Gerlach, Nevada—population 340 full-time residents) to the weekly raves in Tokyo's Yoyogi Park, the real Realm of the Cool marches to its own (currently techno) beat. It's populated by PIBs in SOMA (people in black in San Francisco's South of Market district, for the uninitiated) and PIWs (people in white) hanging out in Tokyo's Harajuku district, especially the ultrahip shops of Takeshita-dori or the seven-level LaForet Harajuku Mall. But whatever the local color scheme, the need for Realm of the Cool denizens to bridge the separation between life and style is a constant. There is even a global niche market for helping the cool stay cool, from New York's *Propaganda* magazine ("Triple-A Rated: Aesthetics, Anarchy, and Androgyny") to *KEROUAC* ("The magazine for eccentric boys and girls"), the bible of Japanese street chic.

Sometimes it may seem hard to distinguish the Realm of the Cool from the stage that precedes it (the Edge) and the one that follows it (the Next Big Thing), but there are critical differences. The first is a matter of scale, and the second is how the devox is portrayed in the media. Sometimes there are examples that on their face appear marginal until you consider additional factors such as market size. Let's take something you might know—assuming you cable surf well after your children are safely in bed. We've selected this next example not for its shock value (which by any standard is high), but rather for what it ought to tell us about exactly how much the world—and the world your customers live in—has really changed. It is an example some may find distasteful since it involves the commercialization of acts that we believe most readers will find extreme to repugnant. Yet this is precisely the point. The commercial world has become so strange that it's possible for people to make money and gain exposure in what you'll see has become a substantial market (now potentially totaling more than 400 global households) doing things that are illegal (in many circumstances) in most civilized nations. We're not saying that these households approve of what they're being exposed to. But we are saying that in a world where personal degradation of the most extreme kind can be translated into a successful business, anything is possible. Clearly, as we are about to see, it's already much later than many businesses think. There's a band loose in the world performing under the endearing stage name of Genitorture that combines death rock and sexual performance art. Audience members at venues such as Brooklyn's L'Amour crawl on stage in order to allow Gen, the band's lead singer, dominatrix, and pierced performance artist, to perform any number of genital tortures on them. On any given night Gen's repertoire may include such wholesome sport as piercing the tongues of French-kissing couples using a twelve-inch needle; domination puppeteering using wires attached to multiple piercings; your garden-variety whipping and piercing of genitalia; torture in the form of sodomy, "water sports," and bondage; hot waxing of nipples; female genital piercing and stitching (don't ask); not to mention the unusual application of a foot-long Pinocchio nose (you really don't want to ask).

Seem a little on the edgy side? Maybe so, but Genitorture tours globally and has been featured on HBO, which brought a small sample of the band's warm-up weirdness into roughly 28 million conventional homes in America alone—probably including yours. Now, if we assume two viewers per household, that would have given the broadcast a potential audience of almost 60 million—60 million people who paid to receive this kind of programming. We could be going out on a limb here, but scale does not seem to be on the side of Genitorture. Try as we may, we can't ever see them doing a double bill with Britney Spears (wouldn't that make a bang-up Pepsi commercial starring Bob Dole) or 'NSYNC. While it's empirically impossible to deny the commitment of Genitorture's fans, we think (maybe we better make that hope) there isn't more than a niche market of exhibitionistic, masochistic human pincushions out there no matter how many times HBO broadcasts this stuff. In addition to its scale problem, Genitorture can't enter the Realm of the Cool because of the way the group is presented by mainstream media. HBO is clearly marginalizing the band and using it for shock value rather than suggesting that it will ever build a broader audience or that it's the tip of some bloodier S&M audio iceberg. Genitorture is big enough to make the radar of the ultrahip, but it will probably never make it to the Realm of the Cool, let alone to the next stage of the devox's journey, a place we call the Next Big Thing. Or maybe they will. This year the band was covered on MTV—the world's most-watched network—which expanded its television exposure by 384 million households.

THE NEXT BIG THING: WHERE YOU NEED TO BE

Success and failure, especially in the entertainment industry, often depend on the ability to move the devox from the Realm of the Cool to the Next Big Thing. Consider the 1998 release of *Godzilla*. Despite a promotional budget in excess of $200 million, the film grossed only $136 million at U.S. box offices. Now compare this with *The Blair Witch Project,* a student art film, which cost less than $60,000 to produce and received only one distribution-rights bid after premiering at the 1999 Sundance Film Festival—a paltry $1 million from Artisan Entertainment. Artisan's investment was apparently worth the risk given that the film has grossed more than $240 million worldwide. Ironically, *Book of Shadows: Blair Witch 2* cost $15 million to make but failed to capture widespread audience support. The success of the original *Blair Witch* was fueled by cowriter and director Eduardo Sanchez, who set up Blairwitch.com, a pseudo-academic and apparently dispassionate site that unemotionally described the "facts" surrounding the Blair Witch. An hour-long television "documentary" on the "disappearance" of the young filmmakers and the "history" of the Blair Witch further built buzz for what otherwise might have easily become a forgotten, grainy B-horror film. Artificially created buzz also helped British author J. K. Rowling's Harry Potter character to cross the Atlantic and dominate North American publishing. Rowling's U.S. publisher, Scholastic Books, began building a carefully orchestrated word-of-mouth campaign months before the first book appeared in America. The approach was so effective that at one point it was seriously suggested that a separate (sans Harry Potter) *New York Times* bestseller list be established to give other authors a chance. In fact, the *Times* eventually moved the books onto the children's bestseller list to open up spots on the general list. We're not saying children don't really love Harry, just that the buzz made it easier for them to find him.

The success of *Blair Witch* illustrates another interesting aspect of the devox—the ability of a rising tide of acceptance to float all manner of deviance. Fifty years ago facts were facts and fiction was fiction and people who confused them were considered not just deviants but liars and frauds. Then, in 1966, Truman Capote blurred the lines separating fact and fiction when he wrote *In Cold Blood: A True Account of a Multiple Murder and Its Consequences,* which told the story of a real crime through a blend of fictional narrative and straight reporting. The technique was edgy, but not for long. In 1974 Carl Bernstein and Bob Woodward made investigative reporting the sexiest career in America with their coverage of the Watergate burglary and the subsequent publishing of *All the President's Men,* a piece of reporting based primarily on the "testimony" of Deep Throat, an individual whose identity still has not been established. Woodward and Bernstein succeeded in moving the artful blending of fact and fiction as a combined entity into the Realm of the Cool, making it hip for news organizations to openly quote unnamed sources, in effect publishing or airing what only a few years before would have been deemed unsubstantiated news stories.

Apparently the idea of deviant journalism is growing in popularity. Hunter S. Thompson has made a career of confusing fact, fiction, and his own fuzzily remembered, psychotropically altered attempts at the coverage of events ranging from presidential campaigns to the Kentucky Derby, chronicled in any number of articles in *Rolling Stone* magazine and a slew of books, including his celebrated (in some circles) *Fear and Loathing* series. Clearly, for the center of the mass market at least, Thompson remains somewhat of an acquired taste (assuming, of course, your taste runs to authors obsessed with heavy-caliber machine guns, large, sharp instruments, and frightening mixtures of alcohol and controlled substances). But the mass market has proved a little more accepting of other authors' efforts.

Bernstein reprised his technique (in what some might have found an over-the-top effort involving allegedly "interviewing" former CIA director William Casey while Casey was in a coma in a hospital) for his *Veil: The Secret War of the CIA, 1981–1987.* Joe Eszterhas's *American Rhapsody,* a fictive chronicle of the Clinton-Lewinsky affair, blurred the line between fact and fiction so badly that even booksellers had a hard time describing what it was. An editor's note on Amazon.com's review of the audiotape version of the book cautions, "This audiobook defies category and convention. It is part journalism and part autobiography." And the technique clearly established itself as the Next Big Thing with the 2000 publication of Edmund Morris's bestselling *Dutch: A Memoir of Ronald Reagan,* which admittedly blended fact and fiction.

The devox's migration from the Realm of the Cool to the Next Big Thing has been well chronicled (in other languages) by a bevy of popular business writers from Seth Godin (*Permission Marketing, The Idea*

Virus, etc.) to Emanuel Rosen *(The Anatomy of Buzz)* and Malcolm Gladwell *(The Tipping Point)*. Sometimes the cycle of the devox repeats itself and items that have been marginalized begin to make their way back across the continuum. Perhaps one of the clearest examples is Gladwell's profile of Hush Puppies.

By 1994 sales of the once popular shoe line were down to 30,000 pairs a year. In 1995, after a few trendy kids starting sporting them in New York's hottest nightspots, the company sold 430,000 pairs. A year later it sold four times that many. "How did it happen?" Gladwell asks. "Those first few kids [who wore the shoes to trendy clubs], whoever they were, weren't deliberately trying to promote Hush Puppies. They were wearing them precisely because no one else would wear them. Then the fad spread to two fashion designers who used the shoes to peddle something else—haute couture. The shoes were an incidental touch. No one was trying to make Hush Puppies a trend. Yet, some-how, that's exactly what happened."

All these concepts seem to be derivatives of ideas first published by Beat Generation icon William Burroughs. In his *Naked Lunch* (1959; first U.S. printing 1966), Burroughs suggested that ideas, indeed words themselves, were viruses that infected the minds of human beings. Of course, Gladwell's examples of renewing the market for Hush Puppies shoes or creating a mass market for books such as *Divine Secrets of the Ya-Ya Sisterhood* clearly are more resonant with mass-market sensibil-ities than Burroughs's graphic description of autoerotic strangulation, homoerotic rape, and/or heroin addiction. But, resonance aside, the fact is that the deviant idea of viral marketing moved steadily from the underground literati to marketing departments across America in less than four decades.

Sometimes you can tell where the devox is at any given moment by watching who signs on. The big-money corporate tie-ins don't gener-ally surface until the devox has entered the Next Big Thing stage. Let's take a look at the unlikely (and some might say unholy) marriage between the hottest form of music in the world and the Ford Motor Company.

Our story begins back in 1981 when Detroit area residents and fellow community-college students Juan Atkins and Rick Davis formed a musical association known as Cybotron, which "embraced the romance of technology, of the city and speed, of the harmony between man and machine, utilizing purely electronic instruments and sounds." By the mid-1980s Cybotron had produced and recorded in its Ypsilanti, Michigan, studio some of the finest electronic music ever made—cuts including "Clear," "R-9," and the mother of all techno songs, "Techno City." During the 1985–1986 period, Atkins teamed up with Derrick May and Kevin Saunderson, recording together and separately as Model 500 (Atkins), Reese (Saunderson), Mayday, R-Tyme, and Rhythim is Rhythim (May). All the songs they produced linked music and the latest developments in computer technology. You might not be familiar with such titles as "No UFOs," "Strings of Life," "Rock to the Beat," or "When He Used to Play," but together they form the bedrock of classic techno.

Techno was discovered by British entrepreneurs, who quickly imported it to Europe and then reintroduced it to America before it made its big splash. Techno supporters managed to convince Detroit city officials to let them stage a festival of what was still largely (and pejoratively) viewed as "Rave music" smack in the middle of downtown. The first Detroit Electronic Music Festival drew 1.5 million people to the downtown area in 2000. Thanks to three days and four stages full of free, nonstop dance music with performances by homegrown and international talent, the festival became the largest music event in history in its inaugural year.

Not one to miss an opportunity to connect with a target market, the Ford Motor Company announced on March 29, 2001, that Ford Focus would be the exclusive automotive, main stage, and title sponsor (read major underwriter) of the 2001 Detroit Electronic Music Festival, which would be renamed the FOCUS:\\Detroit.Electronic.Music. Festival. "We are excited about this integrated sponsorship because our core buyers are continuing to embrace technology and electronic music," Ford Focus brand manager Bob Fesmire proudly proclaimed.

"Techno appeals to a wide, cross-cultural group of people who are all unified by this music and this scene. This music was created partly by the pounding clangor of the Motor City's auto factories." The official Ford version of the sponsorship added, "The Ford Focus and Techno music mirror each other in many ways. Ford Focus owners are influenced by technology, style, music and the idea of change, and Techno was born from the same roots. Focus is a global brand with international appeal, appeal that was developed in Europe. The 'Detroit Sound' has traveled to Europe and reemerged in the U.S."

And, true to our theory, a few real deviants had to be sacrificed in order to advance the devox. Less than two weeks before the 2001 festival took place, Carl Craig, its original artistic director, was informed (via fax) by festival producer Pop Culture Media that his services would be terminated (two years into a three-year agreement) on May 30, 2001, two days after the festival ended, allegedly for his failure to get signed contracts from performers. Contacted on May 16, techno pioneer Derrick May told Detroit media, "Everyone in the community is upset and angry about this, but we have to think about what's best for the music. We are going to go out there and do our shows and be professional. That's what Carl would want." Not all artists agreed. Detroit techno artist Brendan Gillen (aka Ectomorph) said, "The mythology of this festival comes from the fact that Carl Craig is the creative director. To remove him makes me question what is the DEMF." Underwritten, dear Ectomorph, and decidedly big business.

Corporate sponsorship and artistic assassinations demonstrate that techno has moved from the Fringe, through the Edge, out of the Realm of the Cool, and is clearly the Next Big Thing. Can the mass market be far away? We doubt it, unless of course enough people suffer an acute bout of artistic integrity, sadly never a very real threat. By the way, at this point media coverage of the devox shifts from the "Here's what you need to know" world of the Realm of the Cool to "Here's where you need to be."

SOCIAL CONVENTION: THE MAINSTREAMING OF THE DEVOX

Most of us are familiar with what happens next—the mainstreaming of the devox, or the point where it hits the Social Convention stage and moves from "Here's where you need to be" to "Here's what you need to own or do." Examples of mainstreaming are endless. This is where actor Don Johnson's supercool T-shirt-with-the-Armani-suit look from TV's *Miami Vice* is translated into articles of clothing resembling psychedelically dyed shop coats on Kmart racks across America. This is what separates the time when Dennis Rodman makes headlines with dyed hair and tattoos from the era in which major sports institutions like the National Basketball Association begin (in 2001) to have serious discussions of who owns a player's skin since athletes are being approached to wear temporary tattoos endorsing products on their arms. It's the point where the guys who look like the Dennis Hopper and Peter Fonda characters in *Easy Rider* are really your dentist and accountant. It's where Columbine as a noun describing a tragic anomaly becomes an adjective modifying an ongoing aspect of American culture. It's a place where the human cartoons from the World Wrestling Federation get to write *New York Times* bestsellers and the place where stock-car racing, once a redneck art form based in the South, becomes one of the fastest-growing spectator sports in the world. And, of course, it's the place where the devox—often in a thoroughly sanitized and inauthentic form—enjoys its largest commercial success. If you're still in doubt just open *Time, Forbes, Fortune, Business Week,* or, better still, *People* or *Entertainment Weekly.* Look at how the people around you are dressed, or window-shop any mall. If all else fails, most people can figure out what Social Convention looks like just by staring into a mirror. This isn't a slight, just a telling comment on the true power of market formation and exploitation.

There are any number of examples of how business growth and market creation mirror the devox's path of acceptance. Think about the market for foodservice operations aimed at individuals who don't eat meat. At the very Fringe of nonmeat eaters is the orthodox practitioner of Jainism whose overly rigid interpretation of doctrine forbids him from eating anything. Obviously, this view is so extreme that those who hold it die shortly after acting on their beliefs. There's not too much commercial potential for a restaurant serving terminal customers. Vegans (those who eat no meat or meat by-products, including cheese and milk) live on the Edge of the meat-avoiding world. There is a broader market potential here, but nonvegans may or may not find the menu enticing. Vegetarians whose palates are liberal enough to include things like cheese currently reside in the Realm of the Cool. The growing number of vegetarian restaurants and vegetarian selections on more traditional menus speaks to the growing potential of the market. The Realm of the Cool is populated with the "vegetarian aware." These are individuals (generally not full vegetarians) who believe that diets including a number of meatless meals are somehow better than traditional diets. Many vegetarian-aware diners say they are vegetarians but eat chicken and/or fish or even lean cuts of meat. Since many people, including dieters and those concerned about cholesterol, are comfortable with a vegetarian-aware menu, the market for potential clientele more closely resembles that of any restaurant. Vegetarianism hit Social Convention when McDonald's introduced its McVeggie sandwich in America, really a variation on products it had been selling in India and other parts of the world, and Burger King countered with the BK Veggie.

Medicine provides another fairly robust example. We're sure that somewhere out there on the Fringe, perhaps in a swamp someplace, somebody is boiling roots and insects together into a concoction only he or she would consume. Or, a little closer to home, consider Australian skiing aerialist and 2002 Winter Olympian Jacqui Cooper, who regularly downed a mixture of Chinese herbs, ground cockroaches, and Diet Coke in hopes of restoring an injured back.

You can find the Edge of medication out there in botanicas scattered from Spanish Harlem to East L.A. The use of herbal medications like ginseng, gingko biloba, St. John's wort, echinacea, saw palmetto, and valerian is increasingly common in the Realm of the Cool, as hipper-than-thou baby boomers go back to the land for therapies designed to stave off the effects of old age. The market for holistic medications gets broader once you reach the Next Big Thing and its significantly developed market for wellness products. And when you get to Social Convention you find old-line pharmaceutical brands cashing in by marketing their old products with herbal additives.

In the arts, the primitive (to European and American ears) Fringe rhythms of western African slaves gained access to a slightly broader audience in the Edgy cadences of the cotton fields. Later, modified versions of those rhythms fueled jazz and blues clubs in the Realm of the Cool. Wandering farther north, these sounds began to gather broader, whiter audiences and became hailed as the Next Big Thing. Today those same rhythms lie (sometimes deeply) buried on every rock 'n' roll and hip-hop CD released.

It's possible to plot the progress of any idea, invention, or cultural wrinkle through the linear progression that begins on the Fringe and ends at Social Convention. Let's take media in its broadest sense as a vehicle for disseminating content. The person babbling to himself in an alley exists on the Fringe, his message sent and received by the same mind. If he emerges from the alley and graduates to a public soapbox (literally or figuratively) or creates his own Internet forum he has moved to the Edge. When it comes to media, Internet zines, customized newsletters, and broadcast faxes or e-mails represent the Realm of the Cool. The Next Big Thing is downloadability (video and/or audio) that allows the audience to essentially create its own media. That notion of choice, this time in the form of cable television, has clearly reached Social Convention.

It's important to note that while the path from the Fringe to Social Convention is absolute, it is by no means guaranteed. Mapplethorpe photographs continue to command substantial prices in the Realm of the Cool, but we think it will be some time before they grace Cheerios boxes. Bill Gates clearly hoped WebTV could leave the Next Big Thing stage, but alas for him, it never has. For today, at least, quantum computing still exists somewhere between the Edge and the Realm of the Cool, while cryogenics is clearly stuck on the Edge. Internet zines exist on the Edge but sometimes migrate toward Social Convention. The original topless bathing suits were born, and died, on the Edge.

The progression from the Fringe to Social Convention embraces a vast—and often divergent—territory. It's clearly still a long way from solar-powered cars or cars like Ford's Autonomy, a fuel-cell propelled prototype with interchangeable chassis types that debuted at the 2002 Detroit Auto Show, to the soccer mom's SUV. By the same token, the only thing Britney Spears and kids singing for tips on New Orleans' Bourbon Street appear to have in common is that they're all relying on their voices to earn a living. It's critical, though, to remember that in real market terms the distance separating the Edge from Social Convention is continually contracting. After all, today's PDA would have seemed like a science fiction device two decades ago.

The devox's journey isn't necessarily over once it reaches Social Convention. There the devox begins a journey down a more irregular, far less predictable path—one that the forces of convention have difficulty controlling. That path is the subject of our next chapter.

3

From Chic to Bleak:
The Further Adventures of the Devox

Over a twenty-year period, Elvis Presley evolved from the avatar of
American cool to the embodiment of American excess. Almost entirely
confined to bed in his last few months, Elvis devoured pills and fried
banana-and-peanut-butter sandwiches, suppressing the pain of being
Elvis and seemingly trying to lose himself inside his own expanding
girth. . . . There is no better metaphor for the old American dream.
With a few exceptions, we are all Elvis now.

—KALLE LASN, *Culture Jam: The Uncooling of America*

Somewhere on the path from its broadest social acceptance and the
crossroads separating oblivion and immortality, the devox, like
Elvis, wobbles between becoming a cultural standard and a parody of
its original essence. Everything that moves from the Fringe to Social
Convention follows an identical road. The path beyond the mass market, however, is far from linear or predictable. After migrating from
center stage, the devox faces an uncertain path leading to one or more
phases we call Cliché, Icon, Archetype, and/or Oblivion. The step from
Social Convention to Cliché is inevitable, particularly in a world where
sophistry usually triumphs over sophistication and where rationaliza-
tion routinely trumps rationality.

Businesspeople considering the market implications associated with this stage of the devox's journey are well advised to pay attention to the following caveat: When trying to manage the devox to its full potential, never underestimate the ability of Post-Information Age cultures to trivialize the most magnificent accomplishment and sentiments or institutionalize the most banal entity. No matter how "hot" an idea, product, service, or personality may appear as it hits center stage in the mainstream market, it can't stay there forever.

Think fast. Can you recall the name of the first "survivor"? The beaches of the future will be littered with pop cultural ephemera—not just with Richard Hatch, the original "survivor," but with a battalion of boy bands, Pokémon cards, Godzilla tie-in merchandise, the original Spice Girls, *The Weakest Link,* Apple's Newton, WebTV, and, one of our personal favorites, Prince of Thieves cereal. The musical landscape is rife with one-hit wonders, and the business environment isn't all that different. Twenty years from now people are more likely to think of John DeLorean, who founded his own manufacturing empire in Ireland, as a failed cocaine dealer than a maverick of the automotive industry, even though the government's drug charges against him were thrown out in court, and "Chainsaw" Al Dunlop as a vulgar by-product of Wall Street greed than as a once-lionized CEO—assuming, of course, Dunlop and DeLorean are thought of at all. Remember Clifford Irving, who went to prison for attempting to publish a totally fictitious "biography" of Howard Hughes in 1972, behavior that would probably almost guarantee him a spot on *The New York Times* bestseller list today? Back in the seventies, Irving was forced to pay back a publisher's advance of more than three-quarters of a million dollars and spent over a year in jail.

Whole industries have been dismissed in the wake of progress. Can you name America's largest icebox maker, or buttonhook supplier, or celluloid-collar producer? We're guessing the answer is probably no, despite the fact that iceboxes, buttonhooks, and collars were once found in the majority of American homes. More recently, try to remember how much an airmail stamp cost, the product name of the first Texas Instruments calculator, the name of the first Democratic vice president to run against Ronald Reagan, or the last time you Scotchguarded a tie.

Can you name the manufacturer of those heavy, black rotary phones that were a fixture of every baby boomer's youth? How about the leading maker of eight-track tape players?

But, as in every other aspect of the devox's evolution, there is money to be made as the devox moves toward either decline or functional commercial immortality. Even discarded technologies and inventions have some value in the collector's market. The demand for vintage objects—clothing, automobiles, musical instruments, furniture, and even advertising—is huge. So is the market for vintage people. No wonder the Eagles were able to charge $100 a ticket for their Hell Freezes Over tour. The issues, of course, are how much money there is to be made and who makes it.

Many businesses are mismanaging the transition from the mass-market opportunity and allowing other, more entrepreneurial players to profit from their intellectual property. Physical assets determined wealth in the Industrial Age. Technological innovation served as a basis for establishing wealth in the Information Age. Intellectual property or intellectual capital will prove to be the key to capital formation today and in the near future, a period we call the Post-Information Age.

In 1813 Thomas Jefferson wrote to his friend Isaac McPherson, "He who receives an idea from me, receives instructions himself without lessening mine; as he who lights his taper at mine receives light without darkening mine." What Jefferson couldn't have anticipated is that the information or data surrounding a product would eventually be worth far more than the product itself. Ask yourself which you would rather own, the physical assets of the Coca-Cola Company or control of the Coca-Cola trademark?

All of us who have ever lost a laptop or PDA know that the real loss isn't the machine but the information it contains, and most of us would be willing to pay more for the return of an old machine than we would for a new one. By the same token, we believe that the real issue in the Napster debate wasn't whether Jack Ely, Lynn Easton, Mike Mitchell, Bob Nordby, and Don Gallucci (the original lineup of the Kingsmen, the band that first released "Louie, Louie" in 1963) or their heirs should receive royalties every time some kid downloads the song from the Internet, hoping to decipher the "dirty parts." Rather, it was whether the projected 70 million Napster users were going to have free access to the music industry's perceived intellectual property. And in this era of employee free agentry, we've just begun to see the first wave of an endless ocean of lawsuits that will deluge the court every time any employee with access to critical proprietary information quits to go to work for a direct competitor.

Unlike the path from the Fringe to Social Convention, the road away from Social Convention to other phases is polymorphic rather than discrete; that is, the devox can occupy several stages at once. The market for the devox at the Fringe is clearly separate and distinct from the one that exists as it enters the Edge. That separateness exists at every step of the way, from the Edge, to the Realm of the Cool, to the Next Big Thing, to Social Convention. But once the devox has left Social Convention it can exist, and be simultaneously marketed, as Cliché, Icon, and even Archetype. Because the devox is truly polymorphic, it's also probable that more than one of these post–Social Convention stages will be commercially exploitable at any given time.

The chart on the next page continues the mapping of the devox's progress from the point where we left off in Chapter 2, mass-market acceptance. Once the devox has left Social Convention, it has several paths open to it, each of which will be examined in greater depth. It could, for example, move to Cliché and then shuffle off to Oblivion, without ever passing through the Icon or Archetype stages. Or it could achieve Icon status for a moment, only to be replaced by a different devox. Under very specific conditions, the devox might be elevated from Icon directly to Archetype. By the same token, however, it could be jerked out from underneath the bright lights of Social Convention and planted directly in the black hole of Oblivion. We believe specific paths can be engineered but not guaranteed. The devox *makes* markets on its way to Social Convention, but markets *evolve* in the wake of its movement from Social Convention to whatever stage at which it stops.

Let's expand a few of these points to illustrate our premise. It no

THE PATH OF THE DEVOX
FROM SOCIAL CONVENTION TO ARCHETYPE OR OBLIVION

	Social Convention	Cliché	Icon	Archetype	Oblivion
Media Coverage	What you need to own/do	Satirical to scorn	Cultural placeholder	Redefines cultural understanding	Nostalgia to neglect
Audience Size	Mass market	Mass market	Universal	Universal	Niche at best
Who Benefits (Assuming a Benefit Exists)	Mass-market makers	Generally others than those who brought the devox to Social Convention	Champions at the Social Convention and/or Cliché stages	Owners of intellectual-property rights	Tiny niche dwellers
Commercial Potential	70–100%	Less than Social Convention levels	70–100%	40–60%	Less than 1%
Role of Initiating Deviant	Needs to change or be eliminated	Object of satire or ridicule	Image	Reference	Footnote
Authenticity Quotient	10%	Less than 10%	25%	40%	0–100%
Communications Vehicle	Advertising and marketing	Entertainment industry; mass media	Nontraditional applications	Universal applications	Devotees
Relationship to Conventional Society	Acceptance	Amusement	Model	Standard setter	Negative example

longer takes any time for the "in" to become "out." 'NSYNC released its first album in 1998. By 2000, with combined concert revenues and CD sales of $267 million, it was the largest grossing entertainment act in America. On January 2, 2002, *Star Wars* godfather George Lucas's

Lucasfilm announced that some members of 'NSYNC would appear in *Star Wars, Episode II: Attack of the Clones,* which was scheduled for release on May 16. On January 12 NBC's *Saturday Night Live* parodied the band in a *Star Wars* skit, all but sealing the fate of their scenes in the real movie. In this case, the parody was a success before the original ever aired—such a success in fact that nobody outside of a few Lucasfilm editors will ever see the original object of the satire. The Cliché had overtaken Social Convention before the band had any time to enjoy their fifteen minutes of cinematic fame. On January 14, 2002, 'NSYNCer Joey Fatone said the band's scenes had been cut "because people made a big deal about it."

THE EVOLUTION OF THE POST–SOCIAL CONVENTION DEVOX

As society's infatuation with novelty intensifies, most people and products have a shorter and shorter ride at the center of Social Convention. That's not to say there isn't a large, profitable popular demand for Cliché, from celebrity impersonators, to satirical subjects, to nostalgia marketers. In fact, as we'll see in a minute, some products do better from a commercial perspective once they lose their perch astride mainstream acceptance. But whether manifesting itself as Cliché, Icon, or Archetype, or fading into Oblivion, the devox exhibits ten common characteristics.

1. Post–Social Convention devox evolution can operate on more than one level at a time. One person's Cliché is another person's Icon. Norman Rockwell is an Icon of American art at the same time that parodies of his style continue to flood the market. For every one of those "not your father's Oldsmobile"s that isn't moving off a General Motors' lot there's an Olds "classic" being lovingly restored in a garage. The vintage-car enthusiast is a far different breed of cat from the new-car buyer. Individually, they are prepared to spend small fortunes obtaining and restoring or customizing classic autos, almost always far more than the original cars were worth. Collectively, they congregate in venues like Detroit's annual Woodward Avenue Dream Cruise, officially a one-day event that attracted 1.5 million visitors and thirty thousand muscle cars, street rods, customized collectible, and special-interest vehicles.

2. The real commercial opportunity often exists beyond Social Convention. If you want to know the real business opportunities represented by post–mass markets, contrast the number of fully conceived studio albums guitar god Jimi Hendrix released during his lifetime (three: *Are You Experienced?*—1967; *Axis: Bold As Love*— 1967; and *Electric Ladyland*—1968) with the almost ninety Hendrix CDs currently available. Well over 90 percent of all Hendrix's commercial output was assembled after he was dead and his era—musically and socially—was over.

3. Market opportunities continue with or without you. Intellectual property that is not protected will be exploited by others. Xerox owned, developed, or refined most of the technologies that made personal computing practical, but it took companies like Microsoft and Apple to commercialize those advances. From a technological point of view there is nothing revolutionary about radio frequency identification chips, until you put them in a piece of plastic as Mobil did when it introduced the Speedpass. And, as any number of companies have demonstrated, protecting intellectual property can in itself become an independent revenue stream.

4. Clichés, Icons, and Archetypes are value neutral—that is, they can be both positive and negative. The old marketing adage that holds that it doesn't matter what you say about me as long as you spell my name right was never more true. There is a yin and yang to brand building in the era of the devox. For every Yahoo! there is a Yahoo! Sucks! Often the devox discovers restored commercial vitality once it has entered the Cliché phase. This is the basis of the television syndication industry. We got tired of *The Brady*

Bunch and *Star Trek*. We even fell out of love with good old Lucy. But many of these have found new life in places such as Nickelodeon's Nick at Nite and TV Land.

The pattern is always the same. First we love the shows, altering our schedules or setting our VCRs so we won't miss one moment of programming. Then over time the fictional characters who inhabit these shows begin to grate on our nerves. Soon we start to mock the predictable plots and the less-than-inspiring acting. Ultimately our affections run full circle; our gentle mocking is transformed into full-scale rejection. Eventually these shows are banished to the land of Cliché. But strange things begin to happen shortly after they arrive. They begin to acquire renewed vigor and marketability. Syndication deals are signed and soon shows that previously couldn't command enough Nielsen points to remain on the air end up creating residual advertising revenues for decades. Some shows, like *Star Trek,* take on an expanded life of their own offscreen in the form of conventions and other gatherings of the faithful. The actors who were once ridiculed are relionized, and the money just keeps rolling in.

5. There's a significant difference between markets and audiences. Most of the time commercialization begins with the creation of an audience. Market formation occurs when that audience gains sufficient scale. However, there are also any number of products that can resonate with many people and therefore build an audience, but never enjoy enough momentum to represent a viable commercial market. There's a limited, but strong, audience for pianist and composer John Cage's experimental music, for example, but we don't think it has much mass-market potential. In the case of the arts this distinction between audience and market (and therefore the size of the potential payday) is sometimes used to describe the difference between the true artists and alleged sellouts.

Of course, the Internet is changing all of this. Take the example of Quaker's Quisp cereal. Quisp (named, according to its official website—quisp.com—after a character who left Planet Q in 1951 with 12 billion boxes of Quisp cereal, a can of instant soup, a change of underwear, and a spare beanie propeller) didn't sustain enough volume to be kept in mainstream distribution. Quaker's decision to pull the underperforming product met a storm of protest. Quisp, it turned out, has a fanatical (if marginal, from a manufacturing perspective) consumer base. Building a Quisp website where "Quisp-heads" can access their favorite breakfast food proved both an elegant and profitable solution.

6. Authenticity can be regained once the devox leaves Social Convention. Authenticity is often sacrificed in order to make the devox more commercially acceptable. Professional boxing is a classic example. What most fight fans are hoping for is that one of the competitors will decisively damage the other. But in order to be acceptable to society at large, and therefore commercially successful, boxing has had to modify violence through the use of gloves and rules and the presence of trainers and referees. People may have gone to watch Muhammad Ali box, but they go to watch most fighters hurt people or be hurt themselves. Once a fighter has moved out of his—or her—fifteen minutes of fame and entered Cliché they are free to drop the pretense of being a good sport and are allowed to become vicious aggressors.

Mike Tyson provides an excellent case in point. He now gets more attention *before* he gets into the ring than he does when he enters it. Few believe he could ever be the heavyweight champion of the world again, but he's always great theater, and therefore great box office, providing your taste runs to criminal pathos. With the necessity for continuous commercial acceptance removed, there's no reason that the authentic aspects of the devox, honed down as it progressed to Social Convention, can't be restored. In fact, one could argue that in decline the devox becomes the intellectual property of true devotees who tend to obsess about authenticity.

7. Fame is fleeting but infamy lives forever. It's critical to manage these final stages carefully. The task becomes all the trickier when you consider that negative examples seem to have a much longer shelf life than positive ones. Mullet haircuts may have been great (in some circles) in the 1970s, but not even *Joe Dirt,* the 2001 film built almost exclusively around a sight gag involving the main character's permanent mullet weave, will ever bring them back. In fact, we're betting that the mullet image will create smiles and sneers for decades to come. On a grander—and far more sinister—scale, we believe Adolf Hitler has achieved Archetype status, but we don't think he represents a real growth opportunity outside of a few Aryan Nation compounds in Idaho and skinhead bars in white, poor, blue-collar America.

Skinheads aren't the only ones keeping the Hitler Archetype vital. A whole host of groups from militant Zionists to strident civil libertarians use the Archetype as a constant reminder of what can happen to a society that becomes too tolerant of right-wing fanatics or hate mongers. One could argue paradoxically that over time, negative Archetypes like Hitler have the greatest utility to those who stand in the most extreme opposition to them.

8. After the Social Convention phase, intellectual property has to be shared to be controlled. Try as you might like, it's all but impossible to retain *total* control of intellectual property over time. The best advice is to either learn to live with that gracefully or be prepared to employ an army of attorneys. Clichés, Icons, and Archetypes exist in the intellectual property equivalent of eminent domain. Either they are at least quasi-public or they are consigned to Oblivion. There's a fine line here. Point three on this list warned that if you don't exploit your intellectual property somebody else will. That's true, but it's equally true that some external exploitation can increase the value of the portion you do control. The trick is to know when to exercise control.

The commercial world is full of examples of brands that have made a resurgence once their manufacturers learned to tolerate a little teasing and external manipulation. One of the best examples of this is Spam, which, in an era that emphasizes organic, fresh, low-cholesterol, and karmically pure food products, should have been near the top of the endangered brands list.

If it had been up to baby boomers Spam might have gone away, one of the classic American brands sacrificed on the altar of changing fashion. But one generation's poison proved to be another generation's potted meat. Gen Yers and echo-boomers, it seemed, could embrace Spam for one of its least marketed qualities—the fact that the sight of that gelatinous fat oozing out of a tin of compressed pig parts made the back of their parents' teeth hurt. All of a sudden Spam was cool again. Today there's an official Spam website operated by the Hormel Foods Corporation, a Spam Museum, an Official Spam Fan Club, and even a SpamMobile.

The fan club wasn't the brainchild of a marketing whiz in Hormel's hometown of Austin, Minnesota; it was the product of all those Spamheads out there who were busy co-opting a food product into a social statement. As the website explains:

> We didn't come up with the idea of a SPAM fan club. People like you did.
>
> You sent us photos. You wrote touching stories. You came up with tasty recipes.
>
> And more. Why, the only thing left for us to do was organize a fan club. And so, here it is—The Official SPAM Fan Club.

For just $15 a year you too can join the club and "have a front row seat for a lot of fun and cool stuff," including the Official Spam Fan Club T-shirt ("Not just any SPAM T-shirt, mind you. This one's for members only."); the Official Spam Fan Club membership certificate; the Official Spam Fan Club membership card; and a subscription to *A Slice of Spam,* a quarterly newsletter.

9. In all of these stages, a part of the devox may overshadow the whole. This is especially true at the Cliché stage, but even Icons and Archetypes can be startlingly one-dimensional. O. J. Simpson's football career has been obscured by his legal problems. The Edsel is remembered (if it's remembered at all) as a metaphor for bad products, even though it incorporated some state-of-the-art automotive design. Liberace is remembered for his flamboyance rather than his music. And politicians, after they fall from grace, are often defined by a single statement, from "I am not a crook" to "Read my lips, no new taxes."

10. **In a post–Social Convention environment, the devox moves from making markets to making culture, as we'll see in Chapter 6.** McDonald's has added more than 130 words, ranging from Big Mac to Happy Meal, to the global vocabulary. In its post–Social Convention incarnations, the devox moves from a "thing" we purchase or access to an installed part of our personal social and cultural infrastructure. Sure, we still purchase Happy Meals, but when we do we're really buying into a new global food-service culture. McDonald's has the most liberal (from a chicken's perspective) vendor standards for laying hencoops. The eggs in that Egg McMuffin came from happy hens whose coop size standards exceed those of the animal-rights-sensitive European Union. Why? Because McDonald's understands that when you're in the culture construction business, you need to be able to set the standards you—and everybody else—is forced to live by.

CLICHÉ: TRANSFORMING WEIRDNESS INTO MARKET OPPORTUNITY

Cliché is the devox's post–Social Convention evolution. It's here that the devox—whether idea, product, service, or personality—begins to be aggressively satirized and where money is made through parody, ridicule, and even direct attack. Some companies panic as they enter this phase, while others see it as an opportunity to cultivate new business opportunities and expand their already burgeoning kingdoms. And, speaking of kingdoms, the aftermarketing of Elvis Presley provides an excellent case study on how to transform ridicule, satire, flattery, fanaticism and, frankly, outright weirdness into market opportunity.

There is one official Elvis website (www.elvis.com) and 184,355 other Elvis Presley–related websites. Some, such as the site promoting the Flying Elvi (www.flyingelvi.com), the ten-member Elvis-impersonator skydiving team first seen in the movie *Honeymoon in Vegas,* advertise the fact that they are "officially licensed by Elvis Presley Enterprises." Most, we suspect, are not. For example, what about the First Presleyterian Church of Elvis the Divine (http://chelsea.ios.com/~hkarlin1/welcome1.html)? Actually, we loved this site. Sure, they want $13 for "your official laminated membership card and colorful certificate suitable for framing," but where else could you get spiritual advice like this:

> But there's more to good health than just following a sensible, E-approved diet plan. Our physical and mental well-being sometimes requires wondrous substances to ease our aches and pains. Of course, Dristan, Super Anahist, Sucrets and Contact are among the 31 Holy Items, insuring that we are always prepared when a cold strikes. But, once again, just because a medication is not listed as one that must be kept in the home at all times does not mean that we are not free to imbibe a veritable cornucopia of other substances. For Elvis' medicine cabinet is chock-full of goodies to help us along the way during our trying day. Amphetamines give us that extra boost we need when our get-up-and-go seems to have got-up-and-went. On the other hand, there are times when we need a soothing sleeping pill or twelve to enable us to relax and get a good night's rest.

And speaking of spiritual Elvis matters, what about the site devoted to "Elvis Aaron Presley, His Growth and Development as a Soul Spirit Within the Universe"? When we visited the site (http://home.golden. net/~jdmarshall//) earlier this year we were visitor number 20,343, proof to us that even in extremis the devox still has drawing power. The site is hawking a book of the King's thoughts from the afterlife, as channeled by Paula Farmer, on a wide range of topics, including his "true feelings" about "his Mama and Daddy; his stillborn brother, Jesse Garon; and his career, marriage and fatherhood," as well as "his inner-most thoughts regarding life and death; sex and drugs; religion; and his meeting with God." The site notes that "Elvis," "Elvis Presley," and "Graceland" are registered trademarks of Elvis Presley Enterprises, Inc. (EPE) but fails to mention any official licensing deal. The site explains that the book is "a special gift from Elvis and the Universe," but Paula Farmer still wants $12.95 plus $3 shipping and handling before you can be fully enlightened.

The Elvis intellectual property trail was a little easier to follow in the case of Lifestyles International Astrological Foundation's *Elvis Presley's Astrological and Psychological Magazine* ($6, postpaid). According to the website (http://www.lifeintl.com/elvis.htm), the magazine shows "Elvis from within" and explains why he was destined to be trans-formed from a mere mortal to an international legend who will always be the "King of Rock and Roll." At the bottom of the page there's a small note that reads "© Lifestyles Intl. Inc. Elvis and Elvis Presley are trademarks of Elvis Presley Enterprises Inc."

If these last two examples strike you as strange, it's clear you don't understand what a big business afterlife publishing has become. Elvis isn't the only rock star to publish from the "other side." In June 1999 Harmony Books released *In the Spirit: Conversations with the Spirit of Jerry Garcia,* written by Wendy Weir and Jerry Garcia (the Grateful Dead guitarist who died on August 9, 1995). According to the book description on Amazon.com, "through telepathic communication with Jerry Garcia, legendary member of the Grateful Dead, Wendy Weir, sis-ter of Dead guitarist Bob Weir, presents Jerry's deep, loving, and often humorous insights from the realm of spirit and his wishes not only for the band that has become a cultural phenomenon but for each and every one of us." Among the musings of JO (Jerry's Oversoul, to the uniniti-ated) was a small mention of the cosmic good vibrations associated with keeping the band (always one of the Top 10 grossing musical touring acts in America) together. But let's get back to the King.

Elvis Presley Enterprises provides a clear model of how to manage the devox through the Cliché stage. The Elvis image has been satirized in a variety of media for decades and the Elvis persona has fueled the career of a legion of impersonators. Had the King's estate not been so vigilant in actively pursuing licensing agreements, we assume it wouldn't be so large. Elvis himself may have left the building, but his lawyers are everywhere. And with good reason. The King's image adorns everything from bourbon bottles to bedroom wear. Presley's caped, bejeweled, and usually bloated image has become both a near-omnipresent Cliché of faded entertainment glory and a defining American icon. The King appears proudly on postage stamps at the same time that he's made fun of in B movies.

In fact, ubiquitous Elvisness became the subject of a heated legal debate in the United Kingdom. On March 12, 1999, the British Court of Appeals handed down a judgment in the ongoing trademark battle between Sid Shaw of England's Elvisly Yours and Elvis Presley Enterprises, which had applied for the U.K. rights to the marks Elvis and Elvis Presley and the signature mark Elvis A. Presley. For years, Shaw had been trading across a broad range of goods under the Elvisly Yours mark in the United Kingdom. Naturally, he opposed the EPE application on a variety of grounds, including that the marks were not inherently distinctive of Elvis Presley Enterprises's goods and, if used, would create deception and confusion. The court agreed, ruling that both the Elvis and Elvis Presley marks had little distinctiveness and that the signature mark, while admittedly distinctive, bore too close a resemblance to the Elvisly Yours trademark. Perhaps more importantly, the Court of Appeals didn't agree with the American licenser's position that recognition of character merchandising equates in the consumer's mind with any object bearing the character's likeness as having the approbation of, or license from, that celebrity and his or her agents. Apparently not content with his legal victory, Shaw maintains a website devoted to helping other Elvis hawkers overthrow what he clearly perceives as marketing tyranny by Elvis Presley Enterprises.

Of course, not everyone agrees with Shaw's assessment of EPE as tyrannical, and that has allowed the company to grow its business into the protection of other entertainers' intellectual property. The heirs of the late Rick Nelson turned to EPE to protect and increase the value of the Rick Nelson estate based on the success EPE has had with the Elvis estate. On May 8, 2000, Elvis Presley Enterprises and the Rick Nelson Company, LLC, announced in a joint press release that the Presley police had been retained to watch over the licensing sanctity of the late Rick Nelson's estate. Ever vigilant to preserve its image as a Presley purist, EPE explained the deal to (presumably authorized) Elvis fan clubs around the world. The release read in part:

> We have been approached time and time again over the years by the estates of deceased celebrities to perform a role such as the Nelsons are asking us to do. We have always declined. But, the Nelsons are a wonderful family, they are great friends, and the Rick Nelson legacy is fascinating. This does not necessarily signal any sort of expansion of our licensing division to include numerous celebrities other than Elvis. But, who knows what the future could hold?

ICON: MICKEY MOUSE, RAMBO, AND ROCKY

Sometimes there's only a fine line between Cliché and Icon, but that doesn't make marketers any less vigilant. The phrase "Mickey Mouse" practically defines Cliché, but that doesn't stop the Disney organization from being one of the most vigilant guardians of intellectual property on earth. In 1989 Disney demanded—under threat of punitive legal action—that images of characters such as Mickey Mouse, Minnie Mouse, and Goofy be removed from the walls of the Very Important Babies Daycare, the Good Godmother Daycare, and the Temple Messianique daycare centers, all in Hallandale, Florida. The images—so often associated with children, especially in Florida—were still commercially viable in Disney's view. The company argued that letting even good causes reproduce them for free inhibited its future ability to charge licensing fees. The fact that Mickey has been almost endlessly satirized doesn't deter Disney from punishing anyone (even the apparently innocent) who treads too close on its trademarks.

Ironically, of course, Disney itself routinely poaches characters like Aladdin, the Little Mermaid, and Mowgli *(The Jungle Book)* that have moved out of mass-market favor or entered public domain and uses them for movie subjects. The legal lesson is a confusing one: In America, at least, what's good for the Mouse—er, goose—is sometimes also good for the gander—and sometimes not. For example:

- In 1994, the U.S. Supreme Court unanimously held in *Campbell v. Acuff-Rose Music, Inc.,* that rappers 2 Live Crew had a legal right to parody Roy Orbison's "Oh, Pretty Woman," ruling that "a parody's commercial character is only one use to be weighed in a fair use enquiry," and that the rappers were clearly "commenting on the original or criticizing it, to some degree."

- But in 1996, the U.S. Court of Appeals for the Ninth Circuit upheld a federal district court ruling in favor of Dr. Seuss Enterprises' injunction against *The Cat NOT in the Hat!,* an O. J. Simpson murder case spoof by "Dr. Juice."

Clearly one sign that the devox has moved to Cliché is its transformation from salable product to cultural component. As Henry Jenkins, professor of media studies at MIT, has observed, "If something becomes an essential part of our culture, we have a right to draw on it and make stories about it. . . . The core question is whether First Amendment protections include a right to participate in our culture." This is a critical point. If Jenkins is right, anyone can capitalize on the markets created by the devox's migration from Social Convention. This suggests that companies should begin to aggressively manage their product's intellectual property as though it had entered Cliché while it's enjoying the height of its popularity, similar to the approach the Disney organization has taken. Mickey Mouse is a defining Icon of our culture, but God—and a battalion of lawyers—help you if you try to use his image without permission.

Mickey is a great example of how something can simultaneously operate as both a Cliché and an Icon. Mickey Mouse is an Iconic symbol of the Disney empire and popular cartooning. At the same time, he has become a Cliché for the banal, as in "That's a real Mickey Mouse outfit." Mickey isn't alone. Look at Sylvester Stallone. Rambo has become a Cliché domestically for out-of-control Vietnam vets and internationally for American military aggression. At the same time, Rocky is still the Icon of the little guy fighting his way to the top against all the odds. Both characters haunt Sylvester Stallone's career, but they haven't stopped him from making other movies.

In the same way that one person's terrorist is another person's freedom fighter, Bill Gates finds himself simultaneously the Cliché of the New Economy nerd and the Icon of the coldhearted monopolist. The prefix *Mc* is a negative Cliché attached to any number of products and ideas (such as McNews, an early pejorative description of *USA Today*). But at the same time, Ronald McDonald House is an Icon of concerned corporate activity.

The chart on the next page demonstrates how elements of the devox can be taken out of their total context, allowing the devox to simultaneously exist as Cliché, Icon, and Archetype.

The list could go on almost forever. As individuals, Keith Richards and Mick Jagger respectively represent the wretched excess of the rock 'n' roll lifestyle and the most Peter Pan–ish aspects of the genre. But these Cliché and Iconic qualities disappear when the two appear as part of the larger Rolling Stones, perhaps the Archetypal rock 'n' roll band. Similarly, Bob Dylan moved from the Cliché of the young folksinger to the Iconic rock 'n' roll songwriter to the Archetype of the rock 'n' roll tunesmith.

Once the devox has reached the Icon stage, it's less often ridiculed, even if it takes on a fundamentally pejorative connotation. Nixonian politics have an Iconic place in our vocabulary separate from the Cliché

THE DEVOX: CLICHÉ, ICON, AND ARCHETYPE

Object/Person	Cliché	Icon	Archetype
Black Leather Jackets	Outerwear of choice for hoodlums and outlaws	Under Polo, Claiborne, and others, the outerwear of choice for teens and young adults	Under Armani and others, haute couture
McDonald's	McMeals (fast, tasteless, bland food)	Hamburg Index in *The Economist* (a definitive measure of global cost of living)	Global foodservice operator (in fact, the only recognized global foodservice operator)
Star Trek Captains	Kevin Sorbo (line extension)	Patrick Stewart (best of class)	William Shatner (the original)
Blue Denim Pants	Baby boomer uniform	Defines American casual trousers	Uniform of global youth

concepts of Tricky Dick, masks with big noses and drooping jowls, and "I am not a crook" jokes. At the Cliché stage the devox becomes a cultural building block. At the Icon stage it becomes a part of the culture. And at the Archetype stage it defines culture. Think of this example: *to xerox* means to copy; *a xerox* refers to any photocopy; but *Xerox* does not define copiers, just copying. Here's another example: *Kleenex* has become an Iconic phrase for a facial tissue, but the brand Kleenex doesn't define facial tissues. Here's one more: Slick Willy was a Cliché version of President Bill Clinton; Clinton himself became an Icon for America's ambivalence toward the political process; but almost nobody we know (today) would claim Bill Clinton was the Archetype of a U.S. president. However, it may be too early to tell. Two hundred years from now—for better or worse—historians may conceivably judge the Clinton presidency as archetypical of third-millennium presidencies.

Let's expand the examples contained in the chart. Black leather jackets are the Clichéd attire of the stereotypical juvenile delinquent, the outlaw biker, and the B-movie street-corner career criminal. At the same time, under the mass-market crafting hands of Ralph Lauren, Perry Ellis, Liz Claiborne, and others, black leather has become just as strongly identified as an Icon of youth culture as has blue denim. And, under Armani and other upscale designers (with an able assist from non-PETA-supporting celebrities) black leather has also become an integral part of the world of haute couture—Samuel L. Jackson's Shaft moved the black leather coat into the Archetype of cool. By the same token, blue denim jeans, the Clichéd uniform of baby boomers, have come to be the Icon of American casual fashion and are now the Archetypal pants of choice for global youth.

The pattern repeats itself over and over again. For some, McDonald's is a Clichéd metaphor for fast, tasteless, over-processed meals. But McDonald's is also so pervasive that no less of a bastion of originality and intellectual erudition as *The Economist* uses the price of a McDonald's hamburger as an Icon, the definitive measure for determining the relative global cost of living. And, love it or hate it, McDonald's is *the* Archetype for global foodservice operators. It is, in fact, at least from the point of view of global consumers, the only global foodservice operator.

The model even holds true for the Starship *Enterprise.* There's no question that William Shatner is the Archetypal *Star Trek* captain. But, by virtue of being a better actor, Patrick Stewart clearly established himself as the Icon of what a *Star Trek* captain ought to be. By the time poor Kevin Sorbo hung up his Hercules gear, it was clear the closest he could come to the *Star Trek* pantheon was as a Cliché of a captain.

In a general sense, the ability to commercially exploit the devox decreases as you move from Cliché to Icon to Archetype. But some businesses have learned to successfully market their Iconic status to great advantage. Harley-Davidson's image has allowed it to charge nearly double the market price for a motorcycle that arguably has significantly poorer general engineering than bikes produced by Honda, Yamaha, or Suzuki. Mercedes-Benz is not just an automobile maker but an Icon of success, so engineering and service are less important to the image of the brand than they would be to even other luxury automakers like BMW and Lexus.

This notion of Iconography can be tricky. Think about products as basic as coffee and doughnuts. First there's Krispy Kreme, a classic example of an enterprise that's learned the marketing power of becoming not just a company that sells doughnuts but an Icon for the idea of doughnuts. It's also a doughnut company trying to break big time into the coffee business. Dunkin' Donuts, on the other hand, is a doughnut company better known for its Iconic coffee. Interestingly, the company seems to have recognized the important role coffee plays in its operation. Earlier this year, Dunkin' Donuts unveiled a new logo that features a steaming cup of coffee. And, finally, Starbucks is an Icon of the too-hip-for-its-own-good lifestyle in the guise of a coffee company that sells Krispy Kreme doughnuts that aren't "Hot Now" or even necessarily fresh.

· There's really nothing quite as good to many a sweet tooth as a hot Krispy Kreme plucked right out of the oil. We've seen obsessed fans camp out for days to be the first to enter a new Krispy Kreme store. And dozens of times we've seen doughnut devotees huddle over a counter studying just which doughnut will be best as it comes out of the fryer. To the pure of heart—and often large of girth—the Krispy Kreme "Hot Now" sign is like the star that guided the Magi across the desert, and taking that first bite of a hot doughnut is the authentic confection version of finding the Holy Grail. But authenticity is perishable, and we've never found anyone who would argue that those doughnuts taste anything like the real deal after they've been sitting on a Starbucks counter for six hours or so. Nevertheless, Starbuck's Iconic status allows them to get away with selling "Cold Always" Krispy Kremes.

Very often an individual can take on an Iconic position that can then be transferred to an enterprise or even across several enterprises. Willy G. Davidson's presence at rallies and runs clearly helped turn around the flagging Harley-Davidson of the late 1970s and early 1980s, and even inspired a fringed style of black leather riding jacket. And Richard Branson's impact on the Virgin brand has been described by author Jesper Kunde this way: "When consumers buy a Virgin product, they are actually buying Richard Branson, and in this way the core of the company becomes Branson's own personal PR company, which links all Virgin products to the man and his multifarious, adventure-oriented and anti-business approach."

But remember, Icons can be positive, negative, or both. We're sure the fine folks at Mattel think of Barbie as a positive model for young girls, but we're not sure the National Organization for Women would share their view.

Businesses trying to manage the devox through the Icon stage need to remember that the real power of an Icon revolves around its symbolism rather than its content. Is Charlton Heston the best leader the National Rifle Association can find? We don't know, but we suspect the image of him as Moses parting the Red Sea is probably more important to the NRA than his administrative skills. There's plenty of money to be made from symbolism and symbology, provided, of course, that one is willing to accept two principles: First, for better or worse, Icons live in the public domain; and, second, one should never confuse symbolic value with actual content. The power of an Icon to overshadow actual content is well known. As James Joyce wrote in *Finnegans Wake,* "Love my label like myself." Given the proven ability of markets to confuse labels and identities, businesses would be well advised to be careful how their Icons are used.

There's no question that Harley-Davidson has used the licensing of its Icon to create an impressive revenue stream. But we worry that the Icon has been applied so ubiquitously (literally from cleaning products to condoms) that it is in danger of lapsing back into Cliché. On the other hand, the fact that author/artist Garry Trudeau has kept an Iconic Hunter Thompson viable in the form of Uncle Duke in the Doonesbury comic strip has no doubt added to the gonzo journalist's legend and marketability. There are also many business examples of Icons combining to reinforce their own individual positions in a market. Consider Eddie Bauer and Ford or McDonald's and Disney.

One final note on the Icon phase. Which aspects of the devox emerge during the Icon phase can have a critical impact on its commercial viability. For example, Harley-Davidson, once the motorcycle of choice among the unwashed outlaw set, has allowed itself to become an Icon of luxury and indulgence for well-heeled, white-collar baby boomers. It's getting to be too much for Harley's initial customer base. In his autobiography, Ralph "Sonny" Barger, the former president of the Oakland, California, chapter of the Hell's Angels and the living Icon of outlaw biking, admitted that if he had to do it all over again, he might do it on a Honda.

ARCHETYPE: THE ULTIMATE TARGET FOR THE DEVIANT

Generally, if the devox reaches the Icon stage, its journey is complete. Admittance to the next stage, Archetype, is open to only a few incarnations of the devox, those that come not to represent an aspect of culture but rather to define cultural standards. Archetypes share five core characteristics:

1. They set the standards for one or more areas of activity.
2. They enjoy true global presence and share common global definition.
3. They have the ability to sustain themselves over a significant length of time.
4. They endure all challenges to their status.
5. In the same way that they set standards, Archetypes define markets.

These requirements are daunting, which helps explain why there aren't a lot of true Archetypes out there. Microsoft Windows is the Archetype of human-computer interface, although it's clear that open-source supporters would like to see a new Archetype take its place. In terms of brands, companies, organizations, and individuals, there are only a handful of true Archetypes, such as Coca-Cola, Rolls-Royce, Adolf Hitler, and the Vatican.

Our latest vote for Archetype is MTV, which forever changed the way music is sold and promoted across the globe. In 1981 Buggles (Trevor Horn on bass and vocals and Geoff Downes on keyboards) earned itself a permanent place in pop cultural history by being the first group to have a music video ("Video Killed the Radio Star") aired by MTV on its inaugural broadcast. The song (contained on Buggles' 1980 album *The Age of Plastic*) had been a pre-album hit in the United Kingdom. In fact—thanks to radio—the single reached number one on the U.K. charts later in 1979. Prophetically, Horn and Downes seemed to have anticipated the perishability of their band, which released only one more album (1982's *Adventures in Modern Recording*) before disbanding. Buggles may be gone, but MTV has never looked back, expanding its network to include MTV Asia, MTV Brazil, MTV China, MTV Europe, MTV Germany, MTV Italy, MTV Latin America, MTV UK/Ireland, and MTV U.S.A., as well as VH1 Germany, VH1 U.K./Ireland, VH1 U.S.A., SonicNet Germany, SonicNet Japan, SonicNet Switzerland, and SonicNet U.S.

Today, thanks to its global presence, MTV has come not just to stand for a media conglomerate, an art form (music video), or even product lines from rock 'n' roll to hip-hop. Instead, it has come to define mainstream popular youth culture at its best and most commercial. It has even come to define global demographic cohorts (the MTV Generation). But more important, perhaps, is the one common thread running through the lives of members of that cohort. They may not all be able to understand the lyrics of songs played on MTV Germany or Japan, but they always understand what they stand for—the essence and celebration of youth.

MTV's commercial success aside, Archetypes at their hearts are more about culture than markets—defining and limiting our understanding of ourselves, our artifacts, and our world. The great irony is that once the devox has reached the Archetype point, it becomes the final standard by which deviancy is judged, the ultimate target for the deviant.

OBLIVION: THE DEVOX COMES FULL CIRCLE

Oblivion is the devox's final potential resting place. In the wired world, it's almost inconceivable that anything actually *disappears* forever. If you don't believe us, take a quick cyber surf over to http://www.trancenet.org/heavensgate, where the slightly dotty and demonstrably dangerous Heaven's Gate philosophy flows on uninterrupted through the ether. That philosophy, you may remember, caused thirty-nine men to commit mass suicide at their communal home in Rancho Santa Fe, near San Diego, so that they could join a spacecraft trailing the Hale-Bopp Comet. Some of the men were later found to have castrated themselves, apparently so they wouldn't be distracted. Presumably every known aberration will have an extended cyber half-life somewhere on the Internet, which apparently makes it possible for deviance of any and all forms to dance across time. So, bear with us here. We're using a bit of poetic license to make the case that the market for the devox is all but immeasurable at the point of Oblivion.

This is the stage that exists past the world of hobbyist, nostalgia-filled group, collector, and/or aficionado. Somewhere out there in the world there may be a demented fashion victim hoarding all those top-less bathing suits that fashion designer Rudi Gernreich attempted to foist off on the public way back in 1964, but we're not holding our breath waiting for the design (replete with suspenders, if memory serves correctly) to make a comeback.

In a very real sense, if and when the devox reaches Oblivion it has come full circle, returning to the authentic domain of the deviant once again. There, it's free to be anything it wants—except, of course, a commercial success. In the next chapter, we will expand our discussion by examining the progress of the devox through several aspects of life, from media to faith and sex to governance, with a focus on how its journey impacts business.

4

The Abolition of Context and the Post-Information Age

The past, present, and future have never been so moshed together. And since the future seems closer, it seems more malleable. The future is the ultimate plastic medium, for us sculptor wannabes. And we're going to hammer the hell out of it.

—St. Jude

It's relatively easy to trace the path of the devox in areas like technology, where an apparently endless stream of innovations keeps making our lives simultaneously simpler and more complex. People lead different lives today than they did fifteen or twenty years ago, thanks to a string of technodeviants from Alan Kay, the "father" of portable computation, to Bill Gates, Steve Jobs, Larry Ellison, Linus Torvalds, and others. No sooner has a deviant idea appeared in the mind of some cyberfringist than it's making paper millions—even billions—for some Social Convention digital capitalist.

Our attention has been so focused on the collapse of the distance between the Fringe and Social Convention for information and communication technologies that we often lose sight of the fact that the devox is working its strange, twisted mojo on every other aspect of our existence from sex and language to art, science, and governance. And that is a dangerous oversight. Potential markets are being created as fast as our understanding of the forces impacting established markets is eroding. The past is no longer prologue, and the pattern of free-market creation, which has held constant across time and cultures, has irrevocably changed. The world of business you woke up to today will be very different from the one you woke up to yesterday or the one you will wake up to tomorrow. As the careening fortunes of the New Economy should have demonstrated, it isn't always easy, or sometimes even possible, to anticipate the degree of day-to-day market fluctuation. However, by understanding and appreciating the essential nature of the devox—the source of all innovation and the cornerstone of all commercial and cultural progress—it's possible to get your bearings and plot a course to profitability. Let's begin by considering five assumptions about the future:

1. Business has always responded to social or cultural cues.

2. We have entered a new age that—for a placeholder—we're calling the Post-Information Age, the culture of which is characterized by constant, relentless, and all-encompassing change.

3. The scope of this change will accelerate over time and will never stabilize.

4. This constant change has resulted in what we call the Abolition of Context, an inability on the part of everyone and every business and society to find commonly agreed-upon reference points. The Abolition of Context impacts all of the significant aspects of our individual and collective lives.

5. On an individual level, the Abolition of Context creates confusion, anxiety, stress, and depression. On a commercial level, it results in inherent difficulty creating appropriate goods, services, and offerings and makes all commercial offerings increasingly perishable.

Economic historian Fernand Braudel has written that "capitalism could only emerge from a certain kind of society, one which had created a favorable environment from far back in time, without being aware in the slightest of the process thus being set in train, or of the processes for which it was preparing the way in future centuries." For most of human history necessity was truly the brother of convention. Social and commercial change enjoyed a deliberately symbiotic relationship.

The commercial world changed for reasons that are clear and—to a greater or lesser degree—even somewhat predictable, principally in the form of scientific discovery or innovation. These changes created market opportunities and, in a broad sense, both mirrored and dictated equally predictable social responses. Even large-scale economic "revolutions" actually represent more or less measured responses to change.

In agrarian societies, the idea of building a machine to do your work was almost as deviant as the concept of abandoning the land your parents and their parents and their parents before them had tilled to move to cities and work inside all day. Direct contact with the land, bringing forth the bounty of the earth, was seen as the most honest of honest labors. People in preindustrial societies based everything in their lives around the planting, cultivation, and harvesting of the crop. The identity of individuals, their place in their societies, and even their relationship with God were defined by their ties to the soil. But slowly, over more than a century, the deviance known to us as the Industrial Revolution changed the way wealth was formed and identity was defined.

This so-called revolution, actually more like the evolutionary result of an aggregate series of commercial and economic responses to a diverse number of scientific breakthroughs and engineering innovations, didn't just happen one day. It can be traced back to 1698, the year Thomas Savery invented a steam-driven pump to remove water from mine shafts. (Some historians prefer to trace it back to 1701, when Jethro Tull—the man, not the rock band—invented the seed drill, simultaneously freeing up farm labor and lowering crop prices.) The steam engine ambled on the scene sixty-seven years later in 1765, thanks to James Watt. And it took Richard Trevithick another thirty-six years to build a demonstrable steam-powered locomotive.

The societal reaction to the commercial and social changes associated with the devox's championing of industrialization took a century to fully manifest itself in the form of the Luddites. The proto-Unabombers of their day, the Luddites, launched a five-year protest against the economic impacts of technology on everyday life. Mills were burned and eventually dozens of people lost their lives. Henry Ford's moving automotive assembly line—which arguably made work inhuman and clearly transformed life—was still a comfortable 102 years away. Hardly revolutionary for most of its effective life, the Industrial Age lumbered along literally for centuries, a sometimes beloved and other times despised socioeconomic fixture for fifteen human generations—a fairly long and stable run, if you think about it.

WELCOME TO THE POST-INFORMATION AGE

The emergence of the Information Age followed a similar pattern. Consider how the devox subtly began to reshape its twin core pillars—computation and telephony. It took 157 years to move from Charles Babbage's analytical engine (1834), the forerunner of today's computer, to the launching of the World Wide Web (1991). Alexander Graham Bell invented the telephone in 1876. IBM switched to fully transistorized (as opposed to vacuum tube) computers in 1954. Sputnik, the first artificial satellite, was launched in 1957. Nobel Laureate Jack St. Clair Kilby invented the microchip at Texas Instruments in 1958. MIT's Leonard Kleinrock wrote the first paper on packet-switching theory ("Information Flow in Large Communication Nets") in 1961. The first ARPANET connections (which were conceived as a method for facilitating communications between military facilities but were quickly adopted as a system to link up computers at academic institutions) were made eight years later, and the Domain Name System (DNS) was introduced in 1984.

While it took until 1989 for the first commercial services to emerge on the ARPANET (CompuServe through Ohio State University, MCI Mail, and the National Research Initiative), Queen Elizabeth II (hardly the poster girl for technological progress) had sent an e-mail way back in 1976. The fact is, the Information Age had had a wild and woolly history long before the ARPANET was formally decommissioned (February 28, 1990) or the World Wide Web was launched. And at each step of that history markets were established and offerings were created.

The devox—in the guise of the thousands of men and women who refused to take conventional reality for an answer—gradually changed the face of not just technology, but society. As in the case of the Industrial Revolution, most of us went to sleep contented with our now quaint acceptance of Federal Express's idea of what priority looked like or a deskbound definition of when work started and stopped and woke up to information overload and "24/7" connectivity. The Information Age, which had taken better than a century for the devox to birth, hit us with the full force of a collective unplanned, and often unwanted, pregnancy.

Most people's immediate responses to the arrival and impact of the Information Age were generally confined to gripes about computerized billing until the overnight intrusion of fax machines, cell phones, and personal computers in our lives and workspaces. Even Theodore Kaczynski's "Unabomber Manifesto" ("Industrial Society and Its Future") identified the Industrial Revolution rather than the advent of the Information Age as the cause of "a disaster for the human race." As in the case of the Industrial Age, it took society and business more than a century to find an agreed-upon social context or defining framework that could encompass the changes associated with computation and communication. The birth of the Atomic Age in 1945 made it clear that forces we couldn't see (like atoms) were more powerful than those that were visible. The universe, or at least our role in it, was being redefined not just by scientists but by everyone. Science was king, but nobody could define where the borders of the kingdom started or stopped.

We know that it is still fashionable to speak as though we were just entering the really important part of the Information Age, but fashion once again proves as superficial as it is perishable. It's closer to the truth to say we've left the Information Age—psychically, socially, and economically—light-years behind. The Post-Information Age is an era without an empirically perceived, traditionally agreed-upon, or commonly affirmed social context. It is a "present" lacking definition leading to a future that is being constructed using the architectures of uncertainty. The following chart illustrates some of the differences separating the Industrial, Information, and Post-Information Ages.

AN OUTLINE OF THE POST-INFORMATION AGE

	Industrial Age	Information Age	Post-Information Age
Years	1698–1990	1991–2000	2001–?
Dominant Science	Chemistry	Physics	Biology
Dominant Technology	Production • Metallurgy • Engineering • Thermodynamics	Communication • Computation • Telephony • Data storage	Creation • Biotechnology • Sentient software
Reality Proof Source	Tangible goods	Speed and clarity of data transfer	The ability to translate data points into information
Big Questions	How many? How cheap?	How much? How fast?	Why? What?
Media Concern	What happened?	Who's happening?	What will happen?

A PATTERN OF CONSTANT AND RELENTLESS CHANGE

Not only has the pace of change increased, but the distance between the Fringe and Social Convention has been radically truncated. The convergence of this acceleration and compression of time and space—which characterize the Post-Information Age—has created a condition we call the Abolition of Context. Context describes both the collectively defined socioeconomic ecosystem and the rules that define it.

Context is the framework, the structure, the collective common understanding that allows us to live our lives and run our businesses. Take it away and it's all but impossible to know what's the right or wrong action to take. Were you prudent or foolish not to buy New Economy stocks after the NASDAQ crash? Is biotechnology going to define the future of life and business or just make a bunch of patent lawyers rich? Should you invest in the latest new technology, or will it be obsolete before you unpack it? And if you decide to cast your personal fate with an Old Economy company, will you lose your job when it's merged or acquired, or acquires another company?

Even the slickest trend watchers can't keep up. As Todd Cunningham, MTV's senior vice president of strategy and planning, noted on a segment of the PBS show *Frontline* called "The Merchants of Cool," "Today we definitely see the span of time shortened between when a trend is a fad, when it becomes a trend, and then when it becomes mainstream. It's compressed in a really big way." The impact of this convergence cuts through smug cyberchic cliché. Douglas Rushkoff, in his book *Cyberia: Life in the Trenches of Hyperspace,* observed that "in Cyberia at least, reality is directly dependent on our ability to actively participate in its creation. Designer reality must be interactive rather than passive."

Way back in 1993, at what would become the twilight of the Information Age, covert mediaista author Richard Kadrey wrote:

> Nothing interesting ever happens at the center. Everything interesting is out at the edges. . . . Beats, Hippies, Punks—they were the extremists, the monsters, the dangerous edge against which the rest of the culture was judged. But time moves on and the range of acceptable culture has expanded to include these earlier aberrants drawing them toward the center. Punk is now an automobile marketing scheme. William Burroughs is a Gap ad. Jerry Rubin gave up fighting cops to fight cholesterol on his Stair Master. . . . The answer is simple: *there is no edge.* There never really has been. Or rather, there are a thousand edges, at a thousand different angles to each other. . . . The new monsters—zine

publishers, renegade video artists, underground sysops, fashion mob-
sters—have always been there, but they couldn't make themselves
heard over the noise of network TV, MOR radio and glossy magazines.
Now anyone with a computer and a printer can be her or his own magazine, computer bulletin board or recording studio.

Kadrey's argument is directionally right, but it illustrates some of
the problems less avant-garde observers have when they approach the
devox. He saw the Beats, the punks, and others as "the extremists, the
monsters, the dangerous edge," but the truth was these groups had
already migrated to Social Convention. Movements—whether Beat or
punk or born-again Christian—require a noticeable number of members and a public awareness and recognition based on adherence to certain conventions, whether dress codes, hair length, or behavioral. The
Beats, for example, were initially not a movement but just a few
sociopaths (Jack Kerouac, William Burroughs, and Allen Ginsberg and
their immediate drinking buddies and/or sex partners, such as Lucien
Carr, John Clellon Holmes, Herbert Huncke, et al.). By the time the
Beats (as in the movement) had moved from the Realm of the Cool to
the Next Big Thing, they were being satirized by *Mad* magazine and
that bastion of 1960s video veniality, *The Many Loves of Dobie Gillis*,
the 1959–1963 TV sitcom that featured a beatnik, Maynard G. (for
Walter) Krebs, as a regular character. Meanwhile, the Beats (as in the
sociopaths) had all but disbanded. Burroughs was living out of the
country. Kerouac was falling deeper and deeper into an oedipal alco-
holic fog from which he would occasionally emerge to denounce Jews,
gays, and commies. Ginsberg was marketing himself as poetry's answer
to a rock star. And long before he had his Gap ad, Burroughs (and the
master French deviant writer Jean Genet) had covered the 1968 Democratic Convention for *Esquire* magazine, hardly the ripping edge of
journalism even thirty-plus years ago.

The truth is Kadrey just hadn't looked far enough. The real monsters live on the Fringe, not the Edge. He really shouldn't be criticized
for this. It's easy to confuse the faux Edge with what we call the Fringe.

After all, on the Fringe, and even many times on the Edge, there is no audience to appreciate the weirdness. But Kadrey is right about one thing: It takes the devox a lot less time to cross over from the Fringe and penetrate the heart of Social Convention today than it once did.

It might have been hard for Kadrey to imagine just how rapidly time would accelerate and the distance from the Fringe to the center would compress to the point where we'd all end up living through a nonstop series of social and commercial implosions. Today when we discuss individual time starvation or examine corporate races to be first to market we increasingly see that the body of Social Convention is missing the skeleton of collective meaning.

Two years after Kadrey's observations the heat was being turned up. Responding to an atmosphere of constant change, Danny Hillis, former vice president of research and development at Walt Disney Imagineering, cofounder of the Long Now Foundation, and cochairman and CTO of Applied Minds, Inc., has suggested that we have reached a point where even our fundamental understanding of the universe is in chronic need of redefinition. We are approaching life on wholly new and largely unexplored terms. As Hillis expressed it: "We're analogous to the single-celled organisms when they were turning into multicellular organisms. We're the amoebas, and we can't quite figure out what the hell this thing is that we're creating. We're right at that point of transition, and there's something coming along after us."

That "something," we'd argue, is the Post-Information Age and its characteristic lack of reference points. What Hillis, Kadrey, Cunningham, and Rushkoff are describing are aspects of the Post-Information Age. The gap separating the Post-Information Age and the age that preceded it is so wide that we are hard pressed to find words adequate to explain it. This is an age defined by the devox's relentless attacks on conventional understanding, attacks that prohibit us from finding individual, social, cultural, or commercial footholds.

No sooner do we master one "optimum" version of Windows than it becomes obsolete. We finally figure out how to fully optimize our phones only to discover that the newest phones on the market have features and functions, such as wireless connection to the Internet, that were literally the stuff of science fiction when most of you reading this paragraph were younger. And just as the last baby boomer finally masters Graffiti, we're sure PDAs will be routinely marketed with effective voice recognition software. Thanks to the devox, the citizens of the so-called Industrialized World exhibit a range of behaviors from techno-angst to techno-lust inspired by our inability to stabilize our sense of where technology stops (or should stop) and where we begin.

The pace of change has increased exponentially to the point that it's now autocatalytic. Change is literally feeding itself and taking on a life of its own, a life beyond limits or controls. We believe that only a broad global disaster—natural or man-made—can slow its progress. The terrorist attacks on the World Trade Center and the Pentagon on September 11, 2001, weren't enough to slow the pace of change. On the other hand, a long, prolonged, full-scale war on terrorism, accompanied by an anticipated restriction on freedom of communication and mobility and consistent, senseless acts of disruption might, over time, have the same effect as a multinational epidemic or global warming. And, since this is the case, we can only speculate that a change of such magnitude would, in and of itself, launch society and business further into chaos, at the very least altering the direction of change and perhaps even accelerating it in an essentially negative direction.

THE IMPACT OF THE ABOLITION OF CONTEXT

The Abolition of Context touches every private and public aspect of our individual and collective existence. As we will demonstrate in the following chapters, precious little in our lives offers us significant, constant reference points. Even those things that we believe we know end up pointing not to the road ahead, but rather leading us to a series of dangerous detours. By nature we are creatures of habit, rule, order, and law. Disrupt any of those static, constant aspects of our lives, as the devox does by its very nature, and you produce anxiety and stress. Disrupt them all—especially over prolonged periods of time—and you run the risk of inducing individual and social paralysis. Absent a collective context, people begin to fashion minicontexts of their own. The devox's disruption begins to produce an iterative, autocatalytic effect—not only is the commonly accepted reality eroded, but it's replaced by an exponentially changing series of realities. In the same way that adherence to convention built social order, so the devox nurtures higher and higher levels of deviance.

IBM defined computing, only to have its world redefined by Apple and Microsoft. Microsoft clawed its way to the top of the high-technology world just in time to essentially miss the importance of the Internet. And the Internet is about to be transformed, in turn, thanks to broadband connectivity. We routinely do things on our cell phones that most people could barely imagine little more than a decade ago. In 1990 no businesses had websites. Five years later everyone had a website and New Economy stocks were trading at what many believed were obscene levels. Today, the phrase "dot-bomb" is the cliché of choice for describing how those businesses and tens of billions of dollars came and went.

There are numerous examples of how the Abolition of Context feeds itself, but we've settled for one we hope is easily understood. Think of war. World War I redefined what war looked like, how it was fought, its scale, and even what kinds of weapons were used. The trenches, the mustard gas, and the intervention of American troops to resolve what a decade before would have been seen as a European conflict all abolished the historical rules of military engagement. The French responded to the new reality by building the Maginot Line, which may or may not have worked had people been content to fight from trenches. Which, of course, they weren't.

Two decades after the Armistice, airpower, not trenches, defined war. Those rigidly fixed fortifications simply served as great targets. World War II brought with it entirely new rules of war. Rather than use civilians as conscripts to fight, the German and Russian governments opted to murder them by the millions. While no one will ever know for sure, at least 16 million civilians died during the war—noncombatants slaughtered by their own governments. In 1945 the context of war as we had come to know it again was abolished when we dropped the atomic bombs. Suddenly ground troops became almost obsolete. A single atomic weapon could do more damage than battalions of combat troops.

Once war had been decisively redefined, the Abolition of Context took a turn few could have predicted. The most potent weapon in history proved too potent and was semiretired. With a twist of logic only the devox could explain, the nations of the world began assembling huge arsenals of weapons they had agreed never to use while continuing to fight conventional wars in Korea, Vietnam, Bosnia, and the former Soviet Union, as well as across sub-Saharan Africa and other parts of the world. War, which had been defined as a global activity, suddenly became almost tribal. Today, of course, even that context has been abolished. As we write this, the United States and its allies find themselves fighting a war not against nations, but against a series of private citizens. The threat is not that a government will use an atomic weapon on a civilian population, but rather that the civilian population might use atomic weaponry on a government.

It took a century for the successive Abolition of Context of war. We'll revisit this topic in greater depth in Chapter 9. For now, just remember that the changes affecting your world and your business aren't going to wait a hundred years.

MARKETING IN MINDSPACE

The existence of mass markets is the linchpin of our commercial universe. Sure, we're fond of notions like one-to-one marketing, viral marketing, markets of one, subsegmentation, and target markets, but the ability to touch and manipulate markets at scale is essential to our economic well-being. Rhetoric aside, it's just not practical or profitable to actually customize each product or service to every possible mood of every possible customer.

Just as the Abolition of Context creates stress at an individual level, it erodes margins and destroys profits on the commercial plane. It's hard enough to address an increasingly sophisticated, jaded, and suspicious customer, let alone try to determine if your reality matches theirs. How can you possibly meet or anticipate markets you don't or—worse—can't recognize?

Some of you may think we're overstating the case here, which is why we've decided to spend the next five chapters examining a variety of issues, from sex to language, to see exactly how they've been impacted by the devox and how, as a direct result, the things we thought we knew about them no longer apply.

PART TWO

DEVIANCE IN LIFE

We're about to embark on a voyage through waters usually never disturbed by business books. To illustrate exactly how important it is to see how the devox moves, we're going to examine the impact of deviant thinking and the Abolition of Context on areas as diverse as sex, language, art, science, faith, and war.

Why take this approach? First, because it is important to understand that everything around us from the most fundamental instincts to the most esoteric expressions of our aspirations has changed, and those changes represent market opportunity. On a slightly more pragmatic level, think of it this way. Sex is one of the most effective baits in the history of commerce. Language controls the creation and expression of the pitch. Art—from package graphics to advertising—has been used to attract and retain consumers. And science is where business has turned for well over 100 years for its supply of new products and innovations. If any of these things change and you're not aware of when or how, you'll find yourself at a competitive disadvantage.

In Chapter 5, we begin our analysis with sex. We'll see how markets are being formed around ideas as diverse as celibacy, born-again virginity, concealment, and multiple (as in more than two) genders. We'll also see why any product from Palm Pilots to LEGOS can be sexualized.

In Chapter 6 we'll focus on the disintegration of conventional language and the emergence of linguistic forms—from street argot to high art—based on the absence of precise linguistic meaning. We think this is important ground for anyone making a product claim, advertising, or selling things to or employing human beings. Language is the glue that holds society and commerce together. Without it—or more precisely, without a standardized version of it— business just gets very complicated.

Chapter 7 examines art with an eye toward nontraditional artistic expressions ranging from rabbits that glow in the dark to festivals in the desert. The bottom line here is that symbolic manipulation is going in wild new directions, each with the potential to open new markets.

Our look at science in Chapter 8 explores concepts as diverse as gene sequencing and sentient software. Science is becoming increasingly creative, but we're not sure too many people outside the biotech industries are paying enough attention.

Chapter 9 examines the Abolition of Context in areas such as media, religion, and war.

The point of these chapters is not to be exhaustive, but rather to provide an intellectual tasting menu that allows you to sample exactly how strange the world you live in is becoming. There are no protected spaces. Nobody is allowed to call time-out. It's all happening all around you. Your only hope is to remain open to, and aware of, the possibilities.

5

Schwinns to Cyberspace:
Sex and the Path of the Devox

We have conquered otherness with difference, and, in its turn,
difference has succumbed to the logic of the same and of
indifference. We have conquered otherness with alienation (the
subject becomes its own other), but alienation has, in its turn,
succumbed to identity logic (the subject becomes the same as itself).
And we have entered the interactive, sidereal era of boredom.

— JEAN BAUDRILLARD

Since changes in business mirror or follow changes in the human and
social conditions, it is critical to understand how the devox manifests itself in our lives and in society. There is a direct link between the
Abolition of Context in areas ranging from sexuality, art, and language
to belief systems, war, and governance and threats and/or opportunities
for third-millennium business.

We'll start with sex, the cosmic common denominator. Historically,
sex has been nearly universally acknowledged as the world's most effective marketing tool, with good reason. The relationship between technological innovation and changes in our attitudes toward sex has been
well documented. Sex therapist Marty Klein, Ph.D., has observed, "In
every era, new technologies are always adapted to sexual uses." Pottery,
Klein argues, provided a new medium for pornography. Cars naturally

led to having sex in cars; VCRs made it possible to view porn films in the comfort of your own den; telephones gave us phone sex; photography, like pottery, gave pornography a boost; vulcanization empowered the condom industry; hormone research led to oral contraception; and, of course, the Internet made cybersex possible (and apparently profitable).

In fairness, Klein, like Freud, tends to see sex everywhere. He speculates, for instance, that there is a libidinal linkage between the invention of the bicycle and a marked increase in lustful activity in the United States. "Before the bicycle was invented," he wrote, "the average American woman had to wear an average of 37 pounds of clothes just to go out of the house. Once women started to ride bicycles, this wasn't practical anymore, and within two years, women were wearing less than half that amount to go out. Imagine the change that must have been in people's lives." That change, of course, is nothing compared with what's happening today.

It used to be that sexual deviance existed on the Fringe and was diluted on its way to the center. Today even the most conventional objects are being sexualized on the Fringe. How, for example, could those innocent Danes have ever anticipated that the term *sex toy* would take on a whole new meaning when LEGO Porn became available on the Internet (at http://drew.corrupt.net/lp)?

On the other end of the spectrum, while the Born-Again Virgins of America (BAVAM) website (www.sexless.com) has been inactive since July 1, 1999, True Love Waits (http://www.lifeway.com/tlw/index.asp) boasts that "more than a million students have pledged: 'Believing that true love waits, I make a commitment to God, myself, my family, my friends, my future mate, and my future children to be sexually abstinent from this day until the day I enter a biblical marriage relationship.' "

You might question the numbers, but it's clear that somewhere between the inactive Born-Again Virgins and the millions of breathless Americans in True Love's Waiting Room (although the presence of the latter could help explain why the former is increasingly less needed), chastity and celibacy are making a bit of a comeback. Just look at the popularity of books like Elizabeth Abbott's *A History of Celibacy*. There are also those who seriously and passionately argue that sexual activity today and—perhaps far more importantly—tomorrow has moved and will continue to move past the limitations of the biologically defined two-gender model of human sexuality.

In 1993 Anne Fausto-Sterling advanced a model for a five-sex system: males, females, "herms" (true hermaphrodites, i.e., people born with both a testis and an ovary), "merms" (male pseudohermaphrodites born with testes and some aspect of female genitalia), and "ferms" (female pseudohermaphrodites born with ovaries and some aspect of male genitalia). Revisiting her thesis in the July–August 2000 issue of the *Sciences,* Fausto-Sterling admitted, "I had intended to be provocative, but I had also written with tongue firmly in cheek"; but then she went on to add, "One should acknowledge that people come in an even wider assortment of sexual identities and characteristics than mere genitals can distinguish." Exactly how wide an assortment may be just about impossible for even the most prescient marketer to predict.

Consider this quote from cyberculturalist Chris Hables Gray: "But to each their own. After all, there is a virtual space called FuzzyMoo where all the avatars are cute, cuddly little animals with sexual fetishes, like foxes who lust for hamsters, and the like. If the present is confusing, the future will be more so." And how! Just ponder this observation by extropian artist, writer, and speaker Natasha Vita-More, who told the EXTRO 3, the Extropy Institute's third conference, held August 9–10, 1997, in San Jose:

We may become as excited about creating new types of sex as much as "*doing it.*" We may creatively automorph ourselves by actively changing our own psychology and physiology. The new sexual landscapes will bring about different types of sexuality, different types of genders. Put an artist at a drawing board and he may design new types of genitals that attach like replaceable parts, or at least move them around a bit (clitoral relocation) so they are better positioned, or not so vulnerable (internal testicles). Put an inventor to the test and she may come up with new devices to activate arousal and orgasm such as simulated orgasm for learning, mental stimulation, energy or relaxation. . . . In society today there are bisexuals, transsexuals, homosexuals, asexuals and intersexuals. Soon there will be negsexuals, solosexuals, technosexuals, postsexuals, multisexuals, Vrsexuals or even just plain ole' sexuals who remain nostalgic of the 20th century. . . . The possibility is that we might have as many genders as colors in the rainbow or as many types of genitalia as patterns of flowers.

And you thought it was tough keeping up with the Ozzie and Harriet Meets the Sexual Revolution . . . Meets the women's movement . . . Meets gay liberation . . . Meets herpes, AIDS, and other assorted STDs (sexually transmitted diseases) . . . Meets the new celibacy . . . Meets intersexuals . . . Meets the Moral Majority and safe sex! It's clear the devox has been busy, but where exactly is the market opportunity underneath all this gender bending and sexual redefinition?

AIRBRUSHED MADONNAS AND FULL-FRONTAL MARKETING

The core of this book is the idea that the devox moves (at ever increasing rates of speed) from areas nominally defined as deviant or Fringe to Social Convention. In the case of sexuality, free love (how quaint a phrase that now seems) has moved from the Fringe (prostitutes and libertines) to baby-boomer lifestyle. At the same time, celibacy—which in the Agrarian and Industrial Ages was deviant simply by virtue of being a marginalized behavior largely confined to monks and other religious folk—is enjoying a mini Renaissance in the Post-Information Age.

It's no longer PC to speak in terms of husbands and wives. Instead we speak of partners and friends. We are routinely asked to speak at business meetings where the registration materials request "Travel Companion Information," assuming, we suppose, the possibility of relationships even more tenuous than those of partners or friends. Yesterday's "deviant" behavior—traveling (and therefore presumably sleeping) with someone other than your spouse—has become so routine today that it's dealt with not as a whispered scandal, as it would have been even twenty-five years ago, but by preprinted form.

Think about the rapid evolution of pornography. It wasn't all that long ago (in a historical sense at least) that French postcards were considered so obscene they were traded with the same cunning and high secrecy we currently associate with Mark McGwire rookie baseball trading cards.

When Hugh Hefner started *Playboy* in 1953 he was viewed by the center of Social Convention at best as an Edge-dwelling pornographer. The first issue of *Playboy* was released in December 1953 without a date because Hefner wasn't sure when—or if—he'd release another edition. He shouldn't have worried. That initial issue sold more than fifty thousand copies. Today the magazine enjoys a circulation of nearly 9 million. But even though one could argue that Hefner drove the devox from the Edge to Social Convention, the delivered product somehow ended up bearing a closer relationship to his direct (genetic rather than philosophical) ancestors—Puritan leaders William Bradford and John Winthrop—than to the efforts of *Hustler* publisher Larry Flynt or Persian Kitty, an Internet porn portal.

Hef's airbrushed, naughty Madonnas or the silhouette of the Playboy Bunny can't hold a candle (or any similarly Freudian object) to the full-penetration fare routinely found at airports and newsstands across America. You won't find reality (assuming you define reality as *Hustler*'s out-of-shape, stretch-marked Girls Next Door) in the pages of *Playboy.* In an age when a fleeting glimpse of the side of Angelina Jolie's left breast isn't enough to lose *Tomb Raider* its PG-13 rating, *Playboy* seems, well, a bit naive in a sort of retro-chauvinistic way.

What's being sold here isn't sex—in its rawest, most biologically graphic sense—or even sexual fantasies in their most polymorphously perverse form. The product isn't really pornography. Rather, it's one man's terminally adolescent, almost innocently obsessive vision of the idealized woman. Ironically, *Playboy*—which innovated the mass-market "skin book" and was the first national magazine on the World Wide Web, in 1994—doesn't even come close to capturing its fair share of the $1 billion pornography market it helped create. So much for prime-mover, first-to-market advantage.

"I CAN'T COME TO MARKET— I'M TOO TIED UP"

As we begin our discussion of the Abolition of Sexual Context, it may be helpful to think of the word *context* as a sort of cultural GPS (global positioning system) that allows individuals to instantly understand the boundaries separating what is, and is not, acceptable. When it comes to sex, it seems that yesterday's deviance is today's lifestyle preference, generally complete with its own website(s) and very vocal advocacy groups. What you used to have to visit an asylum to witness is being routinely marketed daily on Jerry Springer's show and the Internet.

Everything from child pornography to panel discussions by incest practitioners is readily available to any regular television channel or Web browser. We're witnessing the commoditization of desire—sexual images offered free with any offer to purchase. As Kalle Lasn, publisher of *Adbusters* magazine and founder of the Adbusters Media Foundation and the Powershift advertising agency, notes:

> TV sexuality is a campaign of disinformation, much like TV news. . . . Growing up in an erotically charged media environment alters the very foundations of our personalities. I think it distorts our sexuality. . . . I think the constant flow of commercially scripted pseudosex, rape and pornography makes us more voyeuristic. . . . The commercial media are to the mental environment what factories are to the physical environment. . . . A TV or radio station "pollutes" the cultural environment because that's the most efficient way to produce audiences. It pays to pollute. The psychic fallout is just the cost of putting on the show.

Whether Lasn is fully correct or not—and he readily admits he has no hard facts to back up his claim—or whether the psychic fallout (his words) or the Abolition of Context (ours) is the fault of a vast media conspiracy to exploit sex in order to sell more oatmeal and Buicks, the fact remains that there is no commonly agreed-upon conventional sexual context. Perhaps better said, we are awash in a sensual sea of sexual contexts from the biblical blinders of the Moral Majority to the whatever-you're-into-is-cool-with-us vibe of the live fetish and bondage shows staged at venues such as Detroit's Noir Leather. And no matter whose view seems to win out, for a moment or two that cultural GPS system we referenced earlier is overloaded and sending us off in a hundred different directions at once.

PALM PORN AND BONDAGE BARBIES

So where does all this leave the poor business community? Sex has been the secret weapon in most marketing plans since the first cave people smeared a little mastodon musk on themselves to get a better price for their new and improved chipped-flint arrowheads. We're not saying that sex is going away as either a product or a product enhancement. But we are saying that mass-mediated, one-stroke-fits-all sexuality may have reached the effective end of its life cycle.

After all, we live in a society where people confess their deepest, darkest sexual secrets to total strangers and then sign releases to have those secrets broadcast nationally over cable television (HBO's *Taxicab Confessions*), and download grainy pornography onto their phones and PDAs. For the uninitiated, Palm Porn is available from a variety of companies, including the U.S.-based PalmStories.com, Erotigo.com, and SinPalm, and at least forty European-based WAP sites such as Eurowap.com, XXXwap.net, and Sexyamateur.com. Despite the fact that their product looks, in the estimation of one amateur critic, "like Picasso's gray period," wireless porn's promoters believe it will grow, becoming more user-friendly as technology advances. Who knows?

Perhaps one day—thanks to products like Eruptor Entertainment's (www.eruptor.com) PortaPam (a game where players "manage" Pamela Anderson's career)—PDA may stand for privately displayed aberrations rather than personal digital assistant.

Given the success of the devox in abolishing sexual context, it's increasingly hard to find a niche that hasn't already been commercially exploited. Just look at the number of online erotic greeting card sites, from www.kinkycards.com (for the leather and latex set) to more conventional gay greeting cards (www.condomcards.com, www.ourfrenz. com, etc.).

Based on what's happening, some people may think it's (officially) high time for Bondage Barbie or Lever 2001—the soap that cleans that secret body part that only you know. We can't say, other than to note that what was banned from the movies when most of you reading this book were children is now routinely seen on network television. The bottom line: Good old-fashioned, plain-vanilla sexuality will have its place in marketing—right next to the whips, restraints, and small mammals.

CONCEALMENT AND OTHER THIRD-MILLENNIUM BUSINESS OPPORTUNITIES

The Abolition of Context is only a barrier to companies pursuing a traditional approach to business. For companies prepared to reconsider their go-to-market strategies—or to completely redefine their fundamental understanding of what their market is—new contexts mean new opportunities. All that's required is a rethinking of the offering. Sex used to hide discreetly, provocatively, or wantonly in the shadows of polite society. Today it's part of the infrastructure of public life, illuminated by floodlights and displayed center stage in every available form of popular media. Androgyny permeates MTV, and modified bondage wear is available to suburban preteens and teens at mall shops across America like Hot Topic.

Our sense of appropriate sexual context has moved from obsession with sex (the act) to obsession with sexuality (the expression and meaning of the act to an individual) to sexual fulfillment (the perfection or extension of the act). Pharmaceutical giant Pfizer offers a case study on how to capitalize on changes in context.

Sex has always been viewed as the purview of the young. Previous generations accepted a loss of sexual interest or performance as a normal consequence of aging. However, the significant extension of the average life span and the Abolition of Context of the traditional view of aging have sexualized old age. Parents are now not just worried about the sexual behavior of their children; they're also often just as concerned about the sexual behavior of their parents. Pfizer recognized that older consumers represented a huge market opportunity. Its answer was Viagra, the little blue pill that moved erectile dysfunction from an unspoken shame to a topic of Super Bowl advertising. Pfizer estimates that roughly half of all American men aged forty to seventy suffer from some form of erectile dysfunction. Pfizer has sold well over 300 million Viagra tablets to more than 10 million men in more than a hundred countries. In the year 2000 sales of the drug increased 32 percent to $1.3 billion. Just think what sales would be if they zeroed in on the seventy-and-over market.

The idea of a sexually renewed aging male population only solves half the problem. Many postmenopausal women report a pronounced decrease in sex drive. Enter Procter & Gamble, whose new testosterone patch, Intrinsa (currently in product development), is being touted as a simple restorative for postmenopausal libidos. The nearly transparent patch, which is about the size of an egg, is worn just below the navel and changed twice a week. P&G faces stiff competition from other drugmakers that are currently testing alternative therapies, including battery-operated devices, pills, creams, and other patches.

Intrinsa and Viagra represent two of the product opportunities created by the Abolition of Context, but they aren't the only ones. While it wouldn't have made too much sense in the last few years to launch a *Playboy*-style magazine with its airbrushed bodies shot through gauze filters, new offerings like *Maxim* made a good deal of commercial sense.

Playboy's look-but-don't-touch-anyone (besides yourself) ethos has given way to a new context that assumes that not only will men be touching women but that they can be taught (in fairly explicit detail) how to touch them more effectively. In order to take full advantage of the Abolition of Sexual Context, you need to rethink your assumptions about what's sexy and how sex can be commercially exploited.

In an era during which sexuality is routinely and publicly explored in clinical detail, never underestimate the business potential of concealment. For most people, leaving a little to the imagination may be more attractive than baring all. Covering up (a little) is what launched Frederick's of Hollywood. Refining that formula by toning down the offering, restaging the sales environment, and making sexy chic and sophisticated instead of common and semitrashy was the key to the success of Victoria's Secret. Today Victoria's Secret rates its own television specials; its models are celebrities in their own right; and its catalogs are the pornography of choice for postpubescent males. Sales, by the way, have never been better. Victoria's Secret total net sales in 2000 were $3.3 billion, and the brand commands a 16 percent share of the U.S. lingerie market. Cleverly, Victoria's Secret keeps pushing the envelope. The flight of commercials that began to air in prime time during 2001 for its "Very Sexy" Miracle Bra featured content that would have been barred in regular programming just a few years ago.

Perhaps not unexpectedly in an era of widespread sexually transmitted diseases and easily accessible sexual eye candy, the market for voyeurism (video and otherwise) is well established. This helps explain the popularity of topless bars, Jerry Springer, and Howard Stern and the fact that Internet pornographers were about the only businesses to make any money in the early days of the World Wide Web. Given the Abolition of Context, the subjects of voyeurism apparently need to be exponentially weirder than their predecessors. We've moved from the era of sex as forbidden fruit to the age of the forbidden fruit salad. In the now tame days of fan dancers and striptease artists such as Sally Rand and Gypsy Rose Lee, a flash of flesh was enough to set voyeuristic hearts aflutter. Today voyeurism seems to actively center on what you can't see or hear.

Millions of Americans routinely channel surf over to the E! network to watch Howard Stern order a series of hapless women into taking off their clothes to be rated by a series of variously physically, mentally, or psychologically dysfunctional men or bombard female celebrities with questions ranging from the penis size of their former lovers to their considered opinion of, and experience with, anal sex. When accommodating noncelebrity guests agree to disrobe, their key body parts are obscured by pixels. Stern is, of course, relatively calm compared to Jerry Springer, whose "guests" routinely describe their involvement with various and sundry dysfunctional sexual activities up to and including incest in great detail. Unfortunately (or fortunately), those discussions are usually little more than a series of censored bleeps. So we have salacious visuals that can't be seen and provocative sexual conversations that can't be heard. Some voyeurism!

While we're at it, the market for confession exists as an underexploited dialectic to the market for voyeurism. Some people want to do; some people want to watch; but a lot of people seem to want to confess. Penitent souls or those trying to get a better understanding of the sexual psyche might want to visit such nondenominational cyber-confessional websites as http://yourconfessions.homestead.com/index~ns$.html, http://www.myconfessional.com/, http://www.ulc.net/confession.htm, and http://www.beforgiven.com.

Sexuality may be the prototypical example of what happens when the devox's impact abolishes traditional context. No matter how old you are, we guarantee that the rules of acceptable sexual practice have changed significantly in your lifetime. And we can also agree that they will continue to change—and even more rapidly. But this isn't the only example of how we're impacted by the Abolition of Context. If sex is how global business has traditionally sold its products, language—the topic of the next chapter—is what it has historically used to close the deal.

6

Words Without Meaning

Where would we be without language? It has made us what we are. It alone can show us the sovereign moment at the farthest point of being where it can no longer act as currency. In the end the articulate man confesses his own impotence. Language does not exist independently of the play of taboo and transgression.

—GEORGES BATAILLE

There are people on the Fringe who speak or invent their own language. The devox of language moves from the Fringe to the Edge when that language is adopted by a small group (usually in the context of street culture). Eventually, the language of street culture becomes more widely known and the devox moves into the Realm of the Cool. Often at this point newspapers and magazines begin running articles explaining the new language to the mass market. If the language survives it begins being picked up by scriptwriters and celebrities and eventually the devox moves into the Next Big Thing. At this point, more and more people begin adopting it until one day the language of the devox is the stuff of Social Convention. "Cool," as in Realm of the Cool, is a classic example of this process.

In his novel *City of Glass,* Paul Auster created a dialogue between two characters, Peter Stillman Sr. and Daniel Quinn, in which Stillman explains that he's in the process of inventing a new language, one that will at least say what we have to say. For our words no longer correspond to the world. When things were whole, we felt confident that our words could express them. But little by little these things have broken apart, shattered, collapsed into chaos. And yet, our words have remained the same. They have not adapted themselves to the new reality. Hence, every time we try to speak of what we see, we speak falsely, distorting the very thing we are trying to represent.

Stillman's search captures the essence of the Abolition of Context of Language. But before we examine how the devox has impacted language, let's think about how radically the fundamental nature of language has changed.

SYMBOLS, NOT LETTERS; CODE, NOT WORDS

We live in a time when the majority of information transferred every day isn't communicated in English, or Chinese, or Arabic. The dominant language of the day has no alphabet and only two characters: a 0 and a 1. Binary code—the language of data storage, aggregation, and retrieval—has replaced the mother tongues of Mao, Shakespeare, and Muhammad.

Every second of every minute of every hour of every day a dizzying barrage of code—reminiscent of scenes from *The Matrix*—dances over phone lines and bounces off satellites detailing the ebbs and flow of global commerce and personal finance. At the same time, formal traditional languages from English and Spanish to French and German are devolving through disuse or misuse. The real meaning of most people's lives and certainly most businesses is trapped between a barrage of symbols and eroding linguistic denotations.

But at the very time that code seems to be taking the place of words, words are still critical. Perhaps nowhere is this more acutely felt than in France. Several French organizations have been established to preserve the literal lingua franca, particularly on the Internet. Many Francophones view cyberspace as the digital Trojan Horse that Anglophones will use to deal a deathblow to their language. As Marceau Deschamps, a spokesperson for Defense of the French Language, put it, "It is the role of the association to alert those who edit sites that most of the time there are French words to replace the English and it is unnecessary to use English when there exists a French word. There's also the weight of the keepers of the language."

The French aren't the only ones concerned with the demise of their mother tongue. Just look at the angry Californians—some arguing that English ought to be the only language as passionately as others who believe, just as deeply, that the state should be at least bilingual. Or consider the two sides of the Ebonics debate—whether Black English is a recognized language and, if so, whether it should be accepted and/or taught in public schools. Watch television, listen to the radio, and increasingly read newspapers, magazines, and books and it will rapidly become clear that formal English is under persistent attack. The fusion of English and other languages has given us Spanglish, Denglish (originally German), and a wide variety of other English-based pidgin tongues. Some argue that life, especially technological life, is moving too fast to be constrained by the confines of traditional language formation.

Once you get beyond those 1s and 0s, it seems nothing is sacred or safe. But why should you care? First, while every business uses these digits as the basis for making money or keeping track of it, traditional language is still required in everything from recruitment and training to branding and marketing. Second, because language is increasingly being created by smart businesses that understand how to transform vocabulary into currency.

McDonald's, for example, "owns" 131 words and phrases. Some of these are obvious: Big Mac, Quarter Pounder, Happy Meal, Egg McMuffin, and so on. Others, however, are a bit more obscure, including: "Black History Makers of Tomorrow"; "Healthy Growing Up"; "Gospelfest"; "Hey, It Could Happen"; "McBaby"; "McFamily"; "McMemories"; "McSwing"; "The House That Love Built"; and the ominous "Changing the Face of the World." And, as proof that successful businesses always look ahead, McDonald's also owns "Millennium Dreamers," which ought to be a hot trademark in about a thousand years. All this might make your McHead McSpin if it didn't work; after all, can you name another global foodservice operator? In England—where they eschew Americanisms with the same zeal that they shoot mad cows—McDonald's customers order "fries," not "chips," modest proof that the xenophobes are at least partially correct: America is corrupting world culture. This, we believe, is the whole point. And McDonald's isn't the only corporate language monger.

In the beginning there was "the word," but today there is Word. Not only does Microsoft "do" it, it owns the trademark (Microsoft Windows) on the word. Thanks to the spelling, grammar, and language tools embedded in Microsoft Word, the company is beginning to exert disproportionate influence on the building blocks of written communication, spelling, syntax (arrangements of words into sentences), and grammar (knowledge or usage of the preferred forms in speaking or writing).

A generation of students, freed from the slavery of manual footnoting, can rest content that their reports and term papers are perfectly spelled and grammatically correct. What they can't do is employ any form of improvisational style. Sometimes even basic grammar is a stretch. For example, Word informed us that the correct spelling of the word *their* that appears in the first sentence of this paragraph is actually *there*.

Social commentator Mark Greif has noted that Word allows you to correctly spell such corporate names as SUPERVALU, Twinkies, Monsanto, and Citibank but questions a broad range of cultural references from Gaudi and Pasternak to the Louvre and Dalí. The impact, he suggests, is both subtle and insidious. As Greif has written, "The more natural corporations seem—the more they're a part of our environment, like clouds or trees—the more they get a free ride from consumers. In the end, corporate presence in language helps homogenize opinion; corporate tampering with words pollutes the possibilities of expression."

Language lies at the heart of culture, and if you can co-opt a language you can effectively shanghai a society. Capitalists have always been in the business of making new language—it's called marketing and advertising—often language that didn't make any sense. Could, for example, a product really be simultaneously both new and improved? One assumes if it's really new it never existed before and, if it never existed before, there can be no preexistent version to improve.

One could write volumes on the silliness of advertising and marketing language, but—with deepest and genuine respect for the watchdogs of such things like *Adbuster* magazine and the various Centers for the Public Interest—that's not germane to our current discussion or cultural reality. Like everything else touched by the devox, language is morphing and mutating right before our eyes. For business this is more than just an issue of theoretical semantics. How you speak shapes how you think about yourselves, your employees, your customers, your trading partners, and, most importantly, your market opportunities.

"THE EMPLOYEE IS DEAD. LONG LIVE THE ASSOCIATE."

Historically, language has reflected or chronicled the evolution of the society that produced it. Words were added on a fairly slow and consistent basis to mirror changes in the collectively shared human environment from new inventions to emerging social phenomena.

The language of business, including the selling language of marketing, promotion, and advertising, as well as the corporate-speak of human resources departments, press releases, and annual reports, has always been carefully selected to resonate with the current incarnation of its many publics' zeitgeist. As post-sixties-era boomers entered the workforce, individuals, who had in less democratic times been referred to benignly as employees and less tolerantly as labor, became known as associates, colleagues, highly valued coworkers, and even, in a fit of egalitarian hyperbole, our most valuable assets. The idea that the mailroom clerk was a highly valued coworker of the CEO or chairman didn't make much sense unless you worked in a commune or a monastery, but it sounded good. There is nothing wrong with saying you believe in treating everyone as an equal—unless, of course, you're only paying lip service to the idea of democracy.

In the end, commercial critics argue, that's what the language of business has always been about: pronouncements that sounded good despite their inherent ability to strain credulity. Corporate semiotics has given us polluters who were not just environmentally aware but also environmentally concerned. It allowed Bill Gates to publicly portray himself as a somewhat paranoiac victim, frantic lest some overly cerebral fourteen-year-old came up with an idea in a garage in Iowa that could tumble Microsoft's fortunes, rather than a pragmatic and accomplished monopolist.

The whole lexicon of late-twentieth-century business is full of examples of this approach to language. The person—still, sadly all too often, generally a woman—who has to put up with the silliness of a senior executive—still, sadly all too often, generally a man—is no longer a "secretary." Instead, she's an "administrative assistant," which no doubt makes her feel so much better when the aforementioned senior executive behaves like a twelve-year-old boy overdosing on testosterone. Employees are no longer "terminated" with extreme personal or economic malice. First, they were "downsized" and now, even more appealingly, they are "right-sized" as their employers "reengineer" and "revision."

By the same token, language has been manipulated to create very real opportunities. Words like *new, improved, fresh,* and *reduced fat* have put a spit shine on aging product lines and justified otherwise unconscionable line extensions. Putting the word *pet* in front of the word *rock* transformed otherwise useless pieces of stone into a fad. The devox attacks language like it attacks everything else, abolishing the traditional contextual definitions. Smart businesses are aware of this and guard against the erosion of their position in the public mind as vociferously as they bend new linguistic contexts to their own ends. The danger is that one can easily blur the line between linguistic posture and reality.

MISSION CRITICAL;
VISION AND BELIEF OPTIONAL

Nowhere is corporate-speak more manifest than in mission or vision statements. Just think of all those acres of woodland clear-cut in order to communicate less than clear statements such as this:

> At Global Plutocracy our goal is to provide a strong and nurturing environment in which all our associates can more fully realize their dreams and dimensionalize their possibilities as we bring the highest-quality products and services in the most cost-effective manner possible to our valued customers thanks—in no small part—to the harmonious relationships we enjoy and seek to enhance with our most respected and trusted trading partners.

This is generally more correctly translated internally as:

> You bastards better give us the 16 percent compounded growth the Street is looking for or you're going to find yourselves asking those thieving vendors you play golf with for a job.

We've helped dozens of our clients create what—for lack of a better term—you might have to call vision statements. But we're dedicated to trying to make language mean something. So, out with platitudinous pronouncements on the ultimate perfectibility of man and commerce and in with what we call vision statements with attitude. We counsel our clients never to create vision or mission statements unless they can first draft a *credo* statement that clearly summarizes what they believe as individuals and as an enterprise.

Unless you understand a person's or a corporation's underlying belief system—what they stand for in the present—it's all but impossible to make sense of what they tell you (or themselves) they want to be in the future. Creating a credo statement is a powerful tool for institutional self-analysis and forces organizations to be more honest and focused when they draft a vision. Anyone can create lofty, ambitious statements, but what's the point if those ambitions run counter to what you really believe? Writing credos often forces organizations to look into their own dark corners and ask themselves the tough but critical questions that normally never surface.

We recently worked with Planned Parenthood Federation of America (PPFA) to develop a vision for 2025. Part of that exercise involved having the visioning team create a belief or credo document to accompany a promise statement that differs in a critical way from what's known in the corporate world as a vision or goal statement. An organization's promise—the principle they guarantee will be present in everything they do—is significantly different from a more sweeping statement about who you aspire to be at some point in the future.

The development of a belief statement was critical since PPFA's existence is ultimately tied to the goodwill of a network of volunteers personally energized around a variety of issues ranging from radical ecology to promoting sex education. On a pragmatic note, acceptance of the 2025 vision was subject to ratification by the membership at large, who needed to understand the whys behind the vision's whats.

The final promise and belief statements, found on the following pages, serve as a clear example of how the traditional context of the corporate mission statement has been morphed to include a beliefs platform.

Together the visioning team found out exactly how difficult it is to draft the language of belief. Each of the 429 words of the promise and belief statements was refined, rejected, and reaccepted in an attempt to craft language that best expressed the feelings of a highly diverse membership. PPFA is unilaterally dedicated to the proposition that a woman has an absolute, inalienable right to determine the number and spacing of her pregnancies. But many PPFA members are also deeply concerned with issues associated with overpopulation. So what would happen in

THE PLANNED PARENTHOOD PROMISE

Creating hope for humanity: The freedom to dream, to make choices, and to live in peace with our planet.

The Planned Parenthood promise reflects our core values and deepest aspirations for ourselves and the world. It is a statement of what we want to be that transcends what we will do to fulfill that promise over the next 25 years.

Hope results from our aspirations and dreams. It is the force that can unleash true human potential and bring a people into harmony with themselves, those they love, their communities, society, and ultimately with the earth.

The world we envision is one in which all people possess and pursue their own dreams. We see a world in which people will be free to make life's most profound choices about childbearing and relationships in harmony with those dreams. We have hope that humanity will someday live in peace and harmony with our fragile global environment so that future generations will thrive. The Planned Parenthood promise is to work toward creating the will, the technology, and the enduring political and legal structures to make this vision a reality.

The Planned Parenthood Beliefs

- **We believe** in the right to sexual and reproductive self-determination that is non-coercive, non-exploitive, and responsible.
- **We believe** that the free and joyous expression of one's own sexuality is central to being fully human.

the (impossible) event that every fertile woman opted to give birth to one child a year? By the same token, many PPFAers' gut reaction is to support the principle of the absolute right to sexual self-determination. But, obviously, they didn't want to draft language that appeared to give even tacit approval to things like pedophilia and rape.

Struggling to find the best way of expressing beliefs forces you to admit that they sometimes range between ambivalent and contradictory. This is especially true for voluntary organizations. A person can

- **We believe** in trusting individuals and providing them with the information they need to make well-informed decisions about sexuality, family planning, and childbearing.
- **We believe** that women should have an equal place at life's table, and be respected as moral decision makers.
- **We believe** that children flourish best in families and communities where they are nurtured, honored, and loved.
- **We believe** in passion—for change, for justice, for easing the plight of others, for caring, for living our convictions, and for confronting inhumane acts.
- **We believe** in action—to make things happen and to improve people's lives and circumstances.
- **We believe** in inclusion and diversity—and the power and knowledge they confer.
- **We believe** the future is global and that we are part of a global movement.
- **We believe** in the urgency of creating a sustainable world and living in peace with our planet.
- **We believe** in leadership based upon collaboration rather than hierarchy.
- **We believe** in acting courageously, especially as allies with those who have little or no voice and little or no power.
- **We believe** that every right is tied to responsibility and that the fulfillment of responsibility is itself a source of joy.

volunteer because he or she agrees with one issue or set of concerns yet disagrees about almost everything else associated with the group. Building a viable and meaningful consensus for a group like PPFA forces people, and the organization, to make some hard choices—choices they could normally ignore or avoid. In PPFA's case it meant saying that the group, while concerned in general with sexual freedom issues and opposed to sexual discrimination, was most concerned about the rights of women.

Think about it for a minute. Are your company's beliefs any less complex? True, management has the power to coerce allegiance, but only up to a point. How many interviews have you read or seen with downsized employees who said something like "I worked here for twenty-six years and I never thought this was the kind of company that would betray its employees for a merger opportunity"? Those kind of statements are produced when two sets of beliefs—the company ought to maximize every profit opportunity, and the company owes its primary loyalty to the men and women it employs—come into conflict.

By direct contrast, when we look at the ability of small companies like Tom's of Maine to compete in a commercial space dominated by giants like Procter & Gamble, Unilever, and Colgate, we think we're witnessing the real market strength of aligned belief. So our hard-learned message is this: If you feel compelled to publicly state where you believe you're going, it's usually best to make sure you first know where you really are. What Planned Parenthood and other forward-looking companies are discovering is that words alone are often not enough. The integrity of language—its context, if you will—has been corrupted to the point that one has to go to extraordinary lengths to achieve clarity of communication.

COMMERCIAL-SPEAK AND WALKING BILLBOARDS

Today language in general—and the language of business in particular—is undergoing two critical transitions. First, rather than playing symbolic catch-up with society and culture, language is increasingly inventing cultural icons. Don't believe us? Well, why don't you use a lifeline or phone a friend and ask her or him (in the neolanguage of Anheuser-Busch speakers everywhere), "Whassup?!"

Commercials can be more memorable than the products they're selling. Many of us remember Clara Peller's infamous "Where's the beef?" line, but where exactly was the beef? In a McLuhanesque twist, everyone has become a commercial. We all routinely parade around with language literally on our chests, backs, and heads without understanding we've become human billboards.

Thanks to the Abolition of Linguistic Context, commercials are increasingly ends in and of themselves. "Whassup?! wear" is as popular with people who don't drink beer (or don't drink Budweiser) as Harley-Davidson licensed products are with people who've never straddled a motorcycle. Characters from television commercials like E*Trade's Stuart (the multicolored-haired guy who spends his days xeroxing his face and periodically advising his boss) are often more recognizable than the companies they represent.

This really isn't too surprising when you consider that a frightening amount of contemporary language of commerce was created without meaning and blissfully retains its natal purity despite widespread public acceptance and usage. Words increasingly don't convey meaning outside themselves.

It isn't just that women have become females or that blouses and shirts are now tops. Force yourself to listen to the lyrics of almost any hip-hop song and you'll learn that the individuals formerly know as women have been reduced to females, bitches, shorties, or, even more minimalistically, the ever-popular monosyllabic hos. Make no mistake, there's much more at work here than the dissemination of questionable out-group street argot or the ephemeral verbal by-products of youth culture.

In the streets of America's cities, suburbs, and rural areas, traditional language is devolving into little more than a collection of words whose meaning can't be deciphered outside an audible context. This devolution isn't just a plot by the "boyz in the 'hood." Kid Rock, the multi-platinum prince of ideas ideally communicated in four letters, isn't really from the mean streets of the Motor City. The self-styled "American badass" actually hails from Romeo, Michigan, a rural community twenty-four miles from Detroit whose main products are apples and peaches.

Language used to be emblematic of youth and minority cultures. Now it's an endangered species, and the pebble tossed into the waters of the street is beginning to send ripples into the corporate world. What, for example, do the following sentences mean to you: "So me and my mothafucka was walking down the street when we hooked up with some mothafucka who hipped us to a mothafuckin party that was really happnin. So we went there and mothafucka!, the mothafucka was mothafuckin right. It was a real mothafucka at least until some mothafucka showed up and made a mothafuckin fool out hisself"? *[Translation: "My good friend and I were walking down the street and met somebody we knew, but not well, who told us there was a really good party going on. When we got there, we saw he was right. It was great until some stranger showed up, acted stupidly, and disrupted it beyond repair."]* We've heard hundreds of entry-level and minimum-wage employees— many of them in positions that involve customer interface—whose vocabulary is similarly challenged.

Give it a few more years and we'll be back to grunts and pointing. The bottom line here is that for more and more Americans, from the streets to the boardroom, language increasingly either has no meaning or such vague meanings that we can only approximate understanding. And that makes the job of the marketer both easier and harder. Consumers are attaching themselves to the language of marketing with a fervor and passion formerly associated with the approach of the devout to the language of the church. Mr. Clean could only aspire to become a pop cultural icon in the 1960s, but those cute assorted Budweiser reptiles and ferrets have become not just cultural reference points but cultural fixtures or—dare we say it—culture themselves.

At the same time that language is shaping culture it's having an increasingly difficult time describing the social environment and keeping pace with the changes impacting our lives. This really isn't too surprising when you consider the pace of technological innovation. We need an ever-expanding vocabulary to discuss the common artifacts of our lives—from voice mail, instant messaging, and e-mail, to m-commerce, e-commerce, and, yes, l-commerce (or location commerce), to an encyclopedia of acronyms like PDA and MP3.

We've borrowed words like *spam* (as in the kind you receive as e-mail rather than the kind munched with enthusiasm by members of the greatest generation [itself a classic example of instant culture/language]) and *flame* (what happens in chat rooms as opposed to what is used to warm rooms) to describe features of the Cyber Age. It never seems to stop. We have shaped new meanings for words like *geek* (as in high-tech multimillionaire as opposed to a sideshow freak who bites off the heads of chickens); *wired* (as in those in the know as opposed to that which is electrified); *freak* (as in potential multimillionaire enthusiast rather than oddity of nature); and *nerd* (see geek, rather than social reject or sour candy) to describe the digital Moseses who are happily leading us to the techno Promised Land.

Of course, the problem is that the geeks and nerds are such technology freaks that they keep inventing things—and descriptors for those things, themselves, and the elements of their universe—faster than the rest of us can absorb them. Even wired geeks, nerds, freaks, and the rest have trouble keeping up, which is why they cheat by applying a host of prefixes—including cyber-, nano-, digital-, e-, and techno- —to old language, allowing us to convey thoughts as deep and poignant as this: "The ranting of the digerati about the relationship between the convergence of e-commerce, breakthroughs in nanotechnology, and the accelerated evolution of cyberspace often resembles little more than technobabble." Seems profound, but what—if anything—does it mean?

It appears that Jacques Derrida, the French philosopher who serves as the intellectual godfather of the postmodernists (who somewhat ironically write books explaining why books have no meaning or—more correctly—no fixed or fixable meaning) may be right after all. In a universe fashioned by the devox, the media isn't the message. There isn't any message.

THE GLUE OF CIVILIZATION AND LINGUISTIC POST-IT NOTES

These language-centered transitions—the pace of language formation, the imprecision of linguistic meaning, and the fact that language has become culture rather than reflecting or describing it—have either made language meaningless or imbued it with so many meanings as to render it all but incomprehensible. We are witnessing the functional Abolition of Linguistic Context.

Language has historically been the glue of civilization. But today we find ourselves living in a society increasingly held together by linguistic Post-it notes. Words derive their meaning not from collectively agreed-upon standards, but from physical or verbal clues whose definitions can vary radically depending on context. Our increasing difficulty in establishing linguistic common ground presents a conundrum to marketers anxious to clearly communicate product benefits.

We're not surprised at all by the apparent growing popularity of concepts like Seth Godin's ideavirus, Emanuel Rosen's buzz, or any of the pronouncements of the various proponents of stealth marketing. A unified society demands a common language, a common vocabulary, and a common grammar and syntax. But we don't live in a unified society, so increasingly we favor the language of the tribe over that of the nation-state, and tribal language is all about concealment and exclusion rather than open communication. We're adrift and lost in a sea of acronyms, linguistic shortcuts, and in-group argot.

Walk into any meeting of any professional service or trade association in the United States and—unless you're familiar with the industry—you'll begin to feel as if you've landed on some foreign planet. Whole industries are starting to approach language like teenagers, or at least the teenagers described by author Tom Wolfe in his recent book, *Hooking Up:*

> The typical Filofax entry in the year 2000 by a girl who had hooked up the night before would be: "Boy with the black Wu-Tang T-shirt and cargo pants: O, A, 6." Or "Stupid cock diesel" (slang for a boy who was muscular from lifting weights) who kept saying, "This is a cool deal: TTC, 3." The letters referred to the sexual acts performed (e.g., TTC for "that thing with the cup"), and the Arabic number indicated the degree of satisfaction on a scale of 1 to 10.

Tribalized language almost invariably is accompanied by a breakdown in collective behavior and understanding. The sexual behavior of young people described by Wolfe—where " 'second base' meant oral sex; 'third base' meant going all the way; and 'home plate' meant learning each other's names"—helps in part at least to explain the alarming spread of sexually transmitted diseases, which threatens society as a whole. After all, if you don't think you're having sex, why worry about sexually transmitted diseases?

STDs aren't the only things that are contagious. In 2000 the language of adolescent sexuality and denial found its way to the White House and, thanks to the media, to almost every home and business in America. Think of Bill Clinton summoning all his rhetorical powers and personal charisma to drill through the lens of the camera and tell America he had not had sexual relations with Monica. The same pattern holds true in most people's apparent inability to interpret speed-limit signs.

Most Americans seem to believe that a posted speed limit of, say, fifty-five actually means you're legally entitled to drive at least sixty, if not sixty-five. This also helps explain how the high-flying dot-coms of the 1990s became the dot-bombs of 2000. There simply was not enough linguistic agreement between the starry-eyed residents of Silicon Valley and the jaded denizens of Wall Street.

Nowhere is the tribalization of language more refined than in the world of business and the trade associations that represent it. Consider this passage, which attempts to explain a simple formula for reducing inventories:

> The efficient replenishment maturity index of 38 is the highest of all the five ECR strategies. The current best index value of 63, however, is the lowest of the five strategies and is a result of low scores on ASNs, pallet/case bar-coding, DSD order management and DEX/NEX.

In Silicon Valley the differences between strong potential and strong performance, or between infusions of venture capital and financial health, or between a great idea and a great business model, simply didn't exist. As long as you had a cool T-shirt describing your offering, everything was fine. The crazy thing is that for a moment at least, tribal language works even on the out-group. How else can you explain the mind-numbing enthusiasm of so many Old Economy analysts for New Economy companies?

Language is all about control. It's a story literally as old as the Bible. In Genesis we're told, "In the beginning was the word, and the word was God." A few pages later, when God wants to give Adam and Eve dominion over the animals he does it by letting the humans name them. Call a fetus a child and abortion is murder. Call a person property and it's easy to justify slavery. Call someone a mud person and suddenly you have reason to support murder, rape, arson, vandalism, and even genocide. Nothing much has changed since Genesis, it seems. The word is still God and it's still all about control. That said, the increasing imprecision of language makes it more and more difficult to exercise fixed or precise control—yet another consequence of the abolition of traditional linguistic context.

Communication vehicles are increasingly shaping communication—reducing the wide range of human thought to a relative handful of fixed code phrases so quickly clichéd that they become keys to even more minimalist codes, limiting not just the means and methods of expression but language and thought themselves. Whole new languages are emerging every day, their vocabularies directly shaped by their communications vehicle. These new languages are everywhere, from vanity license plates to the numerically based symbol language of pagers to the linguistic shorthand of instant messaging to the hidden image messaging of the T-shirt.

INTEL INSIDE:
THE MICROCHIP VERSUS THE POTATO CHIP

In a world where the lines separating phrase making and market making are so fragile as to be barely perceptible, business has a unique opportunity to manipulate the Abolition of Linguistic Context to its own commercial advantage. Think of "Intel Inside," which succeeded in building brand awareness in the minds of people who really didn't understand or fully appreciate the difference between a microchip and a potato chip.

Product claims still need to be marginally credible, of course, but increasingly they must also be clever. Purchasers of cellular telephony, for example, must choose between plans encrypted with marketing language about friends and family (in and of itself an interesting distinction) and weekend minutes (somehow different from weekday minutes in a way that's theoretically more desirable). The fact that business people who use cell phones generally use them more during the week is buried by the mention of weekend minutes, the one thing most of us can agree there should be more of.

Of course, you have to be careful when you're inventing or manipulating language. In the 1980s, during the heyday of green marketing, for instance, the consumer packaged-goods industry learned that attractive language (earth-friendly, ecological, and recycled) wasn't, by itself, enough to get consumers to change their purchase behavior, especially when the new language is accompanied by significantly higher prices and reduced quality.

America's fondness for neolanguage has had a fairly profound impact on branding. In the rapidly fleeting days of the final decade of the twentieth century, corporations reversed their historical pattern of doing almost anything and everything to protect the sanctity of their brands, promiscuously renaming, re-creating, and revamping their brands apparently at will. Thirty years ago one of the major issues of mergers and acquisitions was which brand would survive or remain dominant. Today, for every Kraft Foods and DaimlerChrysler there are a dozen Cingulars, Verizons, and Accentures. In any number of industries from high finance to high technology, the rush is on to emerge from the cocoon of old brand identity a new corporate butterfly.

The increasing fluidity of language acceptance has allowed power brands to be birthed as easily as they're bred, perhaps even more easily.

In the public credibility race new brands like Microsoft overran estab-lished brands like Xerox and IBM. Amazon quickly became *the* name in bookstores almost as soon as its website was launched. Overnight thousands of consumers who might never have even heard of Sotheby's became cybertraders thanks to eBay.

At least initially these *neobrands* appear to have an inherent advan-tage over Old Economy competition. For starters, they have no track records and, in this best of all possible marketing worlds, that means carte blanche to make any claims they want (at least until the final round of venture capital fails). Consider Priceline.com, which failed in its attempt to parlay a marginally successful track record of selling dis-counted airfares into a universal formula for selling discounted every-thing; or Webvan, which proved exactly how fast you could fritter away a fortune in start-up financing.

The list of fallen dot-coms is long enough to fill this book. But all these failed companies share a common market denominator. At least for a moment, they were given the ability to eliminate the line separat-ing claim and reality—brand and product, if you will—at the same time that Old Economy firms from NBC News to the Ford Motor Com-pany were being held to increasingly higher standards of public and media accountability.

This fluidity of language creates as many problems as opportunities. The public seems to have increasing difficulty separating the rhetoric from the offering, triggering the law of unintended consequences to birth some decidedly negative outcomes. The success of Anheuser-Busch's commercials has drawn criticisms from educators and children's rights groups who have accused the brewer of targeting underage drinkers. Personally, we would find these accusations laughable if they didn't reflect a disturbing reality.

Like noted psychologist and behavioral expert Konrad Lorenz's goslings, whose imprinting mechanisms led them to follow the scientist around as though he were their mother, consumers of all ages increas-ingly present marketers with a great-unwashed tabula rasa. Apparently any sufficiently clever bit of messaging can successfully imprint itself on this great collective cerebral blank screen. This comes as great news for budding dictators. For the rest of us, it means it's increasingly difficult to get messages to stick in people's minds or even to register much below the instant cliché level.

So how can you practice effective messaging in an era when language seems to be under attack from all angles? An important first step is to learn to pay more attention to *how* you're communicating rather than *what's* being communicated. Anheuser-Busch's "Whassup?!" seems to resonate louder in the public imagination than esoteric claims about things like taste and calorie count. We think that helps explain how Anheuser-Busch managed to wrestle its way to the top of the "lite beer" mountain. *Who* communicates can be even more important than *how* or *what* is being communicated. Spokespeople from the fictional Mr. Whipple to the real, late Dave Thomas touch people in ways that pure language simply doesn't.

It's also critical to understand that a cliché's life expectancy is inherently tied to your ability to keep reinforcing it. Sloganeering isn't the same thing as sales. "M'm! M'm! Good!" was a clever phrase, but it didn't keep people eating Campbell's soup. Given the Abolition of Context, it's easy to lose track of the ownership of what used to be corporate language. Literally millions of people use the phrase "a Kodak moment," but Kodak's market share has declined sharply over the past twenty years.

Rethink branding and any romantic ideas you might still harbor about brand loyalty. A lot of those loyal Crest kids (the Crest generation) switched to Colgate's Total the minute it was introduced. Forget about the Crest Test. Forget about the American Dental Association recommendation. Total's brand promise (complete oral care in a tube) initially knocked the market leader for a loop. In an era of near ubiquitous efficacy across a broad range of goods and services, you just can't keep taking brand loyalty for granted.

In a world where consumers are so bombarded by conflicting advertising claims that they walk around feeling psychically lobotomized, the pitch is the real product. Never mind trying to make sense out of all those confusing telephone rate claims; where does Jamie Lee Curtis keep that cell phone? Making language is a lot easier than creating real breakthrough products. In fact, we now see pitchmen transferring their skills from product to product. Think of Bob Dole's other "little blue friend." There's something odd about mixing the imaging of a cure for impotence and a soft drink, but it apparently works for Bob and Pepsi.

Maybe it's high time to add linguists, cultural anthropologists, mythologists, artists, and other experts in symbolic communication to your R&D teams. In fact, maybe they ought to *be* your R&D teams. We know the idea of staff seems to fly in the face of conventional downsizing wisdom, but conventional wisdom is the problem. To craft effective messaging, it's first necessary to understand how messaging (sending and receiving) has changed and how symbology can benefit marketing and advertising. It's all about culture, after all.

Where does the Abolition of Linguistic Context end? The answer is, it doesn't. Even the creation of language that is deliberately devoid of meaning has now become a product. There is no clearer proof point for the fact that traditional language is in trouble than the success of artist Adib Fricke (b. 1960) and the Word Company.

Among other things, Fricke operates a website devoted to generating nonsense words like *Flogo*. Fricke, who exhibits widely in Europe and staged his first American exhibit in May 1999 at the Busch-Reisinger Museum, extends the Abolition of Context into high art by presenting what he calls "protonyms." Ironically, protonym is a neologism for a neologism. As the *Harvard University Gazette* explained:

Although protonyms such as "smorp," "yemmels," and "ontom" may sound like other words we have heard before, they refuse the comfort of a referent. Part of the fascination with the protonyms lies in the implied parallel to a wholly new, non-referential visual image.... Fricke's protonyms seem to be designed to both annoy and please, combining wry humor and a naïve fondness for the potential beauty of the new word—drawing on the avant-garde dream of a creation that transcends the limits of conventional society, language, meaning.

Fricke uses language as a medium of social and institutional critique. His protonyms are words that don't already exist in another language. "The Word Company can be thought of as an organization which owns the rights to these proprietary neologisms and licenses them temporarily to museums for 'showing,'" according to the *Harvard University Gazette*. "Although this paradigm cannot be fully followed (partly because German copyright law apparently would not consider the protonyms to be worthy of copyright), it raises irritating questions about our current obsessions with originality and intellectual property: just what can one own (genes? words? phrases?), and under what conditions? Can a corporation invent? How does the art museum relate to this mode of creativity?"

Granted Fricke is on the extreme. But his art wouldn't have an audience unless his underlying premise was solid—increasingly, language is just sound, a placeholder for real thought. In the next chapter we'll focus on art and how the Abolition of Context is changing the nature and product of creativity.

7

Art—a Trap with No Exit

Doesn't the paint say it all? What am I after? A long time ago I said
that I want to seduce by means of imperceptible passages from one
reality to another. The viewer is caught in a net from which there is no
escape save by going through the whole picture until he comes to the
exit. My wish: to make a trap (picture) with no exit at all either for you
or for me.

—DOROTHEA TANNING

Art sells products—directly and indirectly. In a society where language is devolving, successful manipulation of symbols is a critical
first step to the successful manipulation of markets. Symbolic communication, whether textual, graphic, and/or auditory, is a prerequisite to
product success and brand building as well as the cornerstone of advertising, marketing, promotion, and merchandising.

Art is one of the most difficult areas to trace the path of the devox
through because at its heart all art appears inherently deviant. Nonetheless, the pattern holds true. Perhaps the best way to illustrate our argument is to examine the work of a single artist. We've chosen Jackson
Pollock because his work is—in a general sense at least—well known
and because it's easy to see how Pollock wrestled with the devox.

Pollock was almost the prototype of the deviant artist. As a troubled
and brooding young man, Pollock had a difficult time reconciling the

deviant notions in his head with the demands of the art establishment of his time. His Fringe vision was too crude, too primitive when compared with those of other artists, including his older brother. When he joined Thomas Hart Benton's Art Students League Pollock moved from the Fringe to the Edge. The early sponsorship of Peggy Guggenheim moved Pollock dangerously close to the Realm of the Cool, and media coverage of works such as *Full Fathom Five* and *Cathedral* (both from 1947) edged him into the Next Big Thing. You could argue that Pollock hit social convention when *Life* magazine did a story on him or that it happened a few years later when no one seemed to see his work as revolutionary anymore. In the deviance-driven world of art, once the devox has hit Social Convention its run is over. Art is one area where the devox is the most perishable.

Dial back to 1969. The devox was driving an entire generation to rewrite the rules of media and experience, and Marshall McLuhan was telling *Playboy* that "the immediate interface between audile-tactile and visual perception is taking place everywhere around us. No civilian can escape this environmental blitzkrieg, for there is, quite literally, no place to hide. But if we diagnose what is happening to us, we can reduce the ferocity of the winds of change and bring the best elements of the old visual culture, during this transitional period, into peaceful coexistence with the new retribalized society."

Assuming somebody in the corporate world of the 1950s had been paying attention to the Edge of academia, they might have been able to profit from McLuhan's insights. His first book, *The Mechanical Bride: Folklore of Industrial Man* (New York: Vanguard Press, 1951), was one of the early attempts to examine modern commercial visual imaging (advertising) in light of a radically changing social and technological context.

A generation later those winds of change were blowing harder than ever. Art reflected that spirit of change, prompting people to expand their definition of art away from the old context of formally trained painters and sculptors. As British author J. G. Ballard wrote, "The paintings of mental patients, like those of the surrealists, show remarkable insights into our modern conventional reality, a largely artificial construct which serves the limited ambitions of our central nervous system." The idea that art was moving toward impermanence, or beyond to chaos, was clearly articulated by Alvin Toffler, the father of modern futuring. His notion that change in the rate of change is a legitimate subject for study and concern remains as vital today as it was when *Future Shock* was first written more than thirty years ago. In 1970, reflecting on his belief that modern art was defined by an impulse toward transience and the creation of perishable environments, Toffler wrote:

> Art, like gesture, is a form of non-verbal expression and a prime channel for the transmission of images. Here the evidence of ephemeralization are, if anything, even more pronounced. If we regard each school of art as though it were a word-based language, we are witnessing the successive replacement not of words, but of whole languages at once. . . . Today, the pace of turnover in art is vision-blurring—the viewer scarcely has time to "see" a school develop, to learn its language, so to speak, before it vanishes.

"In art, as in language," Toffler concluded in *Future Shock,* "we are racing toward impermanence. Man's relationships with symbolic imagery are growing more and more temporary." So temporary, in fact, they aren't just "racing toward impermanence"; they've reached the Abolition of Context. We will focus our discussion primarily on the visual arts because the late twentieth and early twenty-first centuries have been dominated by the visual; or, perhaps more correctly, the marriage of the visual and the audio.

THE TRIUMPH OF THE AUDIOVISUAL

Television, of course, is the best mass example of the marriage of visual and auditory art. Cable giants such as MTV, VH1, and the Nashville Network (TNN) expanded what, in the cases of Dick Clark's *American*

Bandstand and Don Cornelius's *Soul Train,* had been programming concepts into entertainment channels and networks. That expansion changed forever not just how music was sold, but what music was sold. Imagine if Merle Haggard or Neil Diamond had had to compete on their looks against Faith Hill or 'NSYNC. In today's music industry, NTNA (no trolls need apply), no matter how talented they may be. We live in a world where artistic promotion is more important than artistic product. But how did we get here? The answer is partially revealed by a quick review of the idea of modernism and its objectification of the world.

Herbert Read, the renowned art historian, has observed that "there is no doubt that what we call the modern movement in art begins with the single-minded determination of a French painter to see the world *objectively.* There need be no mystery about this word: what Cézanne wished to see was the world, or that part of it he was contemplating, *as an object,* without any intervention either of the tidy mind or untidy emotions." Eventually Cézanne's vision would become translated into Henri Matisse's famous quip, "L'exactitude n'est pas la vérité," or "Exactitude is not truth."

For the last hundred years or so artists wrestled to embrace the devox—devising radically disparate ways to mirror society and the forces driving social change. Dada attempted to shatter all the rules of convention, an early example of the Abolition of Context. Surrealism's obsession with Freudian theory can be seen as a precursor to the devox eroding the borders separating art and social science. Picasso's incessant use of revolutionary modernism to glorify the primitive demonstrates how fast Fringe visual elements (African totems) sped their way from Parisian ateliers to become television sitcom props. Pop artists like Peter Max and Andy Warhol erased the lines between high art and high street commerce. Art and political expression became one in the works of Robert Mapplethorpe, Keith Haring, and Jean-Michel Basquiat.

The Abolition of Context hasn't just radically impacted art's message, it has affected the media used to express that message. Toffler's vision of a future in which art is more ephemeral has come true. The work of modern artists like Larry Rivers is literally physically disintegrating as we write. Other art "objects" like the installations of Christo are deliberately designed to exist only for a brief moment in time. Today's rave DJs and house, techno, and trance "musicians" don't compose new music. They patch together samples of preexisting tracks and even random sounds, preserving not whole pieces of art but only the audio equivalent of brush strokes.

WHEN WE FINALLY GOT TO WOODSTOCK . . . WE FOUND PETER MAX SAWING UP THE STAGE

Throughout his career Peter Max has transformed high modern art into even higher finance. Max has visually sampled everything from a Continental Airlines 777 to Dale Earnhart's racecar as "canvases." His remuneration for the Woodstock II stage offers an interesting example of both visual sampling and planned perishability. As his commission, Max asked for the physical stage itself. He plans on carving the stage up into one-foot-square sections that he'll sell as framed shadowboxes.

The "fine art" of the stage disappeared after the festival, fated to be further deconstructed into pieces of itself so it could be remarketed as a product designed not to be hung in museums but in family rooms, garages, and basements all over the United States, marketed not by Max's gallery agent but rather by QVC or the Home Shopping Network. We've also helped Max explore the possibility of mass marketing his images on even less aesthetically pleasing media—as underwear, a "display space" almost diametrically positioned against the fine art world he entered and helped define in the 1970s.

Why shouldn't Peter Max design underwear? Everyone else from professional athletes to hip-hop and rock musicians have their own lines of ties, shirts, and outerwear. Thanks to the dervish dance of the devox, we've moved from the idea of the artist as celebrity to the notion of the celebrity as artist. The works of convicted mass murderer John Wayne Gacy have been sold in galleries, as have those of "Dr. Death"—

Dr. Jack Kevorkian. Kevorkian's CD sells right along those by Charles Manson and the "spoken word" of Aleister Crowley, the man known as "the Great Beast," perhaps recent history's most celebrated black magician.

The shift in focus from the art to the artist is a boon to business. In the past you needed to go find a genuine artist (almost always by definition a deviant) and then coax (or, as in the case of Michelangelo and Pope Julius II, coerce) him into marketability. No more. Today anyone who has achieved celebrity (in its absolute broadest sense) can sell art. We believe there's an untapped market out there for pastels by Dennis Rodman, figure studies by Mike Tyson, mixed media collages by Monica Lewinsky, and perhaps even an Al Gore still life or two. In this regard, the entertainment industry appears light-years ahead of other businesses.

Remember the Monkees, the band that initially wasn't allowed to play its own instruments but still managed to peddle hundreds of thousands of albums, sell out venue after venue, have a hit television show, and make perhaps the strangest movie ever filmed? The group began a long tradition of bands like the Sex Pistols who were selected more for their look rather than for any musical talent. (In all fairness, at least some of the Monkees, unlike members of the Sex Pistols, had been musicians before they became actors playing musicians.)

We are reeling from the sonic attacks of a whole army of musical mutations from the Backstreet Boys and 'NSYNC to O-Town, which have emerged full-blown from the mind of the third millennium's Dr. Audiostein—Lou Pearlman. Pearlman is the mastermind behind the boy-band phenomenon. Following a variation of Berry Gordy's old Motown playbook, Pearlman has assembled several groups of talented young men and taught them how to dress, dance, and market themselves. The result has been multiplatinum success in the world of pop music, a world where you don't necessarily have to sound good as long as you look good, and where the artist is clearly more important than the art.

It's all about the bottom line here. If you think hanging in the Louvre or MOMA is better than a one-hour slot on QVC selling mass-produced lithographs, you're probably living in a garret. Those who enjoy more luxurious accommodations approach art more like Henry Ford than Henri Matisse. This isn't to say there aren't serious artists out there. Rather, our point is that the lines separating art from commerce are fuzzier than they've ever been. Glance at the area of the so-called fine arts for a moment and you'll notice that the devox hasn't exactly been resting on its deviant laurels.

BURNING MEN AND GLOW-IN-THE-DARK BUNNIES

We've touched on how the devox has eliminated the lines that used to separate fine art from commerce, social science, and politics. There's a growing industry out there scanning the in galleries and the hot clubs for hints about the next big market opportunity. It isn't that these efforts are ill conceived. The problem is that the context of art changes so rapidly that its hottest incarnation lives safely outside the confines of galleries and clubs.

Consider the separation of art and science—a fundamental distinction most of us regularly invoke, at least colloquially, as in "Promotion (merchandising, advertising, product development, etc.) is really still more art than science." Today there is increasingly less and less separating the two worlds. We have artists who use the tools of science to make art, and scientists who prefer to think about science as an art form.

The blurring of these worlds has helped abolish the traditional context of art and had a direct impact on business. Computing, for example, often produces individuals and products that are a hybrid of both worlds, hybrids with high commercial value. Nowhere, at least in a quasi-popular sense, is that blurring more evident than in the work of one artist, Eduardo Kac, and one artistic event, the Burning Man festival.

In 1950, action/drip painter Jackson Pollock lamented, "It seems to me that the modern painter cannot express this age. The airplane, the atom bomb, the radio, in the old forms of the Renaissance or of any past culture, each age finds its own technique." Pollock may have been correct, but it seems that Eduardo Kac, whose work has erased the boundaries between art and biology, has done a fair job of resolving the Pollockian dilemma precisely by using the tools of the age as art. If he were a writer, Kac might well be heralded as the poet laureate of the Biotech Age. His palette is DNA, the *prima materia* of life itself. Kac's vision is simultaneously both unique and the outgrowth of an older tradition.

In *Beyond Modern Sculpture: The Effects of Science and Technology on the Sculpture of This Century* (1968), Jack Burnham noted, "Behind much art extending through the Western tradition exists a yearning to break down the psychic and physical barriers between art and living reality—not only to make an art form that is believably real, but to go beyond and furnish images capable of intelligent intercourse with their creators."

This search for a way to "go beyond," as artist Amy M. Youngs argued in an article titled "The Fine Art of Creating Life," has been an active concern of artists at least since 1936, when Edward Steichen mixed traditional selective botanical breeding, the drug colchicine, and art. The resulting mutant delphiniums were exhibited at the Museum of Modern Art. As a footnote, it took more than half a century for the next exhibition of genetically altered flowers, George Gessert's 1988 Iris Project at San Francisco's New Langston Arts.

BIOART AND BEYOND

If Steichen was bioart's Moses pointing the way to a scientifically enhanced aesthetic Promised Land, then Eduardo Kac is its messiah. In an article titled "Transgenic Art," Kac proposed the creation of a transgenic animal as an artistic statement. "More than make visible the invisible, art needs to raise our awareness of what firmly remains beyond our visual reach but which, nonetheless, affects us directly," Kac explained. "Two of the most prominent technologies operating beyond vision are digital implants and genetic engineering, both poised to have profound consequences in art as well as in the social, medical, political and economic life of the next century."

Kac defined transgenic art as "a new art form based on the use of genetic engineering techniques to transfer synthetic genes to an organism or to transfer natural genetic material from one species into another, to create unique living beings." Initially, Kac hoped to extract what he called the Green Fluorescent Protein and introduce it into a dog.

Kac saw his work—designing what he called chimeras—as a logical extension of the world around him. "Chimeras, however, are no longer imaginary," he wrote; "today, nearly 20 years after the first transgenic animal, they are being routinely created in laboratories and are slowly becoming part of the larger genescape. . . . While in ordinary discourse the word 'chimera' refers to an imaginary life form made of disparate parts, in biology 'chimera' is a technical term that means actual organisms with cells from two or more distinct genomes. A profound cultural transformation takes place when chimeras leap from legend to life, from representation to reality."

In February 2000 Kac's theories became reality with the birth of Alba, an albino "GFP Bunny" who glows green when exposed to specific bands of light, in Jouy-en-Josas, France. Insisting that GFP Bunny is a transgenic artwork and not a breeding project, Kac said, "As a transgenic artist, I am not interested in the creation of genetic objects, but in the invention of transgenic social subjects. In other words, what is important is the completely integrated process of creating the bunny, bringing her to society at large, and providing her with a loving, caring, and nurturing environment in which she can grow safe and healthy."

As to the boundary separating art from science, Kac said:

> The boundary between science and art cannot be defined by media, process and systems. Today this is more the case than ever before, since so many artists work with the very same tools employed by scientists worldwide. Needless to say, computers and the Internet are a case in

point. The boundaries between science and art can only be defined by several factors and their complex interplay: the intention of the artist or scientist, the context in which a given work is presented, the rhetorical strategies employed by the artist or scientist, and the reception given to them by the public. Naturally, these elements can change in time, and their meanings can be reconsidered accordingly (as when a ritual mask is recontexualized in a museum hundreds of years after its creation and use, for example). One of the key differences between science and art rests on their conceptual and pragmatic approaches to tropes: while science erases the origins of its metaphors and metonyms ("gene", for example, is a metonym: the part stands for the whole; "genetic code" is a metaphor first coined in analogy with how Morse encodes messages), art presents a high level of awareness of metaphors, metonyms and other tropes—its very material.

We think the blending of art and science, and the resulting Abolition of Traditional Artistic Context, will help the devox create whole new markets and product lines. Imagine designer pets bred to match the color scheme of your home. Imagine art that was so truly interactive it had to be fed and cared for. The possibilities are almost endless.

BRING ON THE NEO-PAGANS

Establishing a common ground between science—in this case technology—and art also lies at the heart of the Burning Man festival. Darryl Van Rhey chose the following Lucy Lippard quote to preface an article he wrote titled "The Art of Burning Man":

While some artists have never questioned the current marginal and passive status of art and are content to work within the reservation called the "art world," others have made conscious attempts over the last decade to combat the relentless commodification of their products and to reenter the "outside world." In the late '60s . . . many artists became

disgusted with the star system and the narrowness of formal "movements" . . . When they looked up from their canvas and steel, they saw
politics, nature, history and myth out there.

Burning Man may well be the Neo-Pagan, high-technology yin to
Kac's bioenhanced yang. The annual festival, held around Labor Day in
the Black Rock Desert (120 miles north of Reno, Nevada), was dubbed
"the new national holiday" by *Wired* magazine several years ago and is a
must on the social calendars of the Woodstock (II) Nation. Writer Brian
Doherty described it this way: "Burning Man is a quintessentially freaky
West Coast event, appealing mostly to a self-consciously underground
group of artists, digerati and tribally minded hipsters from California,
Nevada and the Pacific Northwest." Doherty ought to be paying more
attention. Burning Man is starting to draw an audience from across the
United States and around the world.

A detailed history of the event is available at the Burning Man website (http://www.burningman.com), but the shorthand version begins
in 1986 when San Franciscans Larry Harvey and Jerry James were looking for a way to celebrate the solstice. They finally settled on burning
an eight-foot figure at Baker Beach (San Francisco) in front of about
eighteen spectators. A year later the crowd grew fourfold, doubling (or
better) a year after that, and reaching over three hundred by 1989.
Thanks to police intolerance the burn site was moved to the Black Rock
Desert in 1990, where it's remained ever since. In 2000 more than 25,000
people attended the event, which is now a highly organized pay-to-
attend gathering.

Attending his first Burning Man event in 1996, science fiction guru
Bruce Sterling wrote in *Wired:* "Burning Man is an art gig by tradition.
Over the long term it's evolved into something else; maybe something
like a physical version of the Internet. The art here is like fan art. It's
very throwaway, very appropriate, very cut-and-paste. The camp is like
a giant swap meet where no one sells stuff, but people trade postures,
clip art, and attitude."

In his essay on the art of Burning Man, Van Rhey described the artist as "a member of a renegade class situated at the fringe of society." Van Rhey's essay is essentially a lamentation on the impact of the devox and the Abolition of Context in art. "The avant-garde," he wrote, "in this latter part of the 20th century, no longer appears to exist. Attempts to shock the middle class undoubtedly exist, but these actions, like so many other cultural elements of our contemporary scene, have been smoothly co-opted by a process of commodification. Madonna now affronts the bourgeoisie, as surely as *Piss Christ* and the concoctions of Jeff Koons, but such transgressive gestures are themselves merely artifacts of a marketing process."

In a posted Internet conversation with Van Rhey, Burning Man cocreator Larry Harvey described Burning Man's art as "immediate and involving." "It's collaborative and it breaks down the barriers between audience and art work. It's based upon participation—it's radically interactive—and it contemplates the facts of life. . . . The point I'm making is this: populist art, the kind we're creating, convenes society around itself."

Burning Man provides an interesting example of how a deviant perspective can render a new sense of order from the devox. "Our technique is to appropriate elements of mass culture, symbols that pervade popular consciousness," Harvey explained. "Our myths have a postmodern twist. It's a kind of guerilla strategy. Pop culture and the media tend to parasitize authentic culture, transforming grass-roots art into commodities. We've simply reversed the process. We turn pop culture back into myth that expresses the life of an actual community. We appropriate the appropriators."

Whatever else it is or isn't, Burning Man is clearly the preferred venue for techno-pagans eager to strut their collective stuff and pretend for a moment that art can build a world. The imagery is simultaneously pre- and posthistoric. Its centerpiece—the Burning Man himself, a postmodern reincarnation of a Celtic nightmare—is presented all tricked out in laser light and quasi high-tech symbolism, his presence heralded by a processional of endless loops of computer-generated and -enhanced techno music. Of course, Burning Man isn't the only example of the erasure of the lines separating art from technology.

Jaron Lanier has a vision of the future that seems to gleefully dart between the shadow of the Burning Man's flames and Kac's obsession with combining hard science and art. Lanier is by turns a scientist, a musician, a visual artist, an Internet pioneer, and—in many people's estimation—the father of virtual reality. Several years ago, the blond, dreadlocked Lanier—who once defined information as alienated experience—explained part of his vision of the marriage of technology and human expression, or what he called post-symbolic communication to *Scientific American.*

"If kids are growing up with an ability to program and make little virtual micro-worlds according to their own thoughts, perhaps some day another generation of kids will grow up with a similar skill but with tools that are much better, so that they can invent the contents of virtual worlds very quickly, at an improvisatory rate," he told the magazine.

> If they can do that, and if they have a shared virtual world interface that's wonderfully inexpensive and of high quality, that they can all participate in, then, as they grow up, they have a possibility to invent among themselves a new form of language.
>
> It's really something different than language. It's a new way to communicate, where people would directly create a shared world by programming it, but modeling it in real time, as opposed to merely using words, the intermediaries that we have to describe things. So it's like cutting out the middleman of words, and finding a new form of communication where you can directly create shared reality—real-time, waking-state, improvised dreaming.

HOW MUCH FOR A THIRTY-SECOND SPOT ON THE BURNING MAN?

The point for business here is that we've entered a period of boundless and fluid symbology. In the same way we've shown that language has been *decontextualized* to the point that its very meaninglessness is a subject for study, we've tried to show how art has been *recontextualized* into a series of new and commercially exploitable media. We doubt many of you will find yourselves dancing naked around a forty-foot-tall Burning Man; or petting a fluorescent green rabbit; or pondering a future in which information and communication technologies free children from the tyranny of language.

We do fully expect that someone reading this book will eventually sponsor some part of Burning Man or use Burning Man iconography to reach targeted consumer segments. We also believe that someone reading this book will launch a major genetically based product, one that could easily have an artistic component. The rest of you may want to consider more pragmatic ways in which the world of art will impact your business.

For example, traditional distinctions between the right-brained and the left-brained are disappearing as fast as the lines between art and science. We may soon see a time when, à la Burning Man, everything is art and everyone is an artist. This means your employees or coworkers will have a different set of expectations than their peers did a generation ago, expectations that may well place a premium on less-inhibited self-expression.

As we become an increasingly visually oriented society, corporate presentations and even the choices of presentation vehicles are going to become more and more important. Perhaps Monsanto should have taken a page from Eduardo Kac's playbook and used a cute fluorescent green Day-Glo bunny, instead of bioenhanced golden rice, to convince people biotech was a good thing. American and European audiences, it seemed, couldn't identify with the image of vast fields of rice, but who can resist a cute bunny?

As fine art and high technology become increasingly integrated into more and more people's daily lives, there's going to be a growing and healthy parallel market for Burning Man–like events that combine art, science, and community.

Dovetailing a bit on Lanier, we agree that both art and science are in the end chasing the same dream—the expansion of consciousness. Expanded consciousness should lead in turn to expanded markets. In fact, it should be a market in and of itself. If you don't believe us just check out the New Age section next time you're in Barnes & Noble or Borders. There's a larger and larger audience of people out there focusing on reaching untapped portions of their brains and/or the universe. They buy books, music, videos, and aromatherapy products, and shell out small fortunes to visit "power spots." Don't overlook them.

We can think of dozens of examples of companies that are already leveraging art as commerce. The Kohler Company, the kitchen and bathroom fixture manufacturer, sponsors a continuous artist-in-residence program in order to stay on the cutting edge of demand. Absolut Vodka's demand that different media create different print ads for them has resulted in a collector's market for its advertising messages. Have you examined the opportunities open to you?

The opportunities for corporate art should never stop at what's hanging on the walls or a slab of marble or hunk of steel outside the corporate headquarters. Art isn't the stuff of elites anymore, it's part of the installed infrastructure of life—or, in Kac's case, it is life itself.

Now it's time to see if the changes the devox has wrought in art are mirrored in science. The answer, it seems, is a definitive yes.

8

Science and the Death of Objective Reality

If we ask, for instance, whether the position of the electron remains the same, we must say "no"; if we ask whether the electron's position changes with time, we must say "no"; if we ask whether it is in motion, we must say "no."

—J. ROBERT OPPENHEIMER

Understanding the devox's impact on sex (the bait) and language and art (the pitch) is important to business. But understanding the changes it has wrought on science (the product) is mission critical. Throughout history, science has been the ally of business, helping it both create and better serve markets. Today, industries as diverse as pharmacology, biotechnology, information and communication technologies, personal and commercial electronics, media, and construction continually comb the frontiers of experimental science hoping to find their futures.

It wasn't all that long ago that science was more art than science—its "truths" dictated by the "facts" of myth, religion, or philosophical artifice. From the fifteenth century through the early years of the twentieth century, however, men and women of science worked hard to make themselves, well, more scientific. For a while, at least, it worked—that is, until the devox came along in the form of interdisciplinary fusion. In fact, you could almost hear the devox echoing in the words of physicist and novelist Nick Herbert when he said, "Reality? We don't got to show you no steeeeenking [*sic*] reality." But more about this in a moment.

We're going to spend most of this chapter examining how the impact of the devox has changed the traditional context of science. But before we do, we want to take a macro look at how the devox moved through the history of science.

On the Fringe of science there was a man or woman who refused to take reality at face value. We don't know that person's name, partially because this all happened so long ago and partially because Fringe dwellers of the ancient world never got noted. But somehow the idea of questioning the nature of physical reality caught on. In the West it was passed from the pre-Socratic philosophers down to Plato and eventually to Aristotle, our vote for the first legitimate scientific Edge dweller. Aristotle and his students took science seriously, attempting to chronicle everything that could be found in the physical universe. Aristotle's student, Alexander the Great, sent his old mentor all kinds of samples from his world conquests.

Even after Aristotle science was not what you'd really call a mass market. Of course, scientific breakthroughs continued to be discovered, but it wasn't until the alchemists that the science devox really entered the Realm of the Cool. The alchemists wrestled natural law away from witches and other Edge dwellers and gave science what it apparently needed most—a profit motive. The alchemists were all about creating wealth, specifically in the form of gold. Their efforts were financed by the most established figures in the world—kings, queens, and other royalty. Their laboratories were housed in castles and they were feted by the aristocracy of their respective nations. Alchemy was hot and, as a result, so was science.

But it took Isaac Newton, a closet alchemist himself, to move the scientific devox from the Realm of the Cool to the Next Big Thing. Newton's mechanical view of the universe made lots and lots of inventions and, as a direct result, commerce possible. If the profit motive is what moved the scientific devox into the Realm of the Cool, it practically shoved it into the Next Big Thing. A whole army of post-Newtonian scientists stewarded the devox into Social Convention, each asking questions not that much different from those asked by Aristotle.

What we've shown is an overview of all science, but the pattern holds true no matter where you look. The pre-Socratic philosophers had a concept of the atom, for example, and atomic theory can be traced right through to the present using the same model of devox evolution. The same could be done for aeronautics, biology, or any science. We could also find any number of modern scientists from Nikola Tesla to Wilhelm Reich whose careers fit the model of the devox's evolution.

In a very broad sense, the devox's work has been aided and abetted by the historical conflict between what British psychiatrist Ian Marshall and American physicist and philosopher Danah Zohar saw as the "old science" and "new science." Under their old science model, "the world was thought to consist of many observable data that could be analyzed and reduced to a few simple laws and principles." These laws and principles were the basis for general theories and hypotheses that could be tested. If they survived the test, the theories formed the basis for a system of scientific predictions.

"Where the old science stressed continuity and continuous, linear change," Marshall and Zohar wrote, "the new science is about abrupt movements and rapid, dramatic change that is off the scale from what came before. . . ." New scientists don't believe in prediction. Newton's clockwork universe has become a madhouse run by compulsive gamblers who have sacrificed their sanity pursuing probabilities instead of truths.

Speaking of old science, old Isaac Newton almost had us all fooled for a while, describing the inner working of a mechanical universe that ran so flawlessly it seemed everything in it was either clearly explicable or could be revealed after rigorous investigation. Thanks in no small part to Newton, the cryptomysticism of the alchemists and the rationalistic platitudes of generations of philosophers and theologians began to collapse under the burden of the idea of physical laws. This is a tad ironic, of course, given that Newton was an acknowledged deviant—a closet alchemist and mystic whose personal passion was the numerology of the Bible.

Newtonian mechanics was the perfect science for the Industrial Age and its physical-production technologies. It might have lasted if the devox, not content with replacing mysticism and subjective empiricism with mechanism and its more ostensibly objective associate disciplines, hadn't introduced interdisciplinary relativism in the first decades of the twentieth century, smashing everyone's sense of scientific social convention for the better part of a century.

During the late nineteenth and early twentieth centuries, the devox was batting three for three in its attack on conventional reality. In the physical sciences, a legion of physicists typified by Werner Heisenberg, whose work in the 1920s demonstrated that particle motion couldn't be accurately observed and described, and Albert Einstein, who proved the whole universe moved to the chaotic beat of relativity, transformed our impressions of time, space, and matter. In the life sciences, the publication of Charles Darwin's *Origin of Species* in 1859 had thrown a monkey wrench (if you'll pardon the pun) into the neat little world of the biblical explanation of the evolution of the universe. Within a few decades, Darwin's ideas blossomed into one of the first primitive fusion disciplines—social Darwinism. And finally, in the social sciences, Sigmund Freud's *Three Essays on the Theory of Sexuality* (1905) began warning us not to smile at our mothers too long, while Carl Jung's work moved "science" back to its alchemical roots. We've all grown up in an era where science—in fact, most sciences—have taught us that we can't really trust everything—or, for that matter, anything—we see or think.

Throughout the twentieth century—and continuing today—the physical sciences, the life sciences, and the social sciences have sometimes battled and sometimes fused in a desperate attempt to make enough objective sense of the devox's progress to provide a coherent and rational explanation of our lives and our world. The results weren't always pretty. As one observer noted, "Science began with the

Promethean affirmation of the power of reason, but it seemed to end in alienation—a negation of everything that gives meaning to human life."

Of course, the success of the devox's efforts to eradicate our collective notions of certitude hasn't ended our search for understanding. Physicist and author Freeman Dyson observed, "In the last 500 years, in addition to the quantum-mechanical revolution that Kuhn took as his model, we have had six major concept-driven revolutions, associated with the names of Copernicus, Newton, Darwin, Maxwell, Freud and Einstein." According to Dyson those same five centuries produced no fewer than twenty "tool-driven revolutions." Explaining the difference, he wrote:

> The effect of a concept-driven revolution is to explain old things in new ways. The effect of a tool-driven revolution is to discover new things that have to be explained. In almost every branch of science, and especially in biology and astronomy, there has been a preponderance of tool-driven revolutions. We have been more successful in discovering new things than in explaining old ones. In recent times my own field of physics has had great success in creating new tools that have started revolutions in biology and astronomy. Physics has been less successful in creating new concepts with which to understand its own discoveries.

The popular imagination tends to favor the life sciences—or deviant versions of the life sciences—over such mechanistic disciplines as chemistry and geology. No wonder! After all, the idea that an ecosystem might evolve in unexpected ways seems easier to accept than the notion that the physical universe is indescribable at best and out of control at worst. Even physical scientists seem to prefer the life sciences.

No less of a scientific guru than Dyson himself has proclaimed with startling certainty (for a physicist), "The dominant science of the twenty-first century will be biology. Two branches of biology in particular, genetics and neurophysiology, present us with an abundance of fundamental unsolved problems that new technological tools will enable us to attack." But biology is itself (if you'll excuse another pun) evolving.

As British biologist Brian Goodwin said, "The 'new' biology is biology in the form of an exact science of complex systems concerned with dynamics and emergent order. Then everything in biology changes. Instead of the metaphors of conflict, competition, selfish genes, climbing peaks in fitness landscapes, what you get is evolution as a dance. It has no goal." No goal versus the less than modest goal of universal explanation would seem a fairly large transition, but it's only the beginning.

The "new" biology Goodwin refers to has spawned a legion of new thinking around issues including chaos, complexity, simplicity, complex adaptive systems, and the like, much of it centered around the Santa Fe Institute and the work of individuals like Stuart Kauffman, Murray Gell-Mann, John Holland, and others.

Intriguingly, the devox's impact on science has also found fertile ground in the corporate community. Consider this from James F. Moore: "Unfortunately, the study of business communities lags well behind the biological. Yet close examination of the history of business innovation and the creation of wealth shows that there are important parallels between these two seemingly dissimilar worlds. While biological analogies are often applied to the study of business, they are frequently applied much too narrowly. . . . In my own work, I have become convinced that the world is more complicated than that, and that we must think in grander terms." Moore isn't alone. Richard T. Pascale, Mark Millemann, and Linda Gioja have attempted to popularize the science of complex adaptive systems in a business context.

Consultant Gary Hamel is another author who has attempted to apply new science directly to business. "Old companies faded away— remember American Motors and Eastern Airlines?—and new companies emerged," he wrote. "But to use a metaphor from biological evolution, it was a world of punctuated equilibrium, where change happened by degrees and seldom spawned entirely new life forms. Today, we live in a world that is all punctuation and no equilibrium. We are witnessing a Cambrian explosion of new competitive life forms. In this new age, a company that is evolving slowly is already on its way to extinction."

Finally, this somewhat ironic note from Susanne Kelly and Mary Ann Allison in *The Complexity Advantage:* "We often see somewhat mystical interpretations of many scientific theories appearing as management science . . . One can be forgiven a certain skepticism concerning the validity of such claims." The authors go on to apply a series of precise scientific concepts and mathematical models to business theory, including nonlinear dynamics, open and closed systems, feedback loops, fractal structures, and coevolution.

SYMBIOTIC MEN AND SPIRITUAL MACHINES

Not everyone sees the fusion of science and business as positive. Joël de Rosnay, director of strategy for the Science and Industry Complex in Paris, has written: "Science, the principal avenue to knowledge, is also subject to power games that undermine its integrity. The desire to dominate, faith in triumphant reason, and the attraction of the business world sometimes distort results and often influence thinking."

The explosive growth of information and communications technologies—particularly computation—have moved science from an activity whose goal is to describe life as it encounters it to an enterprise whose goal is to bring new life-forms into being. MIT's Ray Kurzweil has suggested that within the first three decades of this century humanity would be forced to come to grips with software that—for all intents and purposes—will be sentient.

Whether or not he's correct, Kurzweil has become a poster boy for the new scientists who redefine what the "life" that science is supposed to be studying looks like. And he's got plenty of company. George B. Dyson, Freeman Dyson's son, believes that "we have created a digital wilderness whose evolution may embody a collective wisdom greater than our own."

German Nobel Prize–winning biochemist Manfred Eigen put it this way: "Things we denote as 'living' have too heterogeneous characteristics and capabilities for a common definition to give even an inkling of the variety contained within this term." Any number of scientists have birthed entire universes. Ecologist Tom Ray's "Tierra" is an artificial universe populated by electronic organisms that reproduce, mutate, and evolve—inside a computer or from computer to computer. Since Tierra, any number of artificial life systems have been created. We'd suggest that anyone interested look up Artificial Life Online at http://www.alife.org, a sort of clearing site for the Alife community. Tierra is an instructive experiment on several levels. The work being done by the Alife community provides an interesting way to model evolution and raises difficult questions about what life is and isn't.

We know some of you may be wondering how this impacts your business, so think about this example. Unless you possess some secret cyber-condom that protects your computer system, we're pretty sure you've either been attacked by a computer virus or have invested in Norton Antivirus or some other software to protect your system. If you really want to lose some sleep tonight, consider this: On a practical level, what's the real difference between a physical virus and a computer virus? The answer is that there really isn't much difference. Both "viruses" evolve, mutate, and migrate from host to host.

Think about all those artificial life-forms—whether Alife experiments or viruses—drifting around the Internet. Armed with their neobiological imperative to survive, these "life-forms" could self-evolve into new "life-forms" that, out of the control of their creators, could paralyze your business. We're not talking about some smartbot like Teddy in the movie *AI*—just some relatively dumb pieces of code that could stop your business cold.

Naturally, not every scientist is comfortable with the notion that science is somehow less certain than it used to be, or even that it's operating with a brand-new set of rules. That kind of thinking brings out the orthodox in even the most generally subversive minds. Consider the case of Kary Mullis, Nobel Prize winner, inventor of the polymerase chain reaction that forever changed the face of DNA research and genetics, an accomplished surfer, admitted sampler of various psychedelic substances, author, and one of the few Nobel laureates ever to have described a possible encounter with real ETs.

"The laws of science are demonstrable," Mullis wrote. "They are not beliefs. When experiments in our century showed that Newton's gravitational laws were not quite accurate, we changed the laws—despite Newton's good name and holy grave in Cambridge. Relativity fit the facts better. . . . Scientific method should not be taken lightly."

Mullis's cautions aside, there is a growing body of thought out there that seems to want to do just that—turn the scientific method on its head. Like Mullis, the late Terence McKenna was attracted to psychedelics, so attracted in fact that he came to see hallucinogens as the driving force of history. McKenna honed his thesis in a series of books that included *The Archaic Revival, Food of the Gods,* and *The Invisible Landscape.* McKenna explained humanity's past and future as one giant rave attended by the entire planet. In *Trialogues at the Edge of the West,* McKenna wrote, "The purpose of science should be understanding, not only technique." Science's goal, he argued, should be perspective, not the endless pursuit of data points.

McKenna's is an increasingly popular position. Biologist Rupert Sheldrake has suggested that the shapes and instincts of living organisms are defined and maintained by "morphogenetic fields," molded by the form and behavior of past organisms of the same species through direct connections across both space and time. Other scientists, like Lynn Margulis, have taken a more macro position, arguing that the earth itself is in fact an organism (making you, gentle reader, an infinitesimal parasite) and that she is getting a little tired of us.

For most businesspeople it's far more important to just understand that the new science versus old science debate is going on, rather than to try to make sense of which side is right. To that end we close this section of this chapter with a quotation from Michio Kaku, professor of theoretical physics at the City University of New York: "By the end of the twentieth century, science had reached the end of an era, unlocking the secrets of the atom, unraveling the molecule of life and creating the electronic computer. With these three fundamental discoveries, triggered by the quantum revolution, the DNA revolution and the computer revolution, the basic laws of matter, life and computation were, in the main, finally solved. That epic phase of science is now drawing to a close; one era is ending and another is only beginning." That new phase will be responsible for launching literally billions of dollars of new products.

THE BIOLOGICAL BRADY BUNCH

The move from the Industrial Age to the Information Age shifted our preferred science from chemistry to physics. When we left the Information Age behind, physics gave way to biology. And biology, it seems, has birthed a thousand children, from Eduardo Kac's artificially glowing rabbit, to Rupert Sheldrake's transhistorical memory, to the notion of Gaia. We're not suggesting that science isn't still largely about law and fixed and repeatable patterns. We are saying that the tent of science now shelters a lot more intellectual diversity than it used to, which isn't too surprising given the escalating pulse of the devox.

We rather like being gods, even if we spell god with a small g. So it's only natural that the idea of creating life—especially if there's significant commercial opportunity attached—is almost too attractive to pass up, making the growth of biotech all but inevitable.

The biotech industry provides an interesting mini case study of what happens when the devox, in the form of technological innovation, meets business. In 1971, Ananda Chakrabarty, an Indian microbiologist employed by General Electric, applied to the U.S. Patents and Trademark Office (PTO) for a patent on a genetically engineered oil-munching microorganism. The PTO rejected the application, arguing that American law didn't allow anyone to patent living things. That decision was overturned on appeal by a single vote of the Court of Customs and Patent Appeals, a vote that was in turn appealed. Chakrabarty didn't win his final victory until the U.S. Supreme Court found in his favor in a five-to-four ruling in 1980.

Just a few months after the historic ruling in the Chakrabarty case, which extended patent protection to artificially created life, Genentech, the biotech giant, launched an IPO of more than a million shares of stock at $35 a share. In less than twenty minutes, those shares jumped to $89 a share; and by the time the bell rang and first-day trading closed the company had raised $36 million and was valued at $532 million.

Genentech wasn't alone in trying to capitalize on the market potential of the new biology. Monsanto, for example, reversed gears and bet the corporate farm on a biotechnologically enhanced future, a wager we're sure they'd like a chance to reconsider. The race for bioriches was on with both businessmen and scientists frantic to crack the genome. So far patenting gene sequences hasn't brought us an inch closer to a Brave New World free of hunger, disease, and discomfort, but it has paid for a lot of nice homes for patent attorneys.

Biotech provides the classic example of how market opportunity emerges from the abolition of a traditional view of science. Patenting gene sequences that have no application is a business decision. Presumably, a scientist would rather spend his or her time figuring out what, if anything, those sequences actually do. Additionally, the notion of destroying the established natural order and accepted scientific convention is no longer deviant; it's the basis for attracting venture capital. Apparently, we can't wait to rewrite rules we never fully understood in the first place.

The context of science has also changed in another significant way. We used to draw a distinction between science and technology. Science was seen as a pure understanding of the world, whereas technology was traditionally associated with the tool emerging from that understanding. Using a common business metaphor, we might say science was the strategy while technologies were the tactics. Today we have come to treat technology as though it were a science. We're not absolutely positive what confusing the building tools with the blueprints does for—or to—us, but we ought to think some of these things through a bit more in our collective commercial rush to market dominance.

As businesses and as a society we're juggling some strange juju when we follow the devox's lead in science. For example, we've started to do things like patent gene sequences and create artificial cyberlife forms, not because we should or need to, but rather just because we can. Even though we all grew up being told, "It's not nice to fool Mother Nature," experimentation has become an end in and of itself.

We're not antiscientific, paranoid, or apocalyptic enough to join Jeremy Rifkin and other biotech opponents who believe we're living just one gene splice this side of a biological Armageddon. In fact, we're pretty sure that in the near term, at least, a computer virus has an exponentially greater probability of destroying the sanctity of our life—and your business—than any recombinant gene pool mutantly bubbling away in some petri dish in a lab in Peoria.

Similarly, we're not concerned about a rash of dictators attempting to clone themselves. Actually, we've heard from members of the team that cloned Dolly the sheep that they're deluged by inquiries from people who want to clone not themselves but their parents. On the other hand, we do share some of the concerns voiced by England's Prince Charles and others who worry that in the long term, the rush to biological perfection may negatively and critically impact biodiversity.

There's just no point in putting too many genetically modified eggs in one evolutionary basket. After all, we believe in deviance, and all this talk of engineering a perfect world seems bent on eliminating mutation. And given that the pharmaceutical industry has made literally hundreds of billions of dollars from compounds synthesized from nature, we don't see the validity of deliberately deselecting any species before it's been thoroughly investigated and understood. That underproducing variety of potato may represent the cure for cancer.

We're also just not all that sure that we're collectively ready to live with the consequences of our individual cleverness. It's only a half step from what we've been discussing here to concepts like eugenics and respeciation. Always wanted an Olympic swimmer in the family? Then why not introduce gills in utero? Our track record in dealing with basic differences between people (gender, race, religion, ethnicity, sexual preference, etc.) ought to make us pause a bit. If nothing else, just imagine the EEOC implications of having multiple species on the payroll!

THE BOTTOM LINE FOR BUSINESS

There are five basic take-aways business should consider when evaluating the devox's impact on science:

1. Scientifically based business opportunities will continue to present themselves faster than they can be properly evaluated. That is, after all, what happens when you dance with the devox. But every great Saturday night is followed by a sobering Sunday morning, and we have to understand that the downside of radical innovation—particularly biological innovation—gone wrong could be catastrophic.

2. That said, it's critical that every business do its best to try to stay on the cutting edge of science. Even if you're making something as relatively prosaic as soap, you can't afford to overlook developments in biology that could either improve your product beyond your wildest imaginings or render it obsolete.

3. Over the next two or three decades the combined impact of research in the physical, life, and computational sciences will significantly touch the lives of everyone you work with. At the very least, the effective working life of most Americans—and presumably most citizens of what in a pre-PC world used to be called the developed world—will be extended significantly. We're futurists, not mystics, so we can't be sure what this means, but unless Wal-Mart expands exponentially, creating a chronic need for greeters, we think there might be a growing pool of unemployed and underemployed people.

4. We know some of our discussion of science might have seemed a bit esoteric. But remember, historically science in general, and technology in particular, used to help business better serve markets. Today science and technology are increasingly creating markets. And, as in the case of biotech and even the Internet, these can grow to multibillion-dollar markets well before their commercial viability has been established or we know how to fully control or exploit them.

5. Finally, all this new science is bound to create an opportunity for unemployed philosophers since most scaled businesses will have to wrestle with the ethical impact of scientific and technological development. In the future, a company's ethical position may become even more important than its balance sheet.

In the next chapter we want to throw out some quick "short takes" on the devox's impact on a few other subjects in order to show that we didn't just select models we could easily manipulate to prove our point.

9

Seeing and Believing, War and More

The vehicle for the arrival of the Kingdom of God on earth is *speed,* which is made possible by new technology. . . . As speed increases, time appears to accelerate until it comes to a standstill and everyone and everything seem to be suspended in the eternal presence of a *nunc stans.*

—MARK C. TAYLOR

We've said it before—there are no more protected spaces. The devox's assault on Social Convention is a battle fought on a hundred thousand fronts. Some of them are obvious, as we've shown in our examinations of sex, art, science, and language. Others are so apparently trivial we're not even aware of them until we feel their aggregate weight on those days when "Nothing seems to work like it's supposed to." These changes are reflected—to a greater or lesser extent—by the changes in the lives of enterprises, markets, and economies we will examine in Chapters 10 and 11. And, finally, there are those such as the ones we'll examine in this chapter that are simultaneously both more personal and universal.

But whether the devox's efforts and impacts strike you as profound or just puzzling, it's critical to remember that the context of life—your life, your customers' lives, and your associates' lives—has changed and will continue to change in ways that you likely aren't aware of. Thirty years ago only a handful of devoted science-fiction fans and writers, obsessive worriers, stoned residents of the Woodstock Nation, and outright delusionals seriously discussed extraterrestrial life.

Fifteen years ago you may have been among the legion of sophisticates who occasionally stole a guilty peek whenever a new alien invasion story played across the front page of *The Weekly World News*, but would never buy an issue. Ten years ago you may have found yourself laughing out loud when "genuine abductees" discussed being probed (usually in the oddest places) by gray men on talk radio or television. Try to remember how you felt in 1997 when you read or heard about the mass suicide of the Heaven's Gate cult. Now look around your office. How many of your friends and coworkers or employees are wearing angel pins? People still believe in forces they can't see, but today it's socially acceptable.

Now think about the media, which has invaded almost every aspect of your life. Do you find yourself having conversations with coworkers about characters on television as though they were real? Do you know people who can't tell the difference between news footage and reenactments, or who don't care that there might be a difference? Are you old enough to remember when the news was about the past tense rather than the future tense? Fifteen years ago you may not have needed a personal computer. Ten years ago the Internet was the wild frontier, not a push media. Today hundreds of thousands of people use wireless telephony or their PDA to access the Internet, and we have more bandwidth than content.

Let's talk about war for a minute. How did you feel in the weeks and months following the September 11, 2001, attacks on the World Trade Center and the Pentagon? Did you—like President Bush—expand your previous definition of war to include acts of terrorism? When the president spoke of terrorism being a "new" kind of third-millennium warfare, did he seem prescient or just hopelessly out of touch with modern geopolitics?

And speaking about the president, peel back the veils of memory several months more to recall the time before he was the impassioned leader of an outraged nation, to when he was playing Tweedlepublican to Al Gore's Tweedledumocrat. As we debated the relative importance of dimpled versus pregnant chads, didn't it seem that the devox had a firm grip on the electoral process?

The devox's impact on faith, media, war, and governance demonstrates the same pattern of disruption of the status quo and new-opportunity creation we've seen in the other areas we've examined.

GIVE ME THAT OLD-TIME RELIGION

The English word *religion* is derived from the Latin *religare*, which means "to bind something together in common expression." For the ecclesiastically challenged, here's an approximate breakdown of formal global mass-belief systems. Humanity has witnessed twelve classical world religions. Today eleven religions—Baha'i, Buddhism, Confucianism, Hinduism, Islam, Judaism, the Orthodox Eastern Church, Protestantism, Roman Catholicism, Shinto, and Taoism—dominate the landscape of contemporary faith. But, as the following chart illustrates, there are twice that many serious faith systems active in the world today.

MAJOR WORLD FAITH SYSTEMS
RANKED BY NUMBER OF ADHERENTS

Belief System	Number of Adherents
Christianity	2,000,000,000
Islam	1,300,000,000
Hinduism	900,000,000
Secular/Nonreligious/Agnostic/Atheist	850,000,000
Buddhism	360,000,000
Chinese Traditional Religion	225,000,000
Primal Indigenous	190,000,000
Sikhism	23,000,000
Yoruba	20,000,000
Juche	19,000,000

Belief System	Number of Adherents
Spiritism	14,000,000
Judaism	14,000,000
Baha'i	6,000,000
Jainism	4,000,000
Shinto	4,000,000
Cao Dai	3,000,000
Tenrikyo	2,400,000
Neo-Paganism	1,000,000
Unitarian-Universalism	800,000
Scientology	750,000
Rastafarianism	700,000
Zoroastrianism	150,000

Now, be honest. How many of these belief systems are you familiar with? We're willing to bet that you'll find there are at least millions of people on earth who fervently believe in a truth you're, at best, only remotely aware of. From the Crusades on, religion has been tied to commercial opportunity, and the devox has created a veritable spiritual soup of new religions and belief systems that can easily give rise to new and powerful commercial markets.

Thanks to the devox there are lots of new faiths. In Japan alone, for example, more than five hundred new religions have been established since the end of World War II. Faith-based industries are becoming bigger and bigger businesses as American, European, and Asian baby boomers begin to ease up on the clutches of their psychic Beamers and reluctantly edge toward the admission of their own mortality.

Of course, we're talking about deviance here so some of these new religions are a bit problematic, like the Escuela de Yoga de Buenos Aires (School of Yoga of Buenos Aires), whose leader, Juan Percowicz, was viewed as God by his followers even after he demanded they participate in highly deviant sexual acts. We've mentioned Heaven's Gate, but let's not forget Jim Jones and the People's Temple or Waco. In the twilight of the twentieth century, Uganda's doomsday cults flourished, including the Movement for the Restoration of the Ten Commandments of God and the World Message Last Warning. The list could go on and on, but it wouldn't be complete without a reference to Japan's Aum Shinrikyo (currently renamed Aleph), which staged multiple sarin gas attacks in Japanese cities from 1994 to 1995. But let's focus a bit on the major religions.

A closer examination of the world's two largest religions, Islam and Christianity, reveals a pronounced transition from mainstream worship to the spiritual polarities of fundamentalism and extreme liberalism. For every Hezbollah guerrilla or Taliban member happily smashing Buddhist sculptures, there are a hundred liberal Roman Catholics routinely and without guilt committing acts their parents would have defined as mortal sins. One of the unusual aspects of the devox's influence is its ability to spur contradictory—and even paradoxical—outcomes from a single stimulus.

Perhaps the best examples of this point are the fusion of those historic adversaries science and religion and the rise of New Age, highly idiosyncratic expressions of faith. In the former case we see people looking to science as either a proof source for their faith or even as a faith object. The renewed interest in "scientific" areas as diverse as cosmology and a "general biology" has produced shelves of books ranging from physicist Lee Smolin's *The Life of the Cosmos* to complexity guru Stuart Kauffman's *Investigations.* While these books are not religious works in the classic sense, they seek to use science to answer fundamentally religious questions—an adequate description of life itself and the underlining structure of the world.

In the latter case we have any number of examples from Heaven's Gate to Waco to EST and Gaiaism where, rather than waiting for a religion to come along they can believe in, people are creating religions to match their own personal emotional and psychic needs. Churches have become social centers in affluent communities, places to see and be seen, but are losing attendance across the social board. Church leaders have become a bit more circumspect since the days of Jimmy Swaggart and Jim Bakker, but there's no question that—with the possible exception of

the Dalai Lama, who has become something of a pop-cultural phenomenon—the heads of most major religions have suffered a universal loss
of moral, and consequently political, authority.

At a time of profound and universal change, the Abolition of the
Traditional Religious Context (i.e., I go to church, where God calls
some tough shots, rather than establish a church where God is just one
of my buds) has, if anything, intensified most people's spiritual need.
People "need" some form of understanding about life and its meaning
and assurance that there's more to life than biological definition and
limitation. At precisely the same time, many of the traditional sources
of explanation and assurance are viewed as suspect. We don't think the
future is knowable, at least in a Nostradamus, crystal ball sort of way,
making prediction an intellectually stimulating but inherently limited
pursuit.

That said, we believe that in the immediate future, at least, spirituality will replace sexuality as the most effective marketing tactic available
to business. Don't believe us? Start counting angel pins, Psychic Friends
Network users, tarot-card readers, and Wicca cookbooks, or visit the
Eastern Religion and New Age sections of your local Barnes & Noble.
And there's far more to come as the baby-boomer cohort begins its
inevitable forced demographic march toward old age and death. The
same people who eschewed church and churches may revive their spiritual positions when age ups the ante. Of course, the devox's impact on
other elements of life can influence people's attitudes toward religion.
Consider the Gallup Poll figures in the chart on the following page
measuring the importance of religion that were put together after the
terrorist attacks of September 11, 2001.

Gallup found the same pattern of post–September 11 religious reen-
gagement demonstrated in church attendance. The second chart highlights a decade of responses to questions about recent church
attendance.

In the face of the profound changes the devox is wreaking on faith-
based institutions, our recommendation is that you find a way to build
a spiritual hook into your business, understanding that spiritual is now

"HOW IMPORTANT WOULD YOU SAY RELIGION IS IN YOUR OWN LIFE — VERY IMPORTANT, FAIRLY IMPORTANT, OR NOT VERY IMPORTANT?"

Survey Date	Very Important	Fairly Important	Not Very Important	No Opinion
9/21/01–9/22/01	64	24	12	*
5/10/01–5/14/01	57	28	15	*
8/24/00–8/27/00	57	31	12	*
4/30/99–5/2/99	58	30	11	1
1/16/98–1/18/98	59	29	12	*
11/6/97–11/9/97	58	28	13	1
9/3/96–9/5/96	55	31	13	1
5/11/95–5/14/95	56	30	13	1
6/25/94–6/28/94	55	30	14	1
3/12/93–3/14/93	59	32	9	*
11/20/92–11/22/92	59	28	12	1
11/91	55	29	15	1

"DID YOU HAPPEN TO ATTEND CHURCH OR SYNAGOGUE IN THE LAST SEVEN DAYS?"

Survey Date	Yes	No
9/21/01–9/22/01	47	53
8/24/00–8/27/00	43	57
4/30/99–5/2/99	40	60
1/16/98–1/18/98	39	61
8/12/97–8/13/97	35	65
9/3/96–9/5/96	37	63
5/11/95–5/14/95	41	59
12/16/94–12/18/94	38	62
6/93	38	62
11/92	40	60
11/91	41	59

defined in a much more universal sense than it used to be. Notice we said spiritual, not necessarily formally religious. People are searching for answers that—in the wake of the devox—are not as precisely defined as they used to be. Wearing an angel pin isn't the same thing as going to church, but, at least in some cases, it may deliver the same emotional effect.

It's also important for the people in your organization that you stay attuned to potential impacts of spirituality on your internal operations. It's easy to offend the devout, particularly when you have no idea they exist. The spiritually obscure has an interesting habit of coming home to roost. You also have to be equally cautious of offending those who believe their spirituality has no place in the workplace. The key is to be sensitive to spiritual concerns (such as the issues of life, identity, meaning, etc.) as they impact your internal operations and external publics. The point here is that there are a wide variety of beliefs out there, each as valid to the believer as any other.

GONNA STUDY WAR SOME MORE

Next to sex, war may be humanity's favorite communal activity. Historically, war was the vehicle of choice for grabbing territory, pursuing power, and accumulating wealth. Increasingly, however, it's about making an ideological and, more recently at least, a quasi-theological point. Wars used to be global. Now (with the exception of President George W. Bush's War on Terrorism) they're highly regionalized, almost tribal.

War also used to be an organized activity with formal armies, rules of engagement, and mutually agreed-upon battlefields. Today (as evidenced by the horrors of September 11, 2001) terrorism is increasingly replacing formal warfare—terrorism, whose ultimate goal is disruption rather than conquest. Osama bin Laden and al Qaeda represent the negative side of the devox's impact on warfare.

Residents of Belfast, Derry, London, Munich, Paris, Rome, Tel Aviv, Tokyo, and Spain's Basque country and a hundred other parts of the world from Peru to the Indian subcontinent may have heard a uniquely

American naïveté in President Bush's declaration that the terrorism of September 11 was a new kind of war for the third millennium. Terrorism is, after all, hardly new in most parts of the world. We don't believe the president was overlooking the obvious fact that the World Trade Center had been attacked before by terrorists. What President Bush and hundreds of millions of others around the world were really responding to wasn't the attack itself, but rather the scale of the attack. In his October 11, 2001, address to the nation, the president said that on September 11 we learned there was Evil in the world. We'd say that the devox had finally made its way from the Fringe (in this case a psychotic, orthodox Islamic mind) to the dead center of Social Convention. And, as almost everyone agrees, life will never be the same.

The devox has also abolished the context of traditional warfare. We used to try to isolate civilians from the reality of war. Many believe that the lack of domestic support for the Vietnam War can be traced to the fact that it was the first war piped into America's living rooms. Today— in the spirit of a modern, multimedia Gettysburg—war is routinely broadcast into our homes in a series of sanitized, antiseptic visuals delivered courtesy of CNN.

Several years ago we found ourselves flying across the country with a soon-to-be-very-drunk Raytheon employee who designed missile warheads. We sat in wonder as our intoxicated traveling companion described how tough it was to balance the demands of aerodynamics and the need for a transmitter capable of sending signals to CNN in the same warhead. The Pentagon, it appears, was very concerned that Americans get a clear picture of those smart bombs being deployed. The abolition of the traditional context of warfare and its translation into a media event means everyone—and certainly every business—is a potential terrorist target.

In 1987 science fiction writer William Gibson coined the term *cyberspace* to describe what he called a "consensual hallucination." Nowhere are the fruits of that hallucination more in evidence than in our preference for viewing war through the lens of advanced information and communication technologies. In his 1961 farewell address, President

Dwight Eisenhower warned Americans of the growing dangers of the military-industrial complex. If Ike were delivering that speech today, he'd have to add media to the cabal.

Media is the new handmaiden of war. James Der Derian, an author who teaches international relations at Brown University and the University of Massachusetts at Amherst, has observed, "Technology in the service of virtue has given rise to a global form of virtual violence, *virtuous war.*" Der Derian defines virtuous war as "the technical capability and ethical imperative to threaten and, if necessary, actualize violence from a distance—*with no or minimal casualties. . . .* Along with time (in the sense of tempo) as the fourth dimension, virtuality has become the 'fifth dimension' of U.S. global hegemony." Think of the way American troops were deployed during Operation Enduring Freedom—sent in only after extensive carpet bombing had substantially reduced the potential for casualties. Good strategy and good media. During the entire Gulf War only 270 Americans lost their lives—more than half in accidents. Only 18 Americans were killed during the raid on Mogadishu. And, most amazing of all, barring accidents, NATO forces incurred a remarkable zero casualty rate during the Kosovo air campaign. Now, by contrast think back to Vietnam, where so many Americans died. Every night news footage brought the brutality and horror of combat into the living rooms of Middle America.

"On the surface," Der Derian continued, "virtuous war cleans up the political discourse as well as the battlefield. Fought in the same manner as they are represented, by real-time surveillance and TV 'live feeds,' virtuous wars promote a vision of bloodless, humanitarian, hygienic wars."

In President Bush's War on Terrorism, we see the iterative consequence of the devox's ability to abolish context. On the one hand, you have the now mainstreamed fringe fanaticism of bin Ladin and al Qaeda launching a sophisticated modern incarnation of an ancient Islamic jihad. On the other side, you have the military-media complex attempting to simultaneously fight and broadcast a high-technology war on terror. It's like watching the devox arm wrestling with itself. We suspect

President Bush is correct in his assessment that this will be a long war. We disagree with the idea that the terrorist attacks of September 11 represented a new kind of war. What's happened is that the context of traditional war has been abolished and the response to the attacks represents an ahistorical military engagement.

Today every person on earth is a potential combatant in the new kind of war and every place on earth has become a potential battlefield. The irony is that while this is true, the most direct evidence of the war will be broadcast into people's homes as entertainment, providing us a deviant segue into our discussion of the devox's impact on the media.

THE MEDIA HAVE NO MESSAGE

There have clearly been profound changes in the way we report and broadcast our perceptions of news and other forms of information. Let's start by looking at newspapers and broadcast news media. When most of us were young, news organizations prided themselves on their ability to accurately report what had happened. Today more and more space and time is devoted to what they believe will happen. That's why most of us walk around with a vague feeling of déjà vu. By the time something actually happens, we've read, heard, or seen it, generally several times. We think that's partially what saved Bill Clinton's bacon during l'Affair Monica. How outraged can you be when you're already aware of the elements of a scandal before they're formally made public? Ever since Watergate, significant news stories have been "broken" by news leakers rather than news makers.

The impact of the devox's abolition of the context of what constitutes legitimate news is just beginning to be felt. With CNN, CNBC, and other networks competing for viewership twenty-four hours a day, seven days a week, fifty-two weeks a year, we're literally starting to run out of things to talk about. This may account for the popularity of reenactments. After all, it takes more time to stage and reenact an event than it does to tell you about it. Clearly this content gap has been a boon to the talk-show industry and boosted the television career of dozens of expert commentators on areas from law and finance to technology and war.

One could argue that television is just following the same media evolutionary path blazed by all-news radio. But there is a critical difference—on television the presenter becomes part of the story, something that (with the exception of reporters like Edward R. Murrow and Paul Harvey or commentators like Rush Limbaugh and Don Imus) hasn't always been the case on news radio.

The ultimate deviant media act is to become the story rather than cover it. That's exactly what happened in the wake of the September 11 attacks. The delay in remote live broadcasts between the time a speaker's mouth began to move and the audience actually heard their words became a subject for political satirists. Whether Geraldo should have been carrying a gun was more hotly debated than any of his reports. Whether the speeches (and even choice of apparel) of Taliban leaders, Osama bin Laden, or others should be broadcast (an internal policy decision, after all) became the subject of editorial debate. And the devox's impact doesn't stop there.

We've learned to live on a diet of empty media calories, apparently surprised every time we collapse from information malnutrition. We've all become addicted to McNews thanks to *USA Today* and CNN Headline News. Somewhere along the line we lost the collective desire to dig deeper, to know more. It's not exactly that we want to know less, it's just that we seem happy knowing "enough." This is both good and bad news for business. In a society addicted to headlines, business has to be particularly careful what those headlines say. Since there's little interest in learning in depth, there's little room left for nuance or subtlety.

Naturally this begins to further hone the kind of messaging delivered by the media. President Bush has refined the rhetorical technique used by Churchill and Roosevelt (who didn't have to worry about the problem of sound bites), allowing the complexity of terrorism and global geopolitics to be reduced to a simplistic battle between Good and Evil. It isn't the president's fault he's fallen into what we term media Manichaeanism, or the reduction of complicated thought into two (easily cast and broadcasted) opposing positions. Given the Abolition of Traditional Media Context, it's easier to think in these terms than it is to think. All that most of us remember about the Alar scare is that actress Meryl Streep was convinced that apples were bad for her children. Pesticides are bad. Organic is good. Alan Greenspan can save the economy or pitch it into irredeemable free fall. Communists are always our enemies. Anticommunists are always our friends. Pakistan, which on September 10, 2001, was a rogue nuclear state, was bad, but now it has to be good because its leaders publicly turned their backs on bin Laden.

Finally, the traditional separation between editorial and advertising is disappearing in an increasing number of publications. Some magazines routinely guarantee favorable press coverage in exchange for ad linage. Others have chosen to replace the words "Advertorial" or "Advertising Supplement" with phrases such as "Special Section" or "Educational Section." Some businesses, including Qwest, Sony, and Yahoo!, have sidestepped the whole issue and now publish their own magazines—brands presenting themselves as media. This devolution of media might be a boon to political leaders if it wasn't for the devox's impact on governance.

WHAT'S A GOVERNMENT, ANYWAY?

Government used to make laws and proscribe behavior. Today it struggles for media acceptability and the moral and political authority to enforce them. In an ever-globalizing world the notion that the nation-state's best days are behind it is proving increasingly popular. The clearest evidence of the devox's Abolition of the Traditional Context of Government is the growing number of individuals and entities—from global terrorists to global industry—that simply refuse to acknowledge the right of any sovereign nation to regulate their affairs.

If we're really going to develop truly global businesses, then we need governance bodies with some form of global authority, sort of a European Union on steroids. The United States versus Microsoft is a perfect illustration of the problem modern government has regulating modern business. What other government in history would have been unhappy to house one of the most powerful corporations on earth, especially when that corporation dominated a critical global technology? Proprietary regulation, especially in the form of rigorous antitrust enforcement, is the enemy of global commerce. And commerce, like water, seeks its own level.

We're not sure where the issue of governance will settle out, but we are sure that the issue of who has the right to govern whom will be one of the most critical questions all individuals and businesses will face in the future. Some suggest that the corporation is the rightful successor to government, but this strikes us as economic science fiction. At any rate, the devox's impact on war may change all that. Last year we saw the surge in popularity of President Bush, who until September 11 had been viewed by many Americans as an ineffective leader.

The terrorist attacks on the World Trade Center and the Pentagon were an unexpected, deviant shot in the arm for Bush and the pro–big government lobby. If on August 11, 2001, the president had suggested creating the vaguely ominous sounding Department of Homeland Security, subjecting traveling Americans to inspection by heavily armed guardsmen, and the suspension of certain civil and political rights, we're pretty sure there would have been calls for impeachment. Thanks to the devox, taking those actions allowed him to be perceived as a leader. The more the devox destroys our ability to hold a coherent view of the world and what happens in it, the better it will be for the supporters of traditional strong governance and nationalism to reinstate their authority and control.

Like the chapters that preceded it, this chapter hardly begins to exhaust the cataloging of the devox's impact on traditional context. In Chapter 10 we turn our attention to the impact of the Abolition of Context and the impact of deviance on your business. Just bear in mind our underlying assumption that successful businesses respond to and capitalize on changes in the society around them.

PART THREE

DEVIANCE AND BUSINESS

In Part Three we look at how the devox impacts your business. We'll examine both the Abolition of Context and how business deviants are transforming the landscape of commerce.

We'll start with a quick look at deviant economies in Chapter 10. We'll look not just at the battle between the New and Old Economies but at the growth of microeconomies like the drug economy, corporate economies like Wal-Mart, and the global economy. The important lesson is that in the era of the devox, there's no such thing as a single economic reality.

Chapter 11 looks at deviant corporate cultures. We have come to believe that there are no business problems, rather just dysfunctional business cultures. In this chapter we'll look at the real-world consequences of these dysfunctions.

In Chapter 12 we examine deviant consumers, showing how they can either be unexpected allies or a business's worst nightmare. We'll look at proven tactics for dealing with, and capitalizing on, these new consumers.

Deviant markets and deviant marketing are the subjects of Chapter 13. We'll look at how a colorful cast of deviants from Sigmund Freud to Howard Stern has influenced how markets are made. And we'll see why moving away from deviance can be a costly mistake.

Chapter 14 looks at deviant products, examining such radical ideas as the notion that products should be free to everyone and that by not protecting your intellectual property you might actually stand a good chance of enhancing it.

Chapter 15 looks at deviant brands. Among other topics, we'll look at licensing—a business that's paradoxically booming at a time when brand loyalty is under attack. We'll also look at how to build deviance into your branding efforts.

Specific deviant tools and their use are the topic of conversation in Chapter 16. We'll look at some deviant tools you can begin using today to transform your go-to-market strategies.

Finally, in Chapter 17 we'll take a deeper look at how you, too, can become a deviant, including a detailed examination of some of the most useful forms of deviance available to you.

Our intention in these chapters isn't to offer an exhaustive analysis of any of these topics. It's just to remind you it's already later than you might think.

10

The Deviant Economy

Life, death, preservation, loss, failure, success, poverty, riches,
worthiness, unworthiness, slander, fame, hunger, thirst, cold, heat—
these are the alternations of the world, the workings of fate. Day and
night they change place before us and wisdom cannot spy out their
source.

—CHUANG TZU

Our examination of the devox's impact on the context of traditional
business begins with the cornerstone of all things commercial—
the economy. The best, and ironically the most mediocre, business
minds in the world agree on one thing: Business is anything but usual,
and it's just getting stranger all the time. In less than a decade we've had
the unprecedented opportunity to witness the birth, and some would
argue the death, of an entire economic system.

The so-called New Economy broke most of the conventions of the
system its champions predicted it would replace, only to fall victim to
the very rules it had set out to supplant. It's a story we're all familiar
with, some of us painfully so. Future business school students will
spend countless hours trying to make sense of the years 2000 and 2001,
puzzling over the weird capitalist alchemy that transformed ideas first
into overcapitalized dot-coms and then into grossly underperforming
dot-bombs. What strange monetary mojo, they'll wonder, could be

responsible for the financial yo-yo effect? Our answer, of course, is that one day the devox came knocking on the door of Economic Social Convention.

Since it's so fresh in all our minds, let's see what's to be learned from the rapid formation and dissolution of the New Economy that might help us understand how to leverage the devox to our advantage? We'll begin with a quick recap of how proponents of the New Economy described it: "This new economy has three distinguishing characteristics," wrote author Kevin Kelly, one of the early cyberspace Edge players. "It is global. It favors intangible things—ideas, information, and relationships. And it is intensely interlinked. These three attributes produce a new type of marketplace and society, one that is rooted in ubiquitous electronic networks." Contrasting the traditional economic assumption that the collective human appetite for goods and services will always exceed the availability of those goods and services with what he calls "webonomics," author Evan Schwartz, another shrewd observer of the Internet economy, wrote: "Since the Web is a fast-growing world of intellectual property that can be copied and downloaded ad infinitum, its supply of resources will continue to *soar* past human demand for these resources. Instead of a scarcity of supply, the Web economy exhibits a scarcity of demand."

Encouraging an economic system in which supply exceeds demand (the sound you hear is poor old Tom Malthus spinning in his miserly grave) and which, to steal a phrase from *Fast Company* magazine founder Alan Webber, "begins with technology and ends in trust," was practically anarchistic. It was in a word—yup, you guessed it—deviant. The Old and New Economies begin and end in radically disparate places, and that disparity helps explain in part some of the growing pains "the economy" has experienced attempting to reconcile the two models. It's just too hard—and in many cases too early—to tell the winners from the losers. The context of traditional economics began to be abolished before we had sufficient time to master the disciplines of the new model or learn how to straddle an economic hybrid. At any given time, we're operating with parts or all of both economies, sometimes working and fully functional and sometimes not.

We suspect it will be a little while before a new deviant economic context on the scale of the New Economy emerges and gains anything approaching mass acceptance. Of course, as soon as that happens, the devox can be counted on to pop up and change the rules of economic engagement.

The devox has also been busy launching deviant microeconomies in the shadows cast between the Old and New Economies, and many of these operate completely independent of historical market rules. Barter economics, organized criminal activity, white-collar crime, tax defrauders, and those everyday folks who work under the table all operate on their own frequencies outside the control of, and only tangentially touching, the mainstream economy. In many critical respects, underground economies are healthier and more resilient than the mainstream economy. Organized crime, for instance, appears practically recession proof and seems to flourish in adverse economic environments.

There are also more legitimate microeconomies such as the one we call the mediaconomy—economic tidal waves spawned by the content needs of all-news-all-the-time cable television networks and publishers tying their fortunes to the coattails of change. Much of the enthusiasm for the dot-coms came from cable analysts and a host of journalists tasked with filling the pages of now-defunct magazines such as *The Industry Standard.* Individually, these microeconomies may seem like financial footnotes, but in aggregate they form a powerful force that further challenges the ability of traditionalists to define the economic context in historical terms.

There's yet another economic context out there that we call causenomics, or the exchange of capital and/or volunteer labor for values validation. Causenomics has several subcomponents. It's impossible to accurately assess the economic value of the aggregate volunteer hours donated from causes as diverse as highway beautification and the legalization of marijuana. Cause marketing (in which a percentage of the purchase price or fee structure is donated to a specified cause) is a commercial offering that leverages causenomics and what we call emotional economics, as does values marketing, whereby customers are lured by a shared affinity, from ecological concerns to patriotism.

Emotional economic systems may or may not be cause related, but they share a common characteristic: the exchange of goods and services for a sense of well-being or, at the very least, release of guilt. Characteristically of all Abolition of Context scenarios, these fiscal systems—New Economy, Old Economy, underground economy, emotional economy, and perhaps dozens of other models—coexist rather than supplanting each other. We all participate in one or more of these economies whenever we buy or sell anything. Ironically, perhaps, we're rarely fully aware of which economy we're operating in.

Let's take a case in point. Suppose your favorite music store has sent you an e-mail based on its collaborative filtering of customer data, telling you a bootleg CD version of a live performance by your favorite artist has just been brought in as trade. Anxious to complete your collection, you rush to the store to purchase the CD. You like shopping at the store, not only because of the selection but because the owner donates 1 percent of sales to the local homeless center, which makes you feel as if somehow you're doing your part for the less fortunate. Clearly, in our example, there are multiple economic approaches at work. The truth is most businesses—and most consumers—somehow or another move seamlessly from one economy to another, usually (to steal a phrase) with eyes wide shut.

Ask yourself if you routinely check out the full scope of your supply chain to make sure the products you receive (or the raw ingredients that went into them) weren't made by child or slave labor, or are you just happy that costs appear moderately contained? Do you routinely barter goods for advertising or pay out trade promotion funds that are really nothing more than legitimized kickbacks? Do you worry about how the labor contracts affecting the way in which your goods get to market were negotiated? What would you be willing to pay—or have you paid—to avoid a work stoppage? And how much charitable activity do you engage in every year even if you're not really all that chari-table a soul?

Every day most companies—and almost all individuals—simultane-ously participate in several economies—both macro and micro. Let's say you work for a smokestack industry; invest your money in high-tech or biotech stocks; charge all your meals on a Working Assets credit card because you're concerned about the environment; keep your child in a cooperative daycare program; and occasionally buy bootleg DVDs from your cousin. In the course of a workday you're involved in at least five different economies.

So how should a business deal with the devox's impact on econom-ics and the ensuing abolition of a single, coherent economy with fixed and constant rules? At first blush, it might look as if the economy is just a tad too large to wrestle with, but just think about the economies built by Silicon Valley, the Colombian drug cartels, and whoever it was who created the swap meet and the garage sale, not to mention all the other unconventional economies percolating out there, somewhere on the Internet or in the commercial underground. They're all examples of deviant economies—self-contained financial systems that create wealth on their own, generally very deviant, terms.

Each of these economies shares a common characteristic. They all followed our initial model—that is, they began on the Fringe and suc-cessively progressed from the Edge to the Realm of the Cool, became the Next Big Thing, and finally achieved Social Convention. The drug economy, for example, has been with us, in one form or another, since the first caveman discovered that he could change his consciousness by eating certain plants and then bartered that knowledge among his neighbors. Until the 1960s drug selling would have been seen more as a criminal conspiracy than an economy. Drug users and drug sellers were marginalized at the Edge, scorned, avoided, and prosecuted. Then "the sixties" happened. Use—and abuse—of drugs like marijuana and psy-chedelics became almost de rigueur among baby boomers. The pusher who peddled his products in the back alleys of the Edge became the connection, a sort of blissed-out folk hero.

Changes in the scope and direction of drug use opened the door for big business. Cocaine and heroin dealers—the street sales force for a well-oiled importing ring—quickly replaced the happy hippie backyard pot grower. In the 1970s cocaine was the drug of choice among the high-rolling beautiful people at Studio 54 and other outposts of the Realm of the Cool. Cocaine couldn't be held back. The Ponzi-like exponential growth of user-sellers moved the drug into wider and wider distribution. Freebasing became the Next Big Thing despite incidents like Richard Pryor's accidental attempt at self-immolation. With the development of crack cocaine—which delivered part of the rich man's high to the poor man for only a few dollars—drug use and the drug business moved to become a fixture of Social Convention. No longer were drugs confined to ghettos or urban areas. Suddenly, everyone was a potential customer. And the money just kept rolling in.

We've seen the VW Microbus give way to an armada of smuggling ships, stripped-down aircraft that can fly under DEA radar, warehouses full of contraband, and even an army of human mules who carried the drugs across the U.S. border in their stomachs. What had been a multimillion-dollar cottage industry became a multibillion-dollar global economy. Today the trade in illicit drugs is estimated at $400 billion annually, or roughly 8 percent of all international trade.

No discussion of the devox's impact on economics would be complete without a mention of the most macro market deviation of them all—the emergence of that überdeviant, the global economy, one of the devox's finest efforts. Control is a key to success in most economic systems. Try to trace firm lines around the global economy and you're doomed to failure before you start. By its very nature the global economy creates an endlessly morphing context, self-defined—to the degree it can be defined—and autocatalytic. The global economy is driven by entropy and fueled by the highest order of complex adaptive and emergent behavior. Global markets, unlike those who hope to profit from them most, never sleep.

A truly global economy can't "belong" to anyone. Businesses, new and established, must find ways to exploit the largest market imaginable with a near total absence of fixed economic rules. No ownership means no ability to transfer inheritance. This allows new players to leapfrog their way up the commercial ladder. Old dynasties collapse and new heroes emerge. In 2001, Finland's Nokia unseated American commercial giant Coca-Cola's long-held position as the most recognizable brand name in Europe. The global economy is actually less an economy in the traditional sense than it is a delicate web of networked media, social, cultural, political, financial, transportation infrastructure, information, communication, and financial touch points. It also has a dark side. Despite all the multinational corporate rhetoric about globalism, the global economy has tens of thousands of enemies—manifest in the form of trade restrictions, regulations, nationalism, language, culture, and even time itself.

Today any number of corporations fancy themselves global companies. It's relatively easy to draw up a list of global industries—finance, automotive, certain agribusinesses, media, munitions, telephony, and certain other technologies come quickly to mind. We'd quite frankly have a little more difficulty drawing up a list of authentically global (as opposed to multinational) players. Once you get past Coca-Cola, McDonald's, Sony, Nokia, Oracle, Microsoft, Pantene, and a handful of others, the candidate list thins out pretty fast. Sure, Wal-Mart may become global one day but today it lacks true global scale or even clearly defined global formats.

We've worked extensively with clients in many industries from consumer packaged goods to the postal services of three countries wrestling with the issue of the future of global commerce. Our conclusion: Part of the reason Mount Everest is so dangerous to climb is because its very scale means that it essentially "makes" its own weather. In fact, it makes it so fast that the new weather patterns don't show up on even the most sophisticated high-altitude, computerized, satellite weather-tracking and prediction systems in time to help climbers. Sometimes a storm can be anticipated, and sometimes Everest just throws one at you that you can't see coming even when you're staring it straight in the eye. That's a pretty good metaphor for the global economy. It makes its own storms, some of which can be predicted and manipulated and some of which can kill you.

There are no easy answers to the questions being asked about globalization and its economic consequences. The fact that so many people seem to "know" so much about a concept so new and so massive reminds us a little bit of the initial indiscriminate rush to judgment about e-commerce. As you start to think about what globalization may or may not mean to you, we suggest you consider the following questions:

1. Do you really want to be global or is your corporate country of origin important to you? Microsoft, for example, functions on many levels as a global corporation but chose to burn tens of millions of dollars psychically arm wrestling the U.S. government. As an aside, we suspect a truly deviant global company would have just moved to another country without looking back.

2. If you want to play in the global market, have you conducted a globalization obstacle inventory—that is, are you even aware of the problems that need to be solved in terms of reconciling standards, terms, IT protocols, hardware and software interfaces, and little things such as the impact of currency fluctuations and in what languages e-mails will be sent?

3. What about developing a global understanding? Have you taken a knowledge audit and established some form of knowledge management/communication mechanism? We're reminded of a retiring Unilever chairman whose parting words to the troops were "I only wish we knew what we know."

4. Are you in a position to design global products, services, and brands for global customers? Procter & Gamble managed to build Pantene into a "global brand," but showing a woman in the shower washing her hair is still considered a pornographic image in many parts of the Middle East.

5. Have you asked yourself why you want to be global? Is your effort about real market potential or about collective corporate ego?

6. And, finally, are you really prepared to do business in a world that doesn't have easily understood or even commonly recognized rules or standards?

Inventing a new economic model is a huge challenge, but before you walk away from the idea think about the components of an economy: the existence, or creation, of a set of goods, services, and/or a blend of the two; an agreed-upon standard of value and valuation; common supply-chain protocols that enable and facilitate value exchange; some public marketplace in which trade is conducted; a set of consumers in search of goods, services, or offerings; and, in most cases, the presence of competitors whose activities regulate variables from supply and demand to pricing and innovation.

All of these elements also exist in microeconomies, and creating a microeconomy is not all that far-fetched an idea. Take the Internet, for example. It's clear that early Internet pioneers weren't trying to create the "New Economy." They were just trying to talk to each other. But faster than seems actually possible (really a matter of a few years), connectivity and communication (the Internet, computation, and telephony) proved to be fertile field and seed for an economic model that generated more than a trillion dollars. It's critical to remember that the foundations of new economies—communication media, addiction, barter—aren't in and of themselves "new," but novelty isn't a prerequisite for economic transformation.

In the same way that the Internet is a microeconomy inside the larger global macroeconomy, the rate of change associated with the devox and the Abolition of Context continually births dozens of sub-microeconomic models, some almost too strange to be believed. On August 30, 2001, WDET, the National Public Radio affiliate in Detroit, aired a news feature about "bully insurance," which French schoolchildren are now required to purchase. Bully insurance compensates them against book and other property loss and physical abuse suffered at the hands of bullies. (By the way, just as a footnote to our earlier discussion of deviant language, the word *bullying* now has a more PC linguistic incarnation—relational violence.) Microeconomies focused on marketing items related to the September 11 attack on the World Trade Center sprung up literally before the dust cleared at Ground Zero. A speculators' market in Beanie Babies a few years ago triggered yet another microeconomy, complete with its own media and suppliers.

Thanks to the devox, even companies can create their own microeconomies and can in turn deeply impact the macroeconomy. Let's look at Wal-Mart, which in exactly forty years evolved from a single store into the largest corporation on earth. In 2002, the McKinsey Global Institute, the research arm of McKinsey & Company, released a study suggesting that Wal-Mart has been a substantial contributor to the large increase in American labor productivity in the years 1995 to 2000, an increase many observers might otherwise have ascribed to the growth of high-technology companies. Reporting the findings, the *McKinsey Quarterly* wrote: "Surprisingly, the primary source of the productivity gains of 1995 to 1999 was not increased demand resulting from the stock market bubble, as some economists have claimed. Nor was information technology the source, though companies accelerated the pace of their IT investments during those years. Rather, managerial and technological innovations in only six highly competitive industries— wholesale trade, retail trade, securities, semiconductors, computer manufacturing and telecommunications—were the most important causes." McKinsey estimates that Wal-Mart is responsible for more than half of the productivity acceleration in the retailing of general merchandise. The company also notes that about one-sixth of the improvement in retail productivity came from general merchandise and that the retail trade overall contributed nearly one-quarter of the economy-wide productivity growth jump.

In the era of the devox, we no longer try to change deviant behavior; we just create new economic models to profit from it. So finding ways to create a profitable microeconomy is just one of the side bene-fits of living life on the Edge. If you really think you can create your own subeconomy or microeconomy, here are some strategies to con-sider. You might try studying areas of massive conflict and change, especially those where solutions to perceived problems are not obvi-ously available. One example is the growth of Internet exchanges such as Transora in the food and consumer packaged-goods industry, which is attempting to simplify relations between buyers and sellers while reducing cost for all parties.

It's also important to remember that it takes alliances to build economies. As Bill Gates discovered, no matter how big you are you can't create a whole economic model by yourself. The laptop comput-ing industry offers a marvelous example of how alliances—forced or voluntary—have boosted sales for Microsoft, Intel, Gateway, and Dell, among others.

One way to gain insight is to walk around and listen to what people would be willing to exchange value for. A good cue is to search out opportunities that seem to eliminate complexity—or even choice—for a fairly large group of people. E-ticket check-in kiosks at airports are an example of how one easily detectable behavior (impatience in lines) was parlayed into a market offering.

When you begin to build your model, make sure you're in charge of setting the standards. He who measures, wins. That's why VHS beat Betamax for most consumer applications, and why it's impossible to make a phone call in Europe using most American cell phones (and vice versa).

Remember that economies need to be self-sustainable; that's one of the things that separate them from mere economic opportunities. The market for Beanie Babies couldn't hold. The market for drugs contin-ues to remain robust. Along the way, don't forget that people are the most important ingredient in any economy. If nobody participates, nothing happens. And, finally, remember you can't build an economy without infrastructure—whether it's one you create or one you can co-opt or exploit.

In reality, there are not that many opportunities for most companies to create even microeconomies. In most cases, it's far more practical to concentrate on finding ways of channeling the devox's impact on a slightly lower level, and the corporation seems as good a place as any to begin. If the devox's footprints are all over the economy, they've all but stomped out the formerly clear lines that were the borders of the corporate world.

11

Corporate Cultures—Deviant and Otherwise

It just shows the flexibility of the human organism that people who would willingly sit in the mud and chant "no rain" between badly amplified rock groups turn out to run the economy.

—FRANK ZAPPA

Our experience has led us to a single simple truth. Most companies pay it lip service. Some swear they're executing against it. But the reality is that most run from it with every fiber of their corporate being. Here it is. *All business problems are really culture problems, in more than one sense of the word.*

When it comes to deviants, culture poses both opportunity and challenges. Mass culture continually surfaces new commercial opportunities. The fact is mass culture *loves* the devox. However, in one American company after another, corporate culture acts as an organizational prophylactic, protecting business-as-usual businesses from being infected by new opportunities. Why? Corporate culture *hates* the devox and works tirelessly to eliminate deviant employees. Corporate culture works to discourage deviant ideas. Corporate culture punishes deviant behavior and attitudes. As a result, most large companies lose the opportunity to discover—or create—the future and therefore get to it first.

The two cultural issues are inseparably bound. Despite all their talk about the value of prime-mover advantage, most companies appear trapped in a puzzling—no, make that a deeply disturbing and often fatal—syllogism that they seem institutionally, and constitutionally, incapable of either escaping or resolving: All opportunity springs from deviance. Opportunity is good. Therefore deviance ought to be good—but in reality it's avoided at all cost. No matter how compelling the logic, most of the time deviance ends up being viewed as a negative.

When they find themselves face-to-face with the devox, most established businesses melt down into inactivity, the result of a commercial double blind between their addictive thirst for innovative ideas and breakthrough offerings and their visceral fear and hatred of anyone who refuses to parrot the party line.

WE HAVE MET THE ENEMY AND THEY ARE US

Naturally, it doesn't have to be that way. Deviance and order not only can find a way to coexist but in fact can be profoundly codependent—a lesson that business and business leaders could learn from a quick study of nature. But this can only happen when the internal culture of the company is open to external cultural change. As Walt Kelly said so many years ago in *Pogo*, "We have met the enemy and they are us."

The problem is somewhat different at different levels. Try to solve the problems of what we'll call the human infrastructure (the lower-level employees who ironically control such critical areas as customer contact and internal and external communication) and you might begin by redirecting those corporate Swiss Guards in your human resources department who try to jam an artificially created culture down every new hire's throat. Carefully nurtured corporate cultures act like institutional antibodies, protecting the body corporate from any and all opportunities presented by the devox. So if you're in a "promote-from-the-ranks" culture, the people who advance are going to be those who have best learned the rules of the game. You might as well put a sign on the door reading "No deviants need apply."

There are equal but subtle prescreens the higher you move up the organization chart. Does your company recruit new graduates from a broad range of educational institutions, or do you restrict your preselection to graduates of certain prestigious institutions such as Harvard, Yale, Stanford, and MIT? Or do you instead favor graduates from the school most of the executive team graduated from, or the chairman's alma mater? Of course, that bright deviant you pass over out of school may make a reputation for his or her self and then be recruited by you. But what are they likely to think about a company that wouldn't even give them an interview when they were so desperately looking for that first big break?

Assuming your prescreen doesn't filter out the devox, the initial interview usually does the trick. A few missing years here, a history of insubordination there, a lukewarm reference, or sometimes something as minor as questionable sartorial judgment and even the most subtle deviance can be detected, leaving little else to do but weed out the potential threat of the devox before it has a chance to infect the workplace. Assuming the devox survives the first interview, it can almost always be eliminated sometime between the second interview and the reference checks.

Now, if by some miracle the deviant actually gets hired, a whole network of secondary corporate antibodies goes to work. They take a variety of forms from the employee handbook to those corporate mentors (assigned and informal) who are eager to tell any new hire "how we do it here." The result is predictably the same: Either the new hire conforms to the will of the company, or he or she leaves. Turnover reports are one easy way to see exactly how devox friendly your workplace is. But the real test comes when you analyze your recruitment and hiring processes. Is there a pattern there? After all, the hardest form of diversity to build in and maintain in your company is diversity of opinion.

THE DEVOX-FRIENDLY CORPORATION

The next step to creating a devox-friendly corporation is to blow up all those boards, chairmen, CEOs, COOs, CIOs, CTOs, and CFOs who are better at negation than they are at affirmation. (*"Great idea, but it'll never work here. In fact I think we tried something similar to that in, let me see, yes, it was 1985. Didn't work then. Won't work now."*) The fastest way to encourage positive deviance is to build an affirmation culture that celebrates great experiments, even those that end in failure.

Of course, things are changing on their own as the devox begins to impact the corporation in the same way that it's changing all other social institutions. Dilbert has replaced Babbitt. Corporations are no longer seen as unassailable institutions benignly shepherding the future of consumers, employees, and trading partners. Heritage means little. Corporations routinely change their names, their missions, their scope of operations, and, of course, their leadership. No need to dwell on Enron (the ultimate negative expression of the devox) here, but the Enronization of the business world (pursuit of profit for a few at any cost) has taken its toll on corporate credibility.

We're all familiar with the consequences of the Abolition of Corporate Context. Employees have become disposable. Investment has become opportunistic. The tenure of leadership has been radically truncated. Media management has become as important as management of the analysts, and organizational charts have been flattened.

By the same token, some corporate (or quasi-corporate) institutions are remarkably devox resistant. Go to the official website of the Federation of the Swiss Watch Industry (http://www.fhs.ch) to understand what we're talking about. The site embodies the collective insights of the major Swiss watchmakers. It also explains how a group of companies that once defined an industry lost their market through culture. Navigate over to the glossary and you'll notice there's no entry for digital (or even quartz) watches. It's as if they didn't exist. You can learn all about *assortiment,* the French word for the parts used in making an escapement, the set of parts that converts the rotary motion of the train into to-and-from motions. You can also learn about mainsprings, rotors, repeaters, and regulating elements—in fact, all the parts of a nondigital watch. But you'll find nary a mention on those damned digitals!

The closest thing to a reference we could uncover were a pair of notes in the site's history section. The first read, "In 1967, the Centre Electronique Horloger (CEH) in Neuchâtel developed the world's first quartz wristwatch—the famous Beta 21." The second, slightly more ominous note states, "According to a number of economic analysts, the Swiss watch industry was moribund in the middle of the 1970s, having missed the electronic revolution and being strongly affected by the economic crisis." In other words, the Swiss watchmaking industry missed the electronic revolution it had started because it couldn't see that a watch without movable parts was still a watch. Xerox managed to hand over the benefits of its R&D to Apple and Microsoft in the same way.

Being first with a product, service, or idea doesn't help when you're operating in what we call a Culture of Corporate Containment. Ideas may first surface in Cultures of Corporate Containment, but they rarely survive the corporate gauntlet to become first to market. There's never been a Culture of Corporate Containment that could match the one created by Xerox.

After all, at least in the case of timepieces, Swatch—a prosperous, and apparently deviant, Swiss company—figured out that watches were fashion statements, not just portable clocks, and created a Swiss success story. The federation apparently couldn't stop every Swiss company from benefiting from digital technology; and, in fact, Swatch's financial success is ballyhooed on the official industry website. They could have taken lessons from Xerox.

Michael Hiltzik is the author of *Dealers of Lightning: Xerox PARC and the Dawn of the Computer Age*, the definitive history of the stormy relationship between the troubled copier company and its clearly and self-admittedly deviant Palo Alto Research Center. In his book Hiltzik writes:

Every time you click a mouse on an icon or open overlapping windows on your computer today, you are using technology invented at PARC. Compose a document by word processor, and your words reach the display via software invented at PARC. Make the print larger or smaller, replace ordinary typewriter letters with Braggadocio or Gothic typeface—that's also technology invented at PARC, as is the means by which a keystroke speeds the finished document by cable or infrared link to a laser printer. The laser printer, too, was invented at PARC.

Surf the Internet, send e-mail to a workmate, check your bank account at an ATM equipped with touch screen, follow the route of a cold front across the Midwest on a TV weather forecaster's animated map: The pathway to the indispensable technology was blazed by PARC. There, too, originated the three-dimensional computer graphics that give life to the dinosaurs of *Jurassic Park* and the inspired playthings of *Toy Story*.

So what happened? In large part, culture happened. "The best-publicized aspect of PARC's history is that its work was ignored by its parent company while earning billions for others," Hiltzik continues. "To a certain extent this is true. The scientists' unfettered creativity, not to mention their alien habits of mind and behavior, fomented unrelenting conflict with their stolid parent company. Determined in principle to move into the digital world but yoked in practice to the marketing of copier machines (and unable to juggle two balls at once), Xerox management regarded PARC's achievements first with bemusement, then uneasiness, and finally hostility." Hiltzik is quick to point out that some of Xerox's critics unfairly use PARC as an example of why all large corporations are bad. We tend to agree, at least to the degree that Xerox shouldn't be singled out. It has plenty of company.

THE DEATH OF BIG IRON

We grew up in Detroit, our teen years played out in the shrinking shadows of big Detroit iron and the muscle-car culture. In 1967 Detroit literally exploded from the economic and racial tensions that had built up.

It's no longer PC to call what happened a riot, but from the point of view of two teenage kids, it looked like a pretty good riot, at least until a better one came along. Buildings were burned and looted. People died. Troops were bivouacked in public parks. And, we can assure you from personal experience, you've never really seen your hometown until you've watched tanks rumble their way down its streets; just ask the kids from Prague or Belfast or Tel Aviv or Detroit.

But in affluent Westside suburbs like Dearborn Heights, in the East-side suburbs like the five Grosse Pointes, and in the Northwestern con-claves of Birmingham, West Bloomfield, and Bloomfield Hills—where the heads of the auto industry lived—the view in the late 1960s and early 1970s was still beautiful. No tanks, no rage, no ghettos; just block after block of prosperity. Every day those executives walked to their garages or driveways and saw their brand-new, free muscle cars filled with free gasoline.

As their eyes scanned the driveways of their friends and their neigh-bors they saw the same thing, tons of steel housing some of the most powerful internal combustion engines ever built. Satisfied they were making a positive contribution to the world, the executives jumped in their cars and roared to work untroubled by the thought of an energy crisis, foreign competition, or economic inequality. Our guess? They probably checked the time on one of those swell Swiss watches that only lost a minute or two each day. They never saw the collapse of the American auto industry and the rise of Japan as a car producer coming. The result of their shortsightedness changed the face of Detroit and the global automotive industry forever.

Here's a self-diagnostic that may bring the points we've been mak-ing home. Take out a piece of paper and write down the five most frus-trating things that happened to you on your way to whatever august corporate perch you currently occupy. How many of them had to do with conflicts between you and the culture of the company? Remember the frustration you felt? The anger? Maybe you left a job because of it. We know we have. Now for the tougher question: How many times have you returned the favor by frustrating someone you work for?

Several years ago we were asked to look in on an offshore retail company that had "done everything right" but still managed to post declines in both sales and profits every quarter for five straight years. The stores had tripled their inventory, thereby offering the consumer literally sixty thousand additional choices. They had reduced prices on more than 25,000 items. They had reinvested in physical infrastructure (fixtures and equipment, new retail technology, reconfigured aisles and checkouts). And they had instituted employee training and corporate uniform programs.

The company was involved in a business that tried to use high volume to compensate for low margins. The island was divided, as many islands seem to be, between the affluent (10 percent or maybe 20 percent of the population) and everyone else. Spanish was the native language. The first night we arrived we had dinner with the company's president at a Ruth's Chris Steak House. He ate there every night, he explained, because he hated the local cuisine. We asked him where he lived, and he told us that even though he had been there for years he still preferred to live in a hotel. The neighborhoods, he assured us, weren't safe and the population was inherently untrustworthy. "Half these people have been in prison and another fifty percent of them are on drugs," he assured us. He also took some pride in the fact that he spoke slightly less Spanish than the average Stateside Taco Bell cashier.

The next day we inspected all the "improvements" he had made—all aimed at making a nice, Caucasian middle-class housewife from Iowa happy, and all equally guaranteed to alienate the locals. The stores attracted the island's affluent, but in a highly structured culture attracting the affluent was the same thing as telling the poor they didn't belong. The two groups rarely interacted, so the presence of either one of them was enough to send the other group running. The company's chairman asked us what we thought. "If we were you," we told him, "we'd replace presidents." "I can't," he told us. "Besides, I hired him. How would it look?" Corporate culture—in this case the patriarchal cultural rule that says leaders can't make mistakes—had tolerated all kinds of changes, but precluded the most important, critical, and necessary change of them all.

Here's another variation on the theme. One high-end automotive company retained us to help with their aftermarket sales and service departments. After we got past all the polite conversation, it became clear there was a major structural problem: The company's dealers wouldn't bother to service a vehicle once it went off warranty. The automaker was essentially underwriting certain maintenance costs, and individual consumers simply wouldn't pay the same rates as the manufacturer.

We asked the obvious question: Why not? Well, it turns out the dealers could manipulate the billing system to essentially pad their invoices as long as the cars were on warranty. Why not just change the system, we asked. "Can't" was the answer. Fine, we said. Since these cars had a higher-than-average number of service calls than other cars in their class, why not make better cars? "There's nothing wrong with our cars," we were told. "Why so many problems then?" we asked. The answer was so obvious we couldn't believe we hadn't thought of it ourselves: "It's the customers. They don't know how to drive the cars correctly." Just in case you're getting lost, here's the bottom line: The dealers were crooks, but that wouldn't be such a problem if it weren't for the customers who tried to actually drive the cars.

After a fairly deep piece of research analyzing the future of service, we thought we had the answer. As long as you're committed to policies that essentially all but guarantee that customers have to spend an inordinate amount of time in the dealership, why not concentrate on making that time a more pleasant experience? "Can't use the word experience," we were told. The incoming president had an enemy who once launched an initiative with the word *experience* in the title. Therefore, the use of the word *experience* was considered a personal affront to management. We never had the pleasure of meeting the man, but we bet he checked his Swiss watch every time he walked past the Xerox machine.

CULTURE'S THE ENEMY

Culture's the enemy over and over again. Too often the prime directive of the guardians of corporate culture is to preserve it against threats and, more often than not, reality, even those realities that could enrich it. One last story to drive the point home. Visteon, the Ford spin-off that's gone on to become one of the largest automotive suppliers in the world, asked us to work with them thinking through the future of the automobile. They were looking for ideas that would be a central theme at their booth at the Frankfurt Auto Show, one of the prestige events on the global auto calendar.

We arranged what we call a Cultural Affairs Exchange, essentially a forced exposure to people and ideas you would never think of finding on your own. We populated the room with iconoclastic thinkers, individuals like Chuck Queener, widely recognized as one of the world's leading automotive illustrators, and Steve Barnett, an anthropologist by training who pioneered the use of cultural anthropology as a tool for understanding how businesses operated. Along his career path he has served as director of market strategy for Nissan North America and is the author of *The Nissan Report,* a look at the future of the automobile. We wanted the Visteon group (largely engineers) to begin thinking about cars in ways their culture didn't allow. Why would someone hire Queener, for example, to paint a portrait of their favorite car when a photograph could capture the physical details? We wanted the Visteon team to understand that a car is more than a drive train, engine, and chassis and that understanding this idea was a key to understanding the future of cars—and carmakers.

What eventually turned out to be a great day started on a somewhat rocky note. The initial dialogue went something like this:

BARNETT (with a smile): So when are women going to be allowed to drive cars?

CLIENT (with a cough): Women are allowed to drive.

BARNETT (with a smile): Really, when were they allowed to start driving?

CLIENT (with a more insistent cough): They've always been allowed to drive.

BARNETT (with a smile): So when are you going to design cars for women?

CLIENT (now twitching): We've always designed cars for women.

BARNETT (with a smile): Really? Well, tell me, where in a car can a woman put a purse that is both safe and convenient?

CLIENT (staring at the floor): I don't know. I've never thought about it before.

The session concluded with a general consensus that what they ought to be demonstrating at Frankfurt wasn't the latest telemetric system or Star Wars auto design, but rather just a tape of the day's dialogue. After all, showing that you're capable of truly original thought about cars seems far more profound than demonstrating your ability to prototype a particular feature or function that's still light-years away from release. The future of cars depends more on people than engineering— a formula that helps explain Saturn's success.

At the end of the day, the head of marketing and the project team leader walked up to us and said, "Today helped us see that everything we believe about this industry and our role in it is wrong. We'll be back in touch soon." We smiled at each other, knowing we weren't likely to ever see them again. Hey, we're a couple of kids from the Motor City, we know better than to expect Motown to become Yotown. Even rusting in the sun, Big Iron casts an impressive shadow.

Changing culture is more than a full-time job. It has to be an obsession. Three months later we heard that the team leader had left the company. We weren't surprised. We had given the devox the opportunity to penetrate the otherwise generally impregnable walls of entrenched automotive company culture. Sooner or later it would have happened anyway, but in this case we served as the devox's midwives.

THE CORPORATE MONK

Way back in 1961, in his book *Corporations,* John P. Davis traced the history of the corporation back to ecclesiastical universities and ultimately to the European monastery system. The tie that links monasteries to Microsoft begins when a group of people voluntarily comes together to work toward a common goal and against common enemies. To move the enterprise forward, each of these people agrees to subordinate his or her individuality to the collective will and absolute authority of the institution. The perceived rewards are great—community, stability, order, modest creature comforts, and a form of salvation. But in order to qualify for the rewards, a series of sacrifices—beginning with unfettered self-expression and touching every aspect of life right down to what one wore—are required. There is a simple elegance to Davis's model, right down to the image of the novitiate M.B.A setting aside the frivolity of his youth in order to begin the long, slow, and frustrating road to becoming an abbot.

Monasteries provided places of refuge from the world for men of common faith and preserved the "Truth" against the ravages of pagans, heretics, and sin in all its alluring forms. Sounds a little bit like a corporation, doesn't it. A close friend at Coca-Cola once told us a story that may or may not be the stuff of corporate legend. If it's true, it perfectly illustrates the appropriateness of the monk metaphor. According to our friend, shortly after Doug Ivester assumed the CEO mantle at Coke, he told a group of executives gathered for a planning session, "When I joined this company I realized I had a choice. I could have a family or I could strive to be a leader. I chose the company." Bet he's got a Swiss watch, too.

Corporate cultures are as subject to the ravages of the devox as any other culture. Innumerable businesses have spent the better part of the last fifteen or twenty years flattening the organizational charts; knocking down silos (actually more often than not replacing vertical silos with horizontal ones); building diversity into the workforce (sometimes at court order); and in general trying to give the appearance of becoming more democratic and inclusive and less dictatorial and paternal. The philosophy of the Big Sir was replaced by the philosophy of Big Sur. All of this Aquarian sensibility might have been a tad more effective if it had occurred in a more stable, traditional context. But thanks to the devox, there isn't a common context anymore. As a result, most of these efforts at democratization proved to be too little deviance too late. Rather than being appreciative of the humanistic largesse, thousands of these younger employees rejected large corporations and fled to found their own companies or to work with like-minded souls in start-ups.

Silicon Valley provided a home for many of these refugees and, in turn, spawned more than its share of deviant corporate cultures. In some of these, like Apple under Steve Jobs's first incarnation, the whims of the leaders made it all but impossible to remain a consistently loyal employee. Jobs's early management style was to champion certain projects—and project teams—often at the expense of former favorites, and to question the loyalty of all but a handful of key employees. It might be an overstatement to say that culture was the sole reason Apple stumbled and fell after what should have been an out-of-the-blocks advantage. But volumes have been written (and a docudrama made) chronicling how the Apple culture managed to degenerate into neotribal warfare. One thing is certain: The lack of a coherent culture—or conversely, the existence of a massively incoherent culture—didn't help Steve Jobs, at that stage in his life one of the poster children for deviant leadership. Ironically, thanks to the devox (at least at this writing), Jobs is back at Apple and partially bankrolled by his former nemesis, Bill Gates. Historically, if you left a company under a cloud you were banished for life, but in deviant corporate culture you only have to be gone long enough for everyone's hurt feelings to mend.

Even the devox's disruption of the most superficial aspects of a culture can be unnerving to the residents of a corporate society. "Do you think I'm dressed all right?" used to be a question raised by 1950s housewives going to their husband's annual Christmas party. Now it routinely pops out of the mouths of their grandsons and granddaughters as they're summoned to an impromptu meeting.

It's one thing to morph a culture and quite another to completely kill it off. Most of the oldest Christian churches, after all, are built on former pagan power sites. When Pope Julius I formally declared that Christ's birthday would be celebrated on December 25 in 350, he was no doubt trying to make it easier for converts used to celebrating the feast of the Son of Isis, Saturnalia, Mithras, or some other late December–early January pagan holiday.

A tad more recently, when Durk Jager (who always wore a suit and tie to work) took over the reins at Procter & Gamble, the dress code moved from business casual to business appropriate. "What's that mean?" we naïvely asked one day. "It means if you think you might run into Durk it's appropriate to have a jacket and tie handy," we were told. "And it's never appropriate to wear things he hates, like jeans."

Most companies don't think hard enough about culture building as a conscious activity. Cultures get built all the time, whether or not you intend to build them. Cultures never exist in a complete vacuum. People are skeptical in general, and they don't suspend their disbelief when they come to work. They've learned they can't trust leaders to protect anyone but themselves. Review any high-profile executive hire and you'll see exactly whom the system benefits—the executives and the shareholders. Long-term investments that might end up stabilizing the company are suddenly culturally unacceptable.

CULTURE IS INFECTIOUS

Culture is also infectious. When it comes to creating negative cultures, for both customers and employees, the airlines are the hands-down winners. Not only do customers hate to fly, apparently so do the employees, based on their behavior. We're sure the airline industry really means all that stuff about the skies being friendly, but we can't count the number of times we've sat in first class vainly yearning for that delicious preflight plastic cup of sparkling water, only to watch the flight attendants gathered in the front galley in what appears to be a rugby scrum complaining about their jobs. The whole commercial aviation culture seems bent on conspiring against you.

Next time you're on a plane that's delayed (and you shouldn't have to wait too long to test this), notice the absence of anything approaching a clear explanation of what's going on. The normal response to this is to get surly and take it out on the closest person to you—generally a flight attendant. Flight attendants—being human, after all—return the favor, and by the time the flight leaves there's a danger it might devolve into an airborne version of the Donner party minus the starvation. Add a healthy dose of post–September 11 paranoia into the mix and flying becomes all the more traumatic for everyone involved.

So how can you rewrite the rules of corporate conduct in ways that allow you to prosper in an era of uncertainty? Well, using an "opposites analysis" to develop a deviant view of the corporation might not be a bad place to start. We're not talking about things like allowing people to work at home; shifting production to subassemblers; or even employing virtual workers. We're talking about something far more basic here.

In the case of *Dartmouth College vs. Woodward* (1819), the U.S. Supreme Court defined the qualities and characteristics of a corporation. Among those characteristics were "immortality . . . individuality . . . [and] properties by which a perpetual succession of many persons are considered as the same." Death is the logical opposite of immortality, so why not start thinking about your company (service/brand/etc.) as both mortal and perishable? It could save you lots of money.

Unilever scored a major coup when it introduced its Lever 2000 bath soap. Part of the success of Lever 2000 can be traced back to great marketing and advertising. But the real deviant key was shifting the focus from feature and function to consumer. By advertising that this was a soap designed to clean all two thousand of your body parts (remember trying to figure out where all those body parts were?) and marketing their product exclusively in multipacks, Unilever succeeded in catching its primary competitor, Procter & Gamble, flat-footed. Soap, Unilever argued, wasn't just another household chemical; it was part of a total heath and beauty care regimen.

P&G tried to combat Lever's innovation (real or perceived) on a

number of levels, including attempting to convince retailers to configure existing departments in their stores to house their traditional products. But tradition was part of the problem. Rather than applying the
opposites analysis and saying that it might be time to pull the plug on
its heritage brand—Ivory bar soap, which it sold in a number of packs,
including the (most popular with sanitation-minded shoplifters) single
bar—P&G stuck with tradition and lost market share. We're not saying
that killing Ivory bar soap would have dulled Lever 2000's performance,
just that the tendency of most corporations is to push products and
ideas well past their natural or logical prime.

Most companies institutionalize brands and, in the process, insulate
themselves from changes in consumer taste and behavior. There's no
question that Procter & Gamble is one of the world's best sales and
marketing organizations, yet it let itself get bushwhacked by deviant
products from Lever 2000 to Colgate's Total toothpaste. In fact, P&G
was relatively slow to jump on the peroxide and baking soda dentifrice
bandwagon because its research-focused culture understood that the
ingredients lacked significant oral care efficacy.

Another alternative for making your corporation devox friendly is
to continually reinvent yourself as General Electric did on its path from
being a lightbulb manufacturer to a financial services juggernaut. The
first quality of a deviant corporation is its willingness, when appropriate, to change the rules, in measure or in full, of the culture that made it
initially great. Oftentimes, of course, that's easier said than done. There
are entire industries that appear dedicated to the proposition that
deviance should be resisted, no matter how much it costs. Architecture
is clearly one of them.

BUILDING A BETTER ARCHITECT

A few years ago a leading global architectural firm asked us to help
them think through the future of their profession. One of our goals in
situations like this is to have a client walk out the door asking very different questions than he or she did on the way in. In this case, what the

company really wanted to know wasn't what *the* future of architecture looked like, it was what *their* future in architecture looked like.

The chairman of the company was a charming patrician whose vision of democracy paralleled those of other noble patricians like Mafia dons, Joseph Stalin, and Genghis Khan. He was charmingly dismissive of anyone under fifty with the temerity to believe he or she had an opinion worth listening to. The firm was doing well but had two very specific concerns: the inevitable transfer of power that would result when the chairman finally decided to step down and the company's apparent inability to hold on to its best and brightest new hires.

We set out to understand better the history of architectural companies, consistent with our belief that not only is the past prologue in a metaphorical sense, it often literally holds the key to understanding what the future will look like. What we discovered was a fairly standardized pattern among the global architectural community. Young architects were hired somewhere between twenty-three and twenty-six years old, spent roughly a quarter of a century saying nothing unless being directly addressed, and worked on fairly pedestrian jobs. At fifty or so one was made a partner, allowed to have a voice, and spend the next decade and a half working on just slightly more interesting projects (cathedrals and museums may create headlines, but shopping malls and apartments pay the bills in these companies) and assiduously ignoring younger nonpartners.

We spent some time talking to friends who were independent architects, trying to understand why they chose to leave the security and prestige of large firms for the insecurity of running their own small business. All entrepreneurs are deviants in the best sense of the word, and deviants aren't easy employees to retain or manage. But—even so— some of these refugees from corporate architecture didn't strike us as quite all that flamboyant or daring; they just couldn't stand waiting around for it to be their turn.

We proposed that the firm establish a Myth Museum, built from the finest materials available and designed by the best artists and architects (regardless of seniority) in the firm. The Museum would be used to house the history—and the evolving soul—of the firm. In addition to the records, designs, and photographs of every project the firm had touched, the Myth Museum would house something even more precious: the dreams and ambitions of the past and future.

We further proposed that the firm revisit every building it had ever built, informing the owner (whether he or she had originally contracted for the building to be built) that the firm believed so much in its work it intended to stand behind the building as long as the building stood, regardless of age or ownership. The idea was that a two-person team made up of a senior partner and a relatively young junior member of the firm would visit each building. Both team members would have identical responsibilities—to independently write down and/or visually record their impressions of the building—not just its condition, but their personal response to the design, its use, its evolution, and so on. These observations would be housed in the Myth Museum and made freely available twenty-four hours a day, seven days a week to *any* employee of the company from senior partner to security and custodial staff.

No opinion could be censored or in any other way removed, even after its author had left the company. No revisions would be allowed, no second-guessing, and no coercion. No one could be either rewarded or punished for his or her opinion. You could play politics if you wanted, but your efforts would forever be open to peer review.

We believed this approach would do several things, including providing a valuable HR service. We suggested that potential employees be asked to spend half a day in the Myth Museum, giving them an opportunity to decide for themselves whether they could be comfortable with the spirit of the firm.

There was even a crassly commercial aspect to the plan. Imagine being the only architect in the world to guarantee you'd stand behind every one of your projects, for the life of those projects. Assuming they wanted to, the current owners of each project would also be allowed to visit the Myth Museum to see what generations of the firm had written and observed about the buildings they owned. What a non-cost-added sales enhancement.

Our client loved the idea, with representatives of almost every level of the organization congratulating us on our insights. Like the proverbial blind men describing an elephant, each saw our suggestion through the filter of their own self-interest. The most senior managers saw it as an opportunity for younger associates to pay their homage to the genius of their superiors. Young architects saw it as an opportunity to strut their stuff, be heard, and take shots at designs they secretly saw as more profitable than aesthetically pleasing. Everyone agreed it should be a top priority. Somehow, despite the initial enthusiasm, the Myth Museum never got built. No doubt the failure to implement helped the firm retain its hierarchical lines of control. And without question, it will cause it to continue to lose some of its best and brightest.

We don't want to add any undue weight to bookshelves already overburdened with business texts exploring the arcane meaning of leadership or promising to deliver some secret formula for managing employees. But since leaders and followers are such important ingredients in a culture, we want to at least touch on the topics, especially since the Abolition of Traditional Business Context has decisively changed what it means to be a leader and a follower. Let's start by looking at leaders.

The old adage warns, "A fish rots from the head down." We're not actually sure it's technically true. (Of course, neither is the boiling frog theory—humans are the only creatures stupid enough to stay in a dangerous environment long enough to die. While we're at it, next time you visit an orchard, see if you can figure out that low-hanging fruit cliché; it's almost always the least desirable stuff on the tree.) Whether more metaphorically than physically true, the fact remains that the leader—like the chief abbot of the monastery—bears the final responsibility for the stewardship and integrity of the culture.

Most leaders follow the path of the devox straight to the top. They begin with an Edgy obsessive vision of themselves and/or a corporation. Early in their careers, their ambitions move to the Edge with the gathering of a few initial allies. The rest of their career is spent expanding that core of early supporters or patrons and extending their personal networks until finally enough momentum is built up and they move from being in the Realm of the Cool to the Next Big Thing to the man or woman in charge of operating Social Convention.

Thanks to the devox, there's been a breakdown in the context of leadership. CEOs are more perishable than a bowl of Cherry Garcia ice cream at high noon at Burning Man. That's not because today's crop of senior managers is in any way inferior to their forebears. In almost every imaginable way they're infinitely better prepared for their positions than most of those who preceded them. It's just that the context of traditional leadership itself has been fatally compromised. Let's recall the historical definition of deviance: some measurable increment away from the mean, a departure from an accepted course or standard. By definition, then, one has to be a deviant to lead in a deviant world.

RECRUITING DEVIANT LEADERS

So here are a few hints you might find useful if you're looking for a deviant leader:

- Recruit from the Edge by looking for people with unconventional backgrounds. Outsider perspectives can revolutionize a business. On March 4, 2001, a troubled Coca-Cola company recruited Steven J. Heyer as president and COO of Coca-Cola Ventures. Heyer's background? He was president and COO of AOL Time Warner's Turner Broadcasting System. His mission: shake up the status quo.

- Seeking out generalists rather than specialists. The problem with specialist leaders is that in moments of stress they always revert to their specialty, which may actually destroy a company. In July 1972 IGA, Inc., named Dr. Thomas Haggai to its board. Haggai, an ordained minister, radio broadcaster, author, and lecturer, was the first person from outside the food industry to have a seat on the board. In 1976 he was named chairman, and in 1986 he took on the additional title of CEO. Under this "outsider's" leadership IGA expanded from an increasingly marginalized American franchise to a global food player operating in forty countries.

- Look for someone looking past your company. Several years ago we worked in the United Kingdom with Air Miles, essentially a loyalty scheme operator. One of the things that impressed us most about their new-hire orientation program was that the first thing they said was "Tell us what you hope to do when you leave here so we can help you better prepare for your future." Surprised, most new employees swore they would never leave. Deviant employees, though, offered an answer that allowed Air Miles to help ensure they developed the skill sets that will help them land that other job. Why? Because Air Miles hoped that after they got through with that job, they'd return to Air Miles smarter, better trained, and more experienced. It was not surprising to find someone who had left Air Miles and returned as many as three times.

- Remember that the best qualified shouldn't always lead, all the time. The world *tyrant* comes from the ancient Greek. Tyranny began as a process of selecting the individual best qualified to address a crisis and then giving him absolute authority to deal with it. The authority was handed over with the understanding that the tyrant would give it back and return to being a blacksmith or farmer once the crisis had passed. And also remember that you might have to consider drafting a leader; real deviants might be just what you need, but they rarely volunteer.

Context is defined both internally and externally. Deviant leaders set the internal parameters, but the external boundaries are the result of changes to the broader culture's definition of leadership and what it means to be a follower. Deviant employees have a tough enough time fitting into organizations as it is. Once a company has made it clear that it *really* isn't interested in cultivating dissenting opinions, most deviants are out the door. What our architectural client had missed was the opportunity to create an environment in which deviants felt free to innovate and express themselves.

Deviant employees may be loyal to themselves, a cause, or an idea, but they're rarely loyal to a company, even at the height of a recession. Generations raised to think of serial marriage, serial friendships, serial families, and serial careers as normal can't be expected to do too well in the traditional employment culture. We suspect that's why so many companies had trouble recruiting and retaining the talent they did manage to hire before the collapse of the New Economy and September 11. The veneer of loyalty may appear to resurface during a social or economic crisis. But on balance, through good times and bad, if you want to catch a deviant mouse, you have to build a deviant mousetrap.

The devox's impact on society as a whole and the family in particular has produced generations of employees who have been harder and harder for traditional corporate structures to manage. A pattern of deviance—sometimes in the form of an unwillingness to conform and other times manifested in profound self-interest—started with the sixties generation and moved progressively through Generation X and Generation Y until it reached today's Digital Generation. As these children of the devox continue to pour into—and redefine—the workplace in greater and greater numbers, it gets more difficult for traditional command-and-control-style employers to cope or traditional business culture to survive.

Remember, deviant employees ought to be one of your primary sources of innovative ideas.

Perhaps the classic illustration of this point is offered up by Robert I. Sutton in his delightful book *Weird Ideas That Work: 11½ Practices for Promoting, Managing, and Sustaining Innovation.* Discussing Lotus Development Corporation, Sutton, professor of management science and engineering at the Stanford Engineering School, codirector of the Center for Work, Technology, and Organization, and an active researcher in the Stanford Technology Ventures Program, recalled what happened when Lotus cofounder and (at the time) chairman Mitchell Kapor became concerned that the company was simultaneously enjoying great sales and becoming less innovative. The sales success was the result of hiring key executives from classic marketing firms like Coca-Cola, Procter & Gamble, and other bastions of traditional corporate culture, such as McKinsey and IBM.

Kapor and Freada Klein, Lotus's head of organizational development and training, created an experiment. Klein assembled the résumés of the initial forty Lotus employees (including Kapor). The names were changed and the résumés were edited to both conceal identities and cover the three years they had been with the company. Not one of the team that had built the company, including its cofounder, was even called back for an interview. In retrospect, Kapor's fears seem well-grounded. From the time of its success with Lotus 1-2-3 until its eventual sales to IBM, Lotus enjoyed only one hit product, Lotus Notes, and that was developed twenty miles away from the corporate headquarters. Understanding how the devox manifests itself internally can be a critical step toward capturing valuable external perspectives. And finally, if you don't nurture deviant employees today, you may find yourself competing against them tomorrow.

So where do you start? There are as many possibilities as there are deviant employees, but let's concentrate on the most obvious strategies. It's generally accepted that deviant employees are attracted to challenges and repelled by repetitive assignments. As the open-source movement proves, make the challenge big enough and you can even get a fair number of deviants to work for free.

DEVIANT LOVE AND HATE

Deviants love work and hate jobs. They are perfect for a skunk works project precisely because such activities exist outside what they see as the suffocating confines of traditional employment. Earlier in this book we discussed how the devox's assault on traditional institutions had given rise to neotribalism. Creative managers can channel the impulse to participate in neotribes and give the deviants a sense of belonging. This approach also lets the deviants in your company work at their own (often accelerated) pace. All that's required is the intelligence to trust the lunatics to run their own asylum.

In *Managing Interactively,* Mary E. Boone explores several variations on this deviant neotribal theme. Two of these are what she calls "communities of practice" and "communities of purpose." Communities of practice, she writes, "may cross physical and organization boundaries, but the individuals within them share common professional interests." Intranet formation at IBM or educational institutions are examples of this form of community. Communities of purpose, on the other hand, "often disperse and reform in different configurations around other purposes. Often you'll find communities of purpose embedded in communities of practice." Boone quotes Tom Sudman, president of Digital Av, as saying, "Communities of purpose have goals, time frames, and metrics against which they are measured." Not-for-profit organizations are among the best—and sometimes worst—examples of communities of purpose, but this isn't to say they couldn't exist inside a for-profit corporation.

Deviant employees don't respect chains of command or people who hide behind them. In the era of the devox, authority isn't an entitlement. It has to be earned or it doesn't exist. As Visa founder and CEO emeritus Dee Hock has noted, "Leader presumes follower. Follower presumes choice. One who is coerced to the purposes, objectives, or preferences of another is not a follower in any true sense of the word, but an object of manipulation. Nor is the relationship materially altered if both parties accept dominance and coercion. True leading and following presume perpetual liberty of both leader and follower to sever the relationship and pursue another path. A true leader cannot be bound to lead. A true follower cannot be bound to follow."

Deviant employees are also more loyal to themselves, their families, or some cause than they'll ever be toward you. Get over it. You'll live. Sometimes, as in the case of (the pre-Unilever acquisition) Ben &

Jerry's, Tom's of Maine, Greenpeace, Planned Parenthood, and count-less other organizations, dedication to a cause translates directly into dedication to an organization.

So rather than worrying about *who* deviant employees love, find out *what* they love and embrace it. Celebrate deviance. If you know that you have a number of employees who ride motorcycles, get a bike yourself and sponsor a "run." If you know your deviants like old American film classics, open up the office on a weekend and stage a Bogart film festival.

Deviants of a feather flock together. Hire a visible member of a deviant group, let her be herself, give her a little hiring authority, and she'll likely solve your innovation crisis for you. Even in the current labor market the "right" hire is still tough. There are lots of résumés fly-ing across desks and cyberspace, but that can make it even more diffi-cult to find exactly the right talent. Remember, deviants have their own networks. Some employers may worry about placing the long-term integrity of their intellectual property in deviant hands. It comes down to this: either you trust people not to sell you out or you don't. Chances are your deviant has a deviant friend or life partner at a competitive company. Don't panic. Allow him to pursue the friendship or relation-ship openly and the odds are they'll both be working for you soon.

When it comes to the care and nurturing of the deviant, it's critical to remember that deviants need to stay on the Edge. In fact, the more deviant the individual, the farther out on the Edge they need to be. Properly managed, this irresistible attraction to the Edge ought to help you keep your employees happy and your company sharp. You can begin by facilitating employee access to media, personalities, or venues that help your deviants stay plugged in on their terms.

Never forget your deviants ought to be your first, best line of com-petitive commercial defense. We're still reeling from our experience at a leading foodservice company that retained us to give it an out-of-the-box perspective on ethnicity. We started with the highly deviant idea that the executives who hired us spend time in one of their plants where 95 percent of the employees were Hispanic. Our advice: "Go talk to your own people and find out what they think. If you really want to know what they think, take off the ties and go to work on the line for a month or so with them. Hang out where they hang out, party where they party. After a while, you'll be invited into their homes as a friend. Talk to their families. You'll get better advice than you will from any paid ethnic marketing expert." The company was genuinely concerned about what ethnic consumers thought, provided they weren't on the payroll. This company was much more comfortable with a polished, professional ethnic marketing expert than they'll ever be with the actual ethnic market. The professionals, after all, play by the same rules as the companies that hire them.

BACK TO THE BORG

Collective action is the opposite of individual achievement and often its primary obstacle. We don't want to harp too long on the notion that third-millennium corporations create maximum value when they exist in commercial networks or economic webs. We just want to reinforce the notion that in the face of the devox, a strategy of corporate insularity just might not make as much sense as it once did. But before you run wildly off hoping to plug into the multicorporate equivalent of *Star Trek*'s Borg collective, think for a moment. Rather than forming alliances along traditional lines, why not think about the most deviant partnerships you could establish?

How much sooner, for example, could we reach our collective human goal of finding a cure for cancer if the world's tobacco companies and industrial polluters bankrolled and openly and freely worked in tandem with the American Cancer Society, the Centers for Disease Control, and other global anticancer research teams? Suppose the smoking and antismoking lobbies agreed (in exchange for full or partial indemnity for tobacco marketers) to divert the hundreds of millions of dollars currently going into the coffers of law firms litigating for and against tobacco companies into the accounts of the world's most promising cancer researchers. This suggestion is hardly deviant in a world where the government subsidizes tobacco farmers, onerously taxes tobacco products, and then turns around to use some of those tax dollars to pay for antismoking campaigns. In the developed world, at least, everyone within range of a billboard, a public school, a radio, a television, an Internet connection, or a package of cigarettes for that matter understands the health risks associated with smoking. By funding anticancer research, global tobacco might help keep some of its installed customer base living—and smoking—a few years longer.

By the same token, the haunting question to those African Roman Catholic bishops who in 2001 reinforced their condemnation of the use of any form of birth control other than total abstinence has to be how many African lives could be spared if the church had sought out an alliance with Planned Parenthood or another family planning service that widely disseminates condoms and sex education materials.

Finally, on another note, why would a truly deviant corporation need to own anything at all, including property? The Enron debacle aside, will the ethical deviant corporation of the near future require any tangible assets or just an infrastructure capable of mobilizing enough appropriate assets to capitalize on an opportunity and then move along when the opportunity passes? We suspect these aren't the kind of questions your board of directors is asking you, but they may be the very questions you should be asking your board. The consequences of not asking them are staggering. Wall Street's devaluation of Old Economy companies, which temporarily caught all those asset cadgers way off guard, was just the devox's first shot across the corporate bow. But don't let the collapse of the New Economy fool you; it won't be the last.

Speaking of Wall Street, assuming that the corporation is—or should be—immortal can eventually destroy even the best company. How can Wal-Mart, for instance, continue to sustain the rates of growth analysts demand? A truly deviant Wal-Mart CEO might spend less time worrying about which third- or fourth-choice locations to move into to keep the analysts off his or her back and direct the company's energies into a media campaign assuring shareholders, customers, and employees that the company was—and should be—exclusively dedicated to pursuing profitable growth.

In today's world this approach might be all but impossible to execute. But the first rule of the deviant CEO is "When you can't win playing by the rules, don't break the rules, change them." We suspect that it's more than possible to craft an alternative view of the enterprise, its mission, and the market obstacles. Ross Perot didn't win the presidency, but he did create a viable forum for disseminating his views of how government ought to work. More and more corporate leaders, from Steve Forbes to Mike Bloomberg, have discovered ways to massage the rules of engagement by making what had been private sector concerns public sector issues and even second careers. So, appropriately, we now turn our attention to the targets of all marketing—the new, often deviant, consumer.

12

The Understanding and Care of the Deviant Consumer

You can talk about any intellectual concept, and it is up for grabs, because anything can mean anything, any thought can lead into another thought and thus be completely perverted. But when you get to the actual physical act of sexuality, or of bodily disease, there's an undeniable materiality which isn't up for grabs. So, it's the body which finally can't be touched by all our skepticism and ambiguous systems of belief. The body is the only place where any basis for real values exists anymore.

—KATHY ACKER

Nowhere is the impact of the devox more easily seen than in the change in consumers and consumer markets. A new consumer is being born whose attitudes are completely different from those happy consuming engines of the 1950s through the 1990s. A range of products—from Linux, one of the world's most popular software platforms, to Doom, one of the world's most popular computer games—have been "finished" on the Internet by consumers who turned around and purchased what amount to packaged versions of their own work. Extending political consciousness to food shopping, British and French consumers have literally ripped genetically modified (GM) foods from their grocers' shelves and thrown them into the streets. Wherever you turn, the classic definitions of who consumers are, how they can be counted on to behave, and even basic understandings of what they want and why they want it are being rewritten every day.

At the very Fringe of this new universe are those so opposed to consumption they hate anyone associated with the making and marketing of a good or service. On the Edge this impulse loses some steam but gains some followers—resulting in small boycott or protest groups. One step into the Realm of the Cool and the spirit of corporate criticism begins to resemble engagement and participation. Increasingly, consumer advocates are being recruited by some companies as allies rather than opponents. The Next Big Thing would be to have these concerned consumers seize control of the corporations they are so critical of or form competitive companies. The Next Big Thing, it seems, is already starting to spill into Social Convention.

One of the questions most frequently asked of futurists is "What can you tell us about the future of consumers in the (fill in the blank) industry?" Naturally, the answer depends to a greater or lesser degree on the word that you use to fill in the blank, but the motivation for asking it is remarkably similar across industries. From telephony and high technology to entertainment and consumer package goods, the traditional marketing and research methodologies used to identify consumers and explain their behaviors are failing more and more often. Failing metrics lead to problematic outcomes when dubious marketing data are translated into marketing programs.

In a more homogeneous world, simple demographic indicators were often all you needed to do highly effective target marketing. But in the world of the devox, relying on traditional demography for an explanation of your markets can be akin to commercial suicide. Today's consumers are as deviant as the world they live in and so traditional demographic descriptors—age, gender, education, ZIP code, and income—don't really begin to tell us what we need to know about them to sell products.

Take the case of someone with an address in New York's rapidly gentrifying Tribeca neighborhood. Based on address alone, is that person more likely to be a crack addict, a multimillionaire film star, or both? If your son or daughter has an M.B.A or Ph.D., is he or she more likely to earn $150,000 a year or $30,000 because of a quality-of-life decision? When we were both born (slightly after the midpoint of the last century), a sixty-six-year-old man was statistically either dead or well on his way. Today he may be fathering his second set of children, embarking on his third career, and be in the middle of his fourth marriage. And finally, if someone's surname is Garcia, do they or don't they speak Spanish?

BURN THE DATA

All those filing cabinets loaded with longitudinal studies of consumer behavior provide a great historical record of how traditional consumers used to behave. Increasingly, however, they fall short in terms of their ability to predict or anticipate how consumers will behave. How else can you explain the increasingly high rate of new product failure in an era where we have an unprecedented ability to track and monitor actual purchase patterns? Coca-Cola, one of the world's finest branders and marketers, created two of the best examples of this—OK Cola and New Coke.

The secret shared by all those caffeine-buzzed, black-clad, virus-spreading guerrilla-marketer types is that no matter how bizarre your approach, it's almost always safe to claim (absent supporting concrete evidence) that you're intentionally building a clever consumer-to-consumer campaign. After all, in a world where consumers are so volatile and unpredictable, nobody will ever know if you're right or wrong. You can always blame product or service failure on the economy, the media, improper management, or politics. Whenever any business fails, these are the factors almost universally cited. But products and services that are well matched to clearly defined and viable target markets ought to be better insulated against failure. Kmart's collapse in 2002 had very little to do with the economy or lack of a clearly defined market. Kmart knew exactly who it was aiming at, but the target market refused to purchase according to plan. People still buy goods and services during an economic and political crisis. Just ask all those army-navy surplus stores that made a killing on the Y2K phobia.

The roots of business failure run deep. They begin to grow when an enterprise loses its understanding of who the customer is. Brands like Buick, Kmart, Montgomery Ward, and Oldsmobile struggled precisely because they refused to admit their target consumer had changed. Instead of branching off in boldly deviant directions, they attempted to massage a failed formula back to life—a heroic but fatally flawed effort. In Kmart's case, for example, the target market was clearly lower- and lower-middle-income America. Kmart believed it understood the market and how to create excitement in it. The only problem? Wal-Mart already had the market locked up. Wal-Mart didn't just define its target market; it embraced it and stayed close to it. For years Kmart executives slept content in the knowledge they knew exactly what they were doing. The problem is that they never bothered to discuss those plans with the consumer.

Kmart defined the market in traditional demographic terms—gender, age, income, etc.—while Wal-Mart reflected the market. One key to moving from analysis to understanding is the development of new metrics. Give the notion of developing new metrics to better understand consumers a minute's worth of thought and halfway through you're likely to come to the conclusion that you need to scrap your current thinking and adopt a more creative approach.

We developed fifty questions to help a Fortune 100 client in the beverage business think differently about emerging consumer lifestyles. The company wanted to develop a market-segmentation model that helped it "see" and think about the consumer in nontraditional ways. We started with the assumption that attitudes and values were better predictors of buying behaviors than addresses and age. Our research methodology involved talking with friends, neighbors, and strangers and then listening to what themes kept reemerging. People don't see themselves as members of a marketing cohort. Instead, they more often describe themselves in terms of their hopes, fears, and dreams.

The exercise was useful to the company's managers on several levels. First, it gave them a new quantitative and qualitative research platform. Next, it explored the consumer on a psychographic level, something that really hadn't been done before. Finally, it began an internal dialogue on what questions were important to ask, and what survey instruments had outlived their usefulness. We've included the questionnaire as one example of a new approach to traditional marketing.

1. Whose opinion do you listen to?
2. Whose opinion do you value?
3. Have you ever translated a hobby into income?
4. Are you happy?
5. What constitutes happiness to you?
6. Are you a member of a calling, or e-mail, "tree(s)"?
7. Do you play to win or play to keep from losing?
8. Do you find yourself living in ways that seem superficially contradictory? For instance, do you shop at Bergdorf or Nordstrom and at Wal-Mart or Kmart?
9. Can you explain the difference between influence and control?
10. Does apparent contradiction or paradox bother you? How much? Why?
11. Where do you find magic?
12. Where do you find hope?
13. Where do you find beauty?
14. Where do you find grace?
15. Do you like things that are "different" every time? For example, do you have multiple recordings of the same song?
16. Where are there consequences in life?
17. Is your memory as good as you think it should be? And what do you remember most often?

18. What is authentic today?

19. Can you give us an example of something you believe is phony or inauthentic?

20. How do you define a service?

21. What separates good service from bad service?

22. How do you define the "moment of value" for a product or service; i.e., when does something have its greatest value for you?

23. What makes you unhappy?

24. What personal needs do you feel that you believe nobody even recognizes?

25. Where do you find excitement?

26. Where do you find passion?

27. Where do you find satisfaction?

28. What is your most common source of frustration?

29. Whom do you respect?

30. What do you respect?

31. What do you fear?

32. Whom do you fear?

33. What (in your current life) would you be prepared to sacrifice to "advance" yourself and how would you define advancement?

34. What (in your current life) would you be unwilling to sacrifice under any circumstances?

35. What magazines do you subscribe to or read?

36. What television shows do you regularly watch?

37. How would you describe the kind of music you most frequently listen to at home, at work, and in the car?

38. What is your favorite movie?

39. In which room of your home are you most comfortable?

40. If you had to describe your life stage in one word, what would it be?

41. Do you think you belong to the same generation your parents did when they were your age?

42. Are you more or less comfortable with people your own age?

43. Do you think of yourself as young?

44. What one possession of yours do you believe best defines you?

45. If you were going to learn or do something you've never done, what would it be?

46. Are you safe?

47. Which is more important to you in terms of your self-definition: age, gender, religion, income, profession?

48. Do you ever feel that something is missing from your life, and if so what do you think it is?

49. If you were a time traveler would you rather live in the future or the past? Or would you stay in the present?

50. If you had to describe your lifestyle in one word, what would that word be?

These questions were designed against a specific set of project objectives and are only meant to be illustrative of what can be done. It's easy to make sweeping generalizations about thirty-seven-year-old divorced mothers with incomes under $35,000 a year. But it's a far more difficult task to begin to wrestle with the complex patterns that emerge from this analysis. In fact, modified versions of these questions have been used to do just that—serving as the "content" base for management retreats aimed at getting companies to think about their customers, and therefore themselves, in much different ways.

No one is suggesting that this list is comprehensive, final, or even approximating perfect, but it is a good illustration of one approach to aligning yourself against the ebb and flow of the devox. If you understand how someone's personal context has changed, or her relation to the larger social and cultural context, you can begin to rethink the products she does and doesn't need. We're willing to bet that almost any of you reading this book would be fairly surprised by the answers you'd get if you posed these questions to your customers. At the very least we're sure that asking these questions would force you to rethink some of your current go-to-market assumptions. The company for which we developed these questions used the answers to redefine its understanding of potential future lifestyles and to begin a long-term study of the impact of lifestyle change on a well-established brand.

Call it psychographics if you want to, or perhaps more correctly emotographics, but we believe there is greater value in marketing to a more holistic view of the customer. Most of us understand the power of a concept like comfort food or nostalgia marketing. Ask yourself exactly what cohort you need to belong to to want comfort or pleasant memories. Remember, your consumers are in as much transition as the economy, your company, and every aspect of your personal and commercial life. Their sense of personal context is being abolished, individually as they struggle for meaning in a changing world and collectively as they come to market. This switch from a commercial value orientation among consumers to one that resonates with their personal values has been extensively documented. New consumers demand that business reflect or affirm their personal values. Offering value alone is no longer a sustaining platform for brand loyalty. While the greatest generation sought out tangible value (defined in the relationship between product feature, function, endurance, and price), its children and grandchildren assume transactional value exists and are looking for a deeper sense of values.

Throughout history, human beings have sought affirmation of themselves and their values through their communities and social institutions. Today children routinely grow up not knowing the people who live on their block and, in some cases, even the people who live next door. The breakdown in the traditional sense of community hasn't reduced our need to be social. Instead, it has opened the doors to any numbers of neotribal marketers, companies from Harley-Davidson to Starbucks that understand the value of building community.

One by one the institutions that have traditionally upheld values have failed us. We have come to see our presidents as human beings—often, like Richard Nixon and Bill Clinton, fatally flawed human beings. We used to look to organized religion for direction, but the numbing procession of religious scandals from the Bakkers to Jimmy Swaggart to the widespread revelations concerning child-molesting priests has soured many people on their churches. We used to hope that educational institutions would teach our children values. Now we're happy if they manage to teach them to read and write. We watch in horror as schools from Columbine to Erfurt morph into killing zones. But our need as people for reinforcement doesn't go away just because the sources of that reinforcement have dried up.

The post–Abolition of Context consumer has created a new standard for evaluating businesses—a standard that significantly deviates from the one most traditional businesses are offering. All consumer-facing transactions can be divided into five attributes: access, experience, price, product, and service. In the traditional context, access meant location; experience meant theater; best price was synonymous with lowest price; product usually was expected to be the best; and service usually meant a smile and maybe a handshake. For post-Abolition consumers, access has to do with the ability to locate offerings easily; experience has to do with how I feel about myself; fair and honest prices are preferred; a range of consistently good products is more desirable than best products; and service is measured by how I feel about you.

THE PROBLEM WITH CONSUMERS

While we directly address the issue of brands in Chapter 15, we think it's important to talk about what happens when a deviant brand meets the deviant consumer. Why? Let's face it, the most problematic thing for a consumer-facing business is that consumers just aren't as brand loyal as we'd like them to be. We've already discussed at some length how today's consumers escape traditional demographic conventions. That same pattern is influencing historical marketing assumptions. Just because Mom used Tide and Dad drove a Chevrolet there's no guarantee their children will be lifelong Procter & Gamble or General Motors supporters. In fact, increasingly for a growing number of consumers, brand loyalty (toward product and/or seller) doesn't survive a single purchase experience.

As a result of this rapidly devolving sense of traditional context and the new emphasis on values over value, it ought to come as no surprise that consumers can almost be counted on to leap off trends just about the time you're gearing up to capitalize on them. The situation isn't entirely hopeless. Here are six ideas that just might help you not only survive the devox's assault on consumer context, but actually help you profit from it.

1. Once it has moved from the Fringe to the Edge, deviance, like nature, abhors a vacuum. Deviants seek out other deviants—this is how "scenes" are formed and how "scenes" eventually birth markets. The neotribe (a voluntary aggregation of individuals who join together to form communities, and create unique cultures, around common interests) is the social grouping of choice for the deviant consumer. There's validation in numbers, and validation is remarkably marketable. So keep finding ways to covertly establish neotribes for your customers to join. That way, even if the consumer isn't crazy about you or your product he'll still keep buying it. It's worked for Harley-Davidson and Honda; the Chicago Cubs and Manchester United; *Star Trek* and *Star Wars*. It can work for you.

2. Never underestimate the importance of the therapeutic. Because of the collapse of our collective confidence in institutions, self-realization is one of the goals of the new consumer. Since we are

no longer receiving consistent institutional reinforcement, we have a heightened personal need for individual recognition, affirmation, and understanding—and a perpetual search for a heightened sense of well-being. That's part of what makes neotribal marketing so successful and why the New Age sections of bookstores are so popular.

No matter how bizarre, there's an ongoing market for anything you can do to enhance a person's sense of self-worth and/or self-definition: scents, sounds, and sensations that will—or claim to—make them feel better. This is the era when candle makers have been transformed into aromatherapy manufacturers; massage parlors have morphed into reflexology centers; and the study of Native American flute music and Tibetan Buddhist chants more often falls to middle-aged suburbanites than cultural anthropologists. There's a 900 line for every stripe of paranormal aficionado from tarot-card devotees to astrology buffs. *Crossing Over with John Edward,* a regular feature on the Sci-Fi Channel that claims to link the earthbound with their dearly departed, is a runaway hit—a clear testament to our desire to feel good even after we shuffle off this mortal coil. Even this has evolved. The most popular of these shows now focus exclusively on dead celebrities.

3. Embrace the alienated. The fact that as a society we're finding more and more loopholes in the social contract just gives you more opportunity to capitalize on the cloistered periphery of the hobbyist and crank markets. Look at the booming market for Internet porn or the legions of disembodied souls clicking into chat rooms of every possible description. The alienated are a major market without whom talk radio and shock television would be almost totally devoid of content and audiences. Think what the home security business would be like if people weren't alienated. Who would ever purchase all that survivalist gear? We live in a world where it becomes easier and easier to fade into your own self-made universe. Marketers on the extreme end of alienation produce life-size blowup

dolls, but the tendency to isolate and withdraw into a private reality has also been behind a rash of entertainment products from Sony's Walkman and Discman to the home theater.

Remember that we live in a robustly diverse society, and so we have multiple opportunities to be alienated from something. There are enough people out there who see themselves on the outside of any given issue to build a comfortable market. Youth marketers have always understood the value of helping people express their alienation, particularly musically. Whether it was white youths in the mid-1970s buying punk music from the likes of the Sex Pistols and the Clash or urban and suburban teens eagerly embracing gangsta rap or hip-hop, alienation has always proved a lucrative musical marketing tool.

4. Don't just read about deviants, dance with them. Blow up those traditional longitudinal data sheets you've been hoarding and take it to the streets. Don't hire cool hunters; become a cool hunter. Don't think in terms of "us" and "them"; just become "us." The best way to understand how people live is to go out and live with them. You can't wait for a detailed analysis of the deviant consumers; if they're really deviants they'll have changed significantly by the time the report is shooting out of the printer.

5. Start practicing deviance on a daily basis. As a young man, Peter Drucker decided he would devote sequential decades to the intensive study of subjects he knew nothing about. It was an exercise designed to keep his mind alert and open to new possibilities. There are, of course, less time-consuming approaches. If you see yourself as uncreative, try taking up painting, not just as an exercise but also as a lifestyle. Hang out with artists. Go to gallery openings. Watch films that confuse you.

If, on the other hand, you are loose and creative, find some routine tasks to do (charting euro fluctuations comes to mind). Adopt an anal approach to the project. Devote an uncluttered, ordered space to your research and keep it neat. Attend CPA continuing-education classes and chat with the people on the breaks or go to the data-processing department, and hang out with the data-entry crew. The whole idea is to become what you are not, to deviate from the norm as you define and live it.

6. Finally, quit trying to push products out to the market. Deviant consumers are ill cast in the role of passive commercial sheep. Look beyond the confines of your organization and into your market itself. Pull in consumer ideas and make them into your market realities. The best way to understand what a deviant consumer wants is to listen to her. If she is really deviant, she's generally anxious to tell you. This approach takes away all that wonderful uncertainty, but don't worry; whatever you learn will change just about the time you're ready to institutionalize it.

Understanding the deviant consumer is critical because when you aggregate all those deviant consumers, you end up with deviant markets.

13

Deviant Marketing for Deviant Markets

Gone will be so-called quantitative marketing studies, which will be
useless since so many consumers will be freestyling, or artificially
creating their playsures *(sic)* and new realities, so no two individuals
will make the same purchasing decisions—nor will they stop for a
Netsensor (the on-line future of surveys) . . . Kiss goodbye the stale,
mass-media advertising strategies . . .

—Janine Lopiano-Misdom and Joanne De Luca

Marketing has been an exercise in organized deviance since the
1930s when Edward L. Bernays, the "father of public relations,"
convinced women that cigarettes were really their "torches of freedom." For the record, less than a year later, he deliberately concealed
early scientific evidence linking tobacco use to cancer.

In 1929 Bernays persuaded George Washington Hill, then head of
American Tobacco Company, to hire Dr. A. A. Brill, a psychoanalyst
pal of Bernays's uncle Sigmund Freud, to look into the issue of women
and smoking. Brill's "scientific" conclusion: "It is perfectly normal for
women to want to smoke cigarettes. The emancipation of women has
suppressed many of their feminine desires. More women now do the
same work as men do. Many women bear no children; those who do
bear have fewer children. Feminine traits are masked. Cigarettes, which
are equated with men, become torches of freedom."

Bernays was so taken by the good doctor's analysis he organized a Torches of Freedom march of smoking women for Easter Sunday of that year. It was an unqualified success, leading Bernays to understand exactly how quickly marketing and public relations could move a concept (women smoking on public streets) to the center of Social Convention. "Age-old customs, I learned, could be broken down by a dramatic appeal, disseminated by the network of media," he reported. "Of course the taboo was not destroyed completely. But a beginning had been made."

From the perspective of 2002, Bernays is no longer a deviant. He is in fact the man who began constructing the mold from which most conventional marketing and public relations efforts have been cast. This is the paradox of the devox: It first destroys one context and then creates another that it later destroys. Acceleration in the speed of this pattern and an intensification of the degree of change has created marketing's answer to the Möbius strip (a geometric puzzle transformed into a child's trick in which a deft half twist creates a three-dimensional surface without a front or back)—a commercial reality in which it's increasingly harder to understand where the hype stops and the product starts.

For example, advertising used to be aimed at people. Today people are walking billboards. On the next nice day, get a comfortable seat in a park, on a beach, or anywhere else people gather and count the number of hats, shirts, and bags you see advertising products. Years ago these things were given away. Today they command premium prices. There's even a Marlboro Wear store on Paris's Champs-Elysées. T-shirts with product logos on them have become high fashion and even (in Silicon Valley and outlaw-biker circles) collector's items. That's not the only example of a change in the context of advertising.

Advertising no longer just sells the product, it can *become* a product—sometimes worth more than the product it was trying to promote. Absolut vodka is the textbook case study for deviant marketing. Not only are there websites like the fan-supported Absolut Vodka Advertisement Archive (http://www.absolutad.org) and other sites on which to barter, buy, or sell Absolut ads, Absolut is a mainstay on eBay. Search eBay and you'll find fifteen or so pages (screens) of Absolut items from around the world, including: a stunning Absolut Dad Silk Sperm Tie ($2.99); a smashing Absolut Kurt Vonnegut Ad ($6.00); and even an Absolut Impotent Mock Ad Marked "Rare" (and only $3.50). Think about what's going on out there. People are actually buying old magazine ads and even fake magazine ads. T-shirts and belt buckles are one thing—but used counterfeit magazine ads? Edward Bernays would require years on his uncle's couch to understand this one.

What does this have to do with your business, you ask? Sure, you understand why bikers tattoo the Harley-Davidson logo on their expanded biceps, you've seen people walking around with everything from Joe Camel to car ads on their back, and now we've presented evidence that there's a healthy market for selling ads several multiples over the cover price of the magazines they originally appeared in, but clearly there's a logical limit where this kind of behavior stops.

Or so you might think.

During our stint working for Krispy Kreme doughnuts, we learned some valuable deviant advertising and marketing lessons. In those pre-IPO days, Krispy Kreme's entire marketing and advertising budget was zero. Instead the company relied on a series of guerrilla marketing strategies to push its products, including shipping doughnuts to television celebrities like Rosie O'Donnell, who happily stuffed her face with them on camera. Rather than mass free sampling, Krispy Kreme chose to selectively sample. And when it comes to cult creation, the Branch Davidians and Heaven's Gate crowds have learned a thing or two from Krispy Kreme.

ORGASMS ON ACID

We've seen film footage of actress Susan Sarandon comparing eating a "Hot Now" Krispy Kreme original to having a world-class orgasm while under the effects of some equally world-class LSD. We can't comment from personal experience, but we have seen (apparently in every other way sane) people with the Krispy Kreme logo tattooed on their forearms. We're not sure it's as impressive a tattoo in maximum-security prison circles as, say, a nice Harley "tat" or one of those attractive jailhouse tattoos advertising Folsom or San Quentin, but it's strong evidence of the power of some kind of strange marketing mojo.

The point here is that some of the most successful products of our era—from Tommy Hilfiger's initial line launch to the product giveaway strategies of early cell phone pioneers—have been marketed in ways that are—well, deviant. There is no shortage of marketing theories out there, from the epidemic thesis of Malcolm Gladwell's *The Tipping Point* and Seth Godin's *Permission Marketing* and *Unleashing the Ideavirus.* At the risk of oversimplification, Gladwell and Godin both believe that ideas and trends "spread" through populations in the same way viruses vector through them. Gladwell believes that there is a "tipping point" at which this viral spread reaches critical mass and begins to shape markets. We shouldn't forget the guerrilla marketers and the pragmatic product placement and psychoanalytic subliminal schools. The theory of viral marketing mutates the same way viruses do. The simple notion of an idea or trend spreading from person to person until it creates a market has been modified by Emanuel Rosen, who wrote: "The spread of buzz is complex. People don't rely on any one source of information, whether it be their friends, the media, or manufacturers. They use all of the above. The way all these different sources interact is still unclear. But the fact that such sources of information may be a bit of a puzzle shouldn't stop us from using what we **do** know to stimulate the networks."

The chart on the next page highlights some of the differences between traditional and postdevox marketing. Not only is the assortment of potential media for delivering the marketing message far more robust than it was even fifteen years ago, but the major elements of the marketing equation have changed significantly. Consumers used to read advertising; now they wear it, carry it, or drive it. Marketing used to spend a good deal of effort communicating *how* you should use a product. Today, more often than not, that same degree of effort is put behind the idea of *who* uses the product. And finally, as we showed in the case of Absolut, sometimes advertising becomes the product.

THE ABOLITION OF THE
TRADITIONAL MARKETING CONTEXT

Aspect	Traditional Marketing	Postdevox Marketing
Media	Print and network broadcast	Print, network, and cable broadcast, Internet, PDAs, telephones, fax
Consumer	Target	Walking billboard
License Ware	Promotion	Product
Campaigns	Focused and finite	Viral
Content	Features and functions	Celebrity and lifestyle
Marketer	Master manipulator	At best an enlightened coconspirator
Advertising	Sold product	Can be the product

You could fill a library of dictionaries with the neologisms people create to explain how modern markets perform, or you could accept the facts. The inmates (read consumers) are running the asylum (read commercial markets). They are increasingly demanding that you market to them on their own terms, and when you don't they turn you off. It isn't that one brilliant theory works better than another, it's that in a frenetic universe every marketing ploy works at roughly the same rate that it fails. That's why there's such a growth market for marketing theories and a direct reflection of the absolute Abolition of the Traditional Marketing Context, in which sellers used clever gambits to lure sheeplike consumers to the commercial slaughter. There's always a growth market for those theories because so many of them fail, and companies are desperate to find something that works. Consumers aren't asleep. Quite the opposite, they're more awake than they've ever been. In the dancehall of the devox, nobody gets to stand on the sidelines, marketers or customers.

In a world where ubiquitous distribution is the Holy Grail of consumer packaged-goods companies, deviant marketing creates value by limiting distribution. Hatuey, a brand of beer that began brewing in Cuba in 1926 and that is now brewed by Indian Head Brewery in Baltimore, is a good example of this "only available at" theory of value creation. The brand, which once enjoyed a 70 percent share of the Cuban market, had lain dormant for fifty years until Bacardi revived it in the late 1990s. It was tested in Miami and met with great success. The deviance—which we'll take some credit for—was to keep it contained exclusively to the Miami market and not expand it to every logical, and illogical, market. Today the brand has a significant share of the Miami beer market. Not every Hatuey consumer is Cuban, but keeping the brand close to its Cuban roots has apparently reinforced its authenticity and cemented its position with its target market. We're not sure that would still be the case if Hatuey were suddenly being pushed in Des Moines discos. It takes a deviant to see the value of containing success.

Marketing, essentially the process of convincing people to purchase something they didn't know they needed, is by its nature a pretty deviant activity. Here are some principles that can help you become a world-class deviant marketer.

First, remember that what I believe will always be more important to me than what you tell me. Deviant marketers love to eliminate the distinction between the message and its target. Viral marketing is so effective because the corporate marketer becomes invisible to the target consumer. Suddenly it isn't Sony or Unilever or Microsoft selling you something. This is why liquor companies work so hard to get new products into key clubs and bars through devices such as the creation of drinks with provocative names. Having women bellying up to the bar and ordering a Blow Job, a Slow Screw, a Sex on the Beach, a Screaming Orgasm, or similarly provocatively titled drinks seems to stimulate sales for the ingredients of those concoctions in ways print ads never did.

If you want to send a new message, create a new communication channel or device. By the way, the more that channel or device resembles an objective news source the better. This explains the success of the infomercial industry. It also explains why major marketers like Sony and Yahoo! have their own magazines. You have to be careful here. Digital Convergence had high hopes for its CAT advertising scanners, which were deployed en masse in 2000 by a number of magazines, including *Wired* and *Forbes*. The idea was to get the scanners into the hands of readers who would scan bar codes appearing in the ads. The scanners were mailed free to subscribers and available to any reader requesting them. Scanning would automatically link the reader to an Internet site where they could get more information or qualify for special promotions. To date at least, the idea that consumers really want more out of their ads is apparently still more popular with marketers than customers.

Never try to fire a new gun by tripping an old trigger. You need to continually identify appropriate new consumer motivators. Beauty is a great offer to the young, but looking healthy may be more compelling to an older audience. Cosmetics were once defined as hope in a jar. Perhaps, given the aging of the baby boomers, they are better redefined as dignity in a jar. As skin and hair ages, they respond differently to makeup and hair coloring. We can't see a whole army of boomer women marching toward old age with blue hair and red clown makeup all over their cheeks. The first company to develop an alternative that favors aging hair and skin should have a significant advantage—one that will only grow over time.

As people's life circumstances change, so do the buttons you have to push to motivate a purchase. Levi's learned this lesson the hard way until it figured out those six-pack abs baby boomers had in the sixties had turned into half-barrel stomachs somewhere along the late seventies. Gap also fell on hard times, having failed to realize that its target market was aging and having kids who didn't want to wear clothes their parents were still trying to stuff themselves into.

Real deviants stand out from the crowd, and so does their messaging. Contrast traditional beer ads—picturesque nature scenes, beautiful women, parties, and ski lodges—and those Budweiser amphibians. It's a long way from the ski lodge to the swamp. Anheuser-Busch's consistently memorable messaging has if anything been too effective. Several parent and teacher groups believe the popularity of the company's advertising slogans with young people proves that their ads target children. We disagree, but the success of the campaigns is undeniable.

Find a deviant spokesperson. Snapple's best days were when Howard Stern and Rush Limbaugh endorsed it. Think about the market that was built somewhere between the Dittoheads (Limbaugh's followers) and the Lesbian Love Connection (at the time a regular Stern feature) and you begin to understand the power of the right eccentric spokesperson. From Jamie Lee Curtis's playfully sexual huckstering of cell phones to George Foreman selling grills, the sky's the limit when it comes to deviant spokespeople.

Never underestimate the value of a cliché. Sure, Bob Dole talking about his "little blue friend" is unnerving, but you remember the spots, don't you? And it's all the better when the cliché can be expressed in a slogan like "We try harder" or "Have it your way." These phrases remind us of an additional point. Never forget that deviant marketing doesn't just push products; it also creates culture and language. Take our use of the word *devox,* which we created to explain the spirit of innovation and the personalities behind it.

Whatever you do, don't let your marketing plans get ahead of your customers. Consumers aren't as brand loyal as we'd like them to be. They don't always read, watch, or listen to those cleverly crafted marketing messages. They've been known to toss out direct mail unopened. They're not always impressed that you just spent $300 million to put your name on their favorite sports or entertainment venue, especially when it results in an increase in ticket prices. And, because of everything we've talked about so far in this book, they're likely to leap off trends just about the time you've geared up to tie your marketing campaign to them.

Our discussion of deviant marketing leads us to our next chapter, a look at the deviant product.

14

The Deviant Product

Normality is the route to nowhere. If we are only willing to behave like all the others, we will see the same things, hear the same things, hire similar people, come up with similar ideas, and develop identical products or services. We will drown in the sea of normality. And Normal Inc. is bankrupt.

—Jonas Ridderstråle and Kjell Nordström

Peter Drucker was right when he said that the purpose of a business is to create a customer. And we think most people would agree that the purpose of a product is to create a sale. Since the time when cavemen traded flints for feathers until the 1990s, products had several functions and roles—but the bottom line was that they were created to be sold. Enter master deviant Linus Torvalds and his idea that creating customers really doesn't have to involve a sale at all!

Torvalds has been described as a guy with a passion for wearing mismatched shorts and T-shirts he picked up for free at computer conferences, along with the inevitable white socks and sandals. But underneath those mismatched clothes there's a man whose name appeared with Albert Einstein's on *Esquire* magazine's list of the twentieth century's top geniuses and whom *Reader's Digest* named European of the Year. In an online poll *Time* magazine readers ranked Torvalds number fifteen—just after Madonna—on a list of the most popular people of the last century. Ironically, Bill Gates, the world's richest man and in many respects the living antithesis of Torvalds, came in at number seventeen on that same poll.

For his initial interview with Torvalds, journalist David Diamond invited him to join him for a sauna in a New Age nudist retreat in Santa Cruz, California. Those unfamiliar with Torvalds might find this a tad extreme, but in Silicon circles Torvalds is sort of a god: the man who developed Linux, an open-source computer operating system that creates a framework for expanding markets, developing new products, cutting expenses, saving time, and achieving improved operational control and efficiency—and then gave it all away to anyone who wanted it.

As Diamond explained, "Linus said giving it away was a no-brainer. He was a university student at the time. The operating system took him six solid months to write. He worked on it day and night in his bedroom—some days he didn't even venture out from his mother's apartment. And when it was completed, it made sense for him to post it on the Internet for comments and feedback. That single act may prove to be the most significant innovation in the past decade. Not for the operating system itself, but for the development model it introduced to business."

The philosophic concept underlying open source is simple and well established in academia: Information—in the case of Linux, the source code or basic instructions behind the operating system—should be free and freely shared by anyone interested in improving upon it, and those improvements should also be freely shared. In business circles, however, the idea of sharing is *très* deviant, indeed. Linux currently runs almost 30 percent of all operating systems. By traditional market rules, Torvalds should have had a runaway product hit on his hands.

Why develop a product—especially one as promising and potentially profitable as Linux—if you're just going to give it away? Torvalds had imagined Linux as a project he would complete, launch on the Internet, and, in the fullness of time, move past. But, as Diamond noted, it was, after all, Finland in the dead of winter—so he tinkered with the operating system and netizens from across the planet tinkered with it and pretty soon interest in the operating system began to pick up a life of its own. It wasn't that Torvalds wasn't offered money for Linux. He was. But he was just in it for the fun of it.

Eventually the deviant Finn's deviant product grew into what Diamond describes as possibly "the largest collaborative project in the history of the world." Linux operates the largest share of servers sending information out over the World Wide Web and was the number two ranked operating system sold in 1999 and 2000. Sold? We know, how can a free product be sold? Don't worry; we'll get to this in a minute.

All this activity pits Linux directly against Microsoft's Windows. "One of the benefits of Linux is that—unlike Windows—it doesn't crash. It is stable and adaptable to different platforms," Diamond said. "Unlike Windows NT it lacks fluff—unnecessary features. It saves users the high cost of software licenses, and it ensures that they won't find themselves captive to a vendor's whims." Of course, Microsoft spends a good deal of time, money, and energy trying to "debunk" what it calls the Linux myth.

The list of Linux users includes companies large and small, ranging from Dunlap Company in Ft. Worth, an operator of sixty-five small-to-medium-sized department stores scattered from Maine to New Mexico, to Cendant Corporation, the largest hotel franchiser in America, along with Home Depot, Gap, Burlington Coat Factory, McDonald's, IBM, and Hewlett-Packard. Every one of the Fortune 500 companies uses Linux in one form or another.

Now, back to that question of how you can sell a free system. How *does* anyone make money off a product that's free? "They do it in a number of ways," Diamond explained. "By selling an easy-to-install, shrink-wrapped version of the operating system on CDs, as Red Hat does in the U.S. and SuSe Linux does here in Europe. They do it by selling computers with Linux installed, as IBM does, and offering applications that run on it. In June IBM announced that in the first six months of 2001, the number of enterprise-level applications for Linux offered by IBM and the industry's top independent software vendors grew by 30 percent to more than 2,300 applications. Companies also make money off Linux selling support—that's one of the things VA Linux does. The free operating system has created an industry that not only makes money for companies but perpetuates its use." Linux gets our vote for the perfect deviant product.

And what about Torvalds himself? How does the Don of the Devox keep body, mind, and computer together? He's got a job, working for somebody else. Torvalds is an engineer at Transmeta Corporation, where he moved from the team that developed the low-power Caruso chip to the Advanced Technology Unit, where he helps develop the next few generations of hardware technology. Transmeta also gives him all the time he needs to work on Linux. A few of the Linux companies have given him some stock options.

And what about all those programmers who keep honing Linux for free? More than twenty years ago, Bill Gates revealed himself as an Old Economy wolf in New Economy sheep's clothing when he published an open letter to free software programmers asking, "Who can afford to do professional work for nothing?"

Programmers around the world donate their skills to Linux because the idea of freeware interests them and because they can work on a voluntary basis. No surprise here; Linux programmers are part of a global neotribe, a voluntary group polarized around the creation of ever more elegant versions of software and an ideological assumption that software should be made freely available to everyone. Deviants like to group together to work, and not always with people employed by those who employ them. Part of the appeal of Linux is that it lets like-minded souls who may have different employers work together. The implications of the deviant product extend well beyond the product itself. Borrowing a line from open-source chronicler Eric Raymond's book *The Cathedral and the Bazaar* (which started as a series of essays distributed over the Internet), Linux volunteers do what they do "to scratch a personal itch."

"The geeks who participate in open-source projects may be lacking in social graces," Diamond continued, "and unable to get dates, but they aren't lacking in ego. They thrive on getting recognition for being good at what they do. When programming contributions are made, only the best ones get adopted. Getting one's work adopted means gaining prestige in the hacker community." The word *hacker* is being used in the way hackers themselves use it: to describe anyone who programs with a certain attitude.

Despite the mass corporate paranoia over retaining control of intellectual property, the deviant notion that products ought not be owned and that the intellectual property surrounding a product should be openly shared seems to be gaining traction. Austria's Dresden Bank has opened up development in one of its projects—an internal system to glue together a number of the back-end systems it had bought—to outsiders, in part as a way to attract new programmers to the company. Harvard University Law School's Open Law Project relies on volunteer lawyers, law students, and the Internet as it mounts its challenge to the United States Copyright Extension Act.

In April 2001, the Massachusetts Institute of Technology announced plans for a 2002 launch of MIT OpenCourseWare, through which almost all of its courses are available—at no charge—over the World Wide Web. This is high deviance, indeed, even for academics. It's also right in keeping with MIT's recent history. In the 1980s, MIT computer scientist Richard Stallman set up the Free Software Foundation to head off the co-option by business of research in the area of artificial intelligence. He then launched the GNU Project to develop technology under the Free Software Foundation umbrella. Torvalds used a GNU Project creation—the GCC compiler—to get his operating system working.

Palm Computing made not only its source code but also its development environment open—opening up its platform to vendors and individuals who wanted to write programs for the Palm. The result? Anyone had access to Palm's core technology, opening the doors to product cloning. Palm is looking at it differently, though, and believes that by opening up its Application Programming Interfaces and making it easy to get development tools for free, it will end up expanding the market. And that's what's happened. Other companies wrote games that work on Palm Pilots, and more advanced calendar programs than what

Palm itself offered. Palm has in effect launched a cottage industry, one whose sole product is finding new Palm applications.

Handspring, Palm's principal competition, has adopted the same strategy for its Visor line but has gone Palm one better by allowing for hardware plug-ins like GPS receivers and mobile phone attachments. So how big is the market for free or open products? No matter what business you're in—or how far you believe yourself to be insulated from the ravages of high technology—check out SourceForge.net. Source Forge.net bills itself as "the world's largest Open Source development website, with the largest repository of Open Source code and applications available on the Internet," providing "free services to Open Source developers, including project hosting, version control, bug and issue tracking, project management, backups and archives, and communication and collaboration resources." The day this chapter was written, the site boasted 230,410 registered users and 24,992 hosted projects.

Open sourcing has obvious benefits to any company since it inherently broadens the talent pool attacking a problem. As Diamond said, "They get to leverage an entire development community, not just their own employees. They can speed up the development of a product they are trying to get out. With so many eyes at work, they can find bugs more quickly. They can strengthen an existing product. They can create new markets."

Take out your cell phone. Is it a Nokia or an Ericsson? One of the reasons non-American cellular manufacturers have a global jump on U.S. producers is because they rallied behind a common, open-standard GSM while American companies attempted to control the market through the use of old predevox, traditional context proprietary standards. By the way, at least on Nokia's European models, you can now play Doom on your cell phone, thanks to software developed by one of the game's enthusiasts and given to Nokia for free.

In the spring of 1998, Netscape saw the benefit of opening its browser technology to the open-source development community. On one hand it wanted to stabilize and, it hoped, increase its market. On the other it wanted to drive innovation and improve its product. At first it was slow going. "One of the reasons for the slow start," Diamond said, "was that Netscape—like most corporations—had no experience in turning over an internal project to the world. It poses a tricky management challenge. Suddenly there are two camps of people—developers inside the company who are working for a paycheck and developers outside the company who are working for the fun of it. The company needs to make sure its project is being managed by someone who can be trusted by both groups on both a technical level and a political level— in other words, someone who knows good technology and will not favor the contributions of insiders versus outsiders."

So what's the moral of this deviant product story? "The rules have changed," Diamond argues. "Control is destined to backfire. If we've learned anything from the recent past, it's that the Internet—the printing press of our age—and rapidly advancing technology have given us a new approach. The approach is called openness, and it will dictate the future." Of course, IP paranoids will quickly point out that the profits from Linux have been accrued by companies like IBM and Red Hat that haven't given anything away.

Open sourcing is a dramatic story, but it's only one example of how the Abolition of Context is impacting products. John Naisbitt has observed: "In a world where technology can transform nature as never before, it is no wonder that we repeatedly ask, 'Is that real?' 'Is that fake?' Authentic or simulated? Genuine or imitation? Original or copy?" Naisbitt's rather utopian take on all this: "In a time when it is difficult to distinguish the real from the fake, businesses are latching on to authenticity. Authenticity can be commercially very successful. It is no longer viable for companies to get their product ideas from a middle market, such as designers, hence the new profession of 'cool hunters.' . . . In a time when technology is obscuring the real while simultaneously exaggerating it, we are reassured by the authentic."

We think authenticity is a moot point. Once the cool hunters (trend watchers hired by companies to tell them what trends or products are about to become hot) have stumbled across the latest incarnation of the devox, it's probably well on its way to respectability. So "new" products really aren't as Edgy as they seem. As we've already established, there might not be a mass market for true deviance. The sanitized—and by definition less authentic—product often represents the biggest commercial opportunity. It's hard to imagine exactly what authenticity looks like in a world where Lara Croft—the "real" one, not Angelina Jolie—has been interviewed by *Esquire* (October 1997), has more than a thousand websites associated with her, and has appeared on two hundred or so magazine covers.

It's a trifle hard to see any headlong rush to authenticity, especially in the Milli Vanillized universe of Pamela Anderson Lee's breasts, the World Wrestling Federation, Jell-O in flavors not found in nature, boy bands, momma's boys sporting menacing faux prison tattoos, and Caucasian gangsta rappers from affluent suburbs. Rather than craving authenticity, people seem to crave the appearance of authenticity. They're perfectly willing to have cosmetic surgery—provided, of course, that it doesn't make them look like they've had plastic surgery.

You can prove our point from anywhere in the United States. Start wherever you live and plan a drive through the campgrounds of the closest state park. What you'll see are huge RVs replete with generators so the inhabitants won't miss a single installment of *ER* or those *Seinfeld* reruns. We've personally seen people bring lawnmowers to mow nature into a more orderly pattern, and once we watched somebody carefully unroll Astroturf over the grass before they set up their folding chair and portable television. America—and the rest of the world—is awash in inauthenticity. We just hate to be reminded of it. Naisbitt's right; there will always be a significant market for the authentic, but it remains to be seen if it will ever be a mass market.

The spirit of the devox impacts products in other ways as well. We have, for example, products that are really placeholders for some psychic, emotional, or social statement. Take a look at all the Harley-Davidson licensed ware purchased by people whose last experience on two wheels was with a Schwinn, or the Eddie Bauer products bought by individuals in more imminent danger of contracting Jungle Fever than jungle fevers. These products really aren't ends in themselves—they point to some real or imagined quality of the owner's self. If Linux (in its purest form) is a product that can't be sold, these are products that represent abstractions that can't be bought.

The following chart illustrates a few of the transitions that have led to the Abolition of the Traditional Product Context.

TRANSITIONS IN THE CONTEXT OF PRODUCT

Characteristic	Old Products	Deviant Products
Essence	An end in themselves	Pointing to something else
Makeup	Goods and services	Goods, services, and information
Goal	Sale	Relationship
Consumer Preference	Authentic	Authentic and faux
Obsolescence	Calculated by manufacturer	Inherent at purchase
Life Cycle	Handed down generation to generation	Disposable
Product Evolution	True innovation	Line extension
Value to Consumer	Tangible	Emotional/psychological
Designer	Manufacturer	Manufacturer and/or end user

Let's look at some practical examples of what this means. Starbucks isn't selling coffee; it's selling self-image to coffee drinkers. You wouldn't want to spend too much time on a basketball court wearing Skechers shoes, but you might not want to be caught dead in the stands without them. The Marlboro Man is pushing rugged individualism, not lung cancer and emphysema.

Products used to be ends in themselves; now they're door openers for longer-term relationships. Look at your cell phone. Odds are you got it for free, or what you thought was free, in exchange for a two-year service agreement. There are dozens of similar examples, from free plants tied to office plant maintenance services to free carpeting given away as long as you sign a cleaning agreement.

Our relationship to products—especially high-technology products—has also changed. Our parents and grandparents purchased products they expected, and hoped, would last a lifetime. Today, whether we're purchasing a computer, a television, a sound system, or a PDA, our expectation is that the product we purchase today will be inherently inferior to one we could purchase tomorrow. We've come to view products, from lease cars to fax machines, as disposable. We form no emotional attachment to them because we realize we won't have them long. This in turn has opened the doors to yet more deviant products that promise to bridge that connectivity gap. Call a candle pink and it's worth about $0.49. Call it serenity, it's suddenly worth $5.49. There's no tangible difference in the product, but we feel better owning the label.

From the pet rock to Napster, deviant products create markets, they don't meet them. Nobody needed a pet rock, but once they appeared thousands flew off store shelves. Sometimes, as in the case of Pringles (a potato chip so deviant it was uniform rather than variable and came in a canister rather than a bag), it takes a couple of decades or so, but markets can be made. Of course—as in the case of WebTV—it doesn't always work.

People who create deviant products understand that efficacy isn't always a critical issue. Consider all those clever but unbranded hydrogen peroxide makers who figured out they could profitably put their product in toothpaste despite the fact it had no apparent dental benefits. By the same token, one of our absolute favorite products is Arm & Hammer baking soda. Now, with all due respect, baking soda is essentially little more than crushed rock in a box. Its primary intended use is (as the name implies) as an ingredient in baking, an activity that—in an era where "oven" really means microwave—is becoming increasingly more deviant in its own right.

The Arm & Hammer folks follow their market. They understand those boomers are becoming empty nesters. They also know regular baking is becoming a culinary endangered species. So they started thinking like a deviant. Rather than clinging to tradition or historical uses, they just threw the book out and began to speculate on all the things you might be able to do with baking soda.

The result was an old product with a brand-new raison d'être. The former baking ingredient is now a carpet freshener, a dentifrice, and a refrigerator deodorizer. How does it work? Simple. In the first case, open the box, sprinkle the contents all over the floor, vacuum them up, and—oops!—time to go buy another box. The third use is far subtler. Open a box, stick it in a refrigerator (a damp, moist environment where the porous aforementioned crushed rock can absorb water), and throw it out when it begins to clump. Oops! Time to restock again. Nobody questions what's going on and everybody's happy—especially Arm & Hammer.

We don't know if the world could have survived without all the elements of the high-technology rainbow from Red Hat to Blue Tooth to Blackberry, but we suspect civilization would have found some way to muddle through. But deviant products have a way of insinuating themselves into our lives. Fifty years ago nobody needed a second oven in their kitchens, and today there's (at least) one microwave in almost every home. There are increasingly two dishwashers in those kitchens as well—not the result of old-fashioned demand creation, but a reflection of home builders understanding that emptying the dishwasher and remembering if the dishes are clean or dirty is too taxing to a significant, and affluent, segment of the market. No builder could have ever convinced home buyers they needed two dishwashers; he or she just needed to understand that the way people related to dishwashing had changed.

Just think of these (at one time) counterintuitive products that are now found in many homes: paid-for television; office equipment (computers/fax machines/copiers); bagged salads; disposable lighters; low-strength adhesives (from school glue to Post-it notes); bottled water; bottled iced tea; various weeds (in the form of teas and supplements); electronic phone books (PDAs); the aforementioned second dishwashers; five- or six-figure seasonal transportation; and plastic composters. Look around your own life. How many of the things that you routinely use or purchase are really things you actually need, and how many are there just because they exist?

Take the concept of "extremeness" out of extreme sports and apply it to packaged goods to create lines of extreme food products or, at the very least, traditional food products with some extreme characteristic—color, taste, or even odor. Heinz now offers ketchup in green and purple varieties. Hot foods can't get hot enough for a growing number of consumers, forcing traditional products like Tabasco to add line extensions. Special wide-circumference pickles have been developed that completely cover our burgers. Candies aren't just cloyingly sweet anymore; now many of them are almost unbearably tart and bitter. This isn't about surfing hot trends. It's about looking deeper and understanding how waves form so you can anticipate when they'll hit the beach.

Of course, deviant products require a deviant approach to branding, the topic of the next chapter.

15

The Deviant Brand

When the going gets weird, the weird turn pro.

—Hunter S. Thompson

Generations of consumers and marketers alike have seen brands as destinations, trusted signposts guiding the public safely through the vagaries and dangers of the commercial swamp. In the era of the devox, however, brands are increasingly vestiges of tradition and habit at best and at worst convenient placeholders for a range of generic purchase decisions. When in doubt, buy Brand A. When Brand A isn't available, buy Brand B.

Ask for a Coke on a Northwest Airlines flight or in a Marriott hotel and you'll likely be asked, "Pepsi okay?" Wander into a bar and ask for an O'Doul's (Anheuser-Busch's nonalcoholic beer) and the odds are pretty good you may be served a Sharp's (Miller's nonalcoholic brew). Question why you received the Pepsi or Sharp's and you're likely to be told, "That's the one we have."

It doesn't stop there. Chances are that "Xerox" you read yesterday really came from a Canon copier and that the "Kleenex" you're using is actually a Puffs. Research has shown that consumers, who a generation ago would have demanded the "best" brand, are now satisfied with a range of choices they see as essentially interchangeable. This might not be a big deal to you unless you've spent millions of dollars trying to build brand equity. We are still big believers in brands, but even we're forced to concede that the Abolition of Context has rendered many established branding concepts obsolete.

Brands used to be the proud possessions of the companies that brought them to market. Today, after twenty-odd years of intense mergers, acquisitions, and consolidations, brands have become free-standing, portable entities whose legacies are available to the highest bidder. Brands used to reside with the companies that developed them. Now they move around like pawns on a great commercial chessboard. Several years ago Kraft sold its signature caramels business to Favorite Brands. Favorite Brands was later purchased by Nabisco, which in turn was purchased by Philip Morris, Kraft's parent company. So, three sales later the brand was back home.

Brands are also used in many cases as guarantors of superior quality. Lucrative licensing agreements and the proven cost effectiveness of introducing line extensions (versus launching truly new items) have conspired to dilute historic brand promises. Most mass-distribution manufacturers are far more concerned with gaining or protecting shelf space than they are interested in investing in original research and development.

Thanks to the devox and the instability of consumer markets, branding (in the form of licensing) is itself a product. Take Eddie Bauer, for example. You probably knew you could buy an Eddie Bauer Expedition truck from Ford, but did you also know you could buy Eddie Bauer Lifestyles wooden furniture from Lane; Eddie Bauer wallpaper and borders from the Imperial Home Décor Group; Eddie Bauer diaper bags from Baby Boom Consumer Products; or Eddie Bauer play yards from Cosco?

Harley-Davidson goes Eddie Bauer several better in the licensing department. One can, if so inclined, purchase Harley-Davidson condoms, plush toys, panties, lighters, key chains, and, in fact, almost anything large enough to attach a Harley logo to. In 2000 Harley enjoyed sales of $2.9 billion, $151.4 million (or 5.2 percent of total sales) of which came from general merchandise sales, a 14.1 percent increase over 1999. Licensing has always been a lucrative business, but in the era of deviant branding there doesn't necessarily have to be a direct connection between a product and the licensed logos that appear on it. The consumer wants total identification with a brand, no matter how far-fetched an individual application might be.

Brands have come to live outside their traditional context in any number of ways. The apparent ease of creating "overnight" brand sensations such as Amazon, eBay, CNN, Orange (the once British, now French telco), and countless others is a testament that the rules of conventional branding have changed. As we saw in the case of Kraft caramels, brands can thrive away from the companies that birthed them. In a world where the distribution channels tend to blur products, as in the case of Sharp's and O'Doul's, brands increasingly guarantee an adequate rather than exceptional standard of performance. In this case it is a property (the lack of alcohol) that is more important than the vehicle that delivers it.

As we saw in the rise of the dot-coms, innovation has replaced tradition as a way to create brand buzz. This emphasis on innovation may help explain the popularity (at least in commercial terms) of line extensions and clones. There's a downside as well. Brands used to command premium prices. Today they are often used as loss leaders. As any honest brand marketer will tell you, brand loyalty is no longer an inheritance. It has to be re-earned every day. This is especially true in a commercial environment where innovation trumps tradition almost each and every time.

No one cares that Compaq has a long tradition of making portable computers—they want the newest and hottest box. Kmart is more than one hundred years old, but that didn't slow Wal-Mart down one bit. Holiday Inn is one of the oldest brands of hotels appealing to road warriors, but when was the last time you stayed in one?

Sometimes the brand isn't so much applied on a product as it is a product in its own right. Take the case of a deviant brand that began life as a licensing gimmick that was never attached to any product. The brand is Hello Kitty and licensing is still the product. In fiscal 1999 Hello Kitty, which started out as nothing more than a rudimentary sketch of a cat, was a $1.2 billion business. Here's the ultimate brand: something that's never existed in any tangible form and is still powerful enough to generate more than a billion dollars' worth of sales every year.

The Hello Kitty brand appears on more than fifteen hundred licensed products, which appear on the market at the rate of one hundred new items a month. In addition, the brand's parent company has licensing agreements with five hundred companies globally. Not bad for a company that started life as a graphic representation of a cat. According to the official website of Sanrio, Hello Kitty's master licenser (http://www.sanrio.com), "Sanrio is a world-wide designer and distributor of character-branded stationery, school supplies, gifts and accessories. We are perhaps best known for Hello Kitty, our star character and corporate symbol. Hello Kitty, however, is only one of the many Sanrio characters and designs that bring [the] Sanrio merchandise line to life. Others include Pochacco, our athletic young pup, and the slightly naughty Badtz Maru."

Sanrio, which remains headquartered in Tokyo, was founded in 1960 by Shintaro Tsuji. Tsuji created a line of character merchandise designed around gift-giving occasions; four decades later, he heads a licensing empire with distribution throughout Japan, Southeast Asia, the Americas, and Europe. Hello Kitty merchandise is available in four thousand retail stores in the United States alone, including two hundred Sanrio boutique stores, forty of which are corporately owned.

Hello Kitty has become a cultural icon. Artist Tom Sachs's Hello Kitty Nativity Scene, with Hello Kitty as the Baby Jesus surrounded by some very Simpsonesque wise men, created a storm of protest when it debuted in Barney's New York Christmas windows in 1994. Just in case you find the idea a tad hard to swallow, the Hello Kitty Nativity lives for-Internet-ever (that is, until somebody abandons the site) at http://www.geocities.com/Tokyo/Garden/3313. Sachs explained his fascination with the character to *Wired* magazine this way: "Hello Kitty is an icon that doesn't stand for anything at all. Hello Kitty never has been, and never will be, anything. She's pure license; you can even get a Hello Kitty car! The branding thing is completely out of control, but it started as nothing and maintains its nothingness. It's not about the ego, and in that way it's very Japanese."

Sanrio won't put its license on everything (although when you see all the Hello Kitty items that's a little hard to believe). For instance, the company won't license sharp objects like letter openers. However, perhaps consistent with the company's motto, "Small Gift, Big Smile," you can buy a Hello Kitty vibrator. You have to hand it to the Japanese. When it comes to branding, it's hard to beat them. Pokémon has sold more than $15 billion in global merchandise since its 1996 debut, and we shudder to think what the Godzilla brand in aggregate is really worth.

There's a difference between brands that are deviant on their face, such as Burning Man; brands that want to appear deviant, such as FUBU and Phat Farm; and brands like Arm & Hammer that are traditional but succeed in a deviant manner. The danger in the former case is that as soon as a deviant brand becomes a success it loses its deviant appeal. It's a principle that's underscored over and over again in the entertainment and apparel industries. Last year's outlaw is seen as a sellout as soon as he or she—or they—sign a recording contract. Last season's daring style is cloned, and suddenly the very people who popularized it wouldn't be caught dead wearing it. It's a principle that underscores our entire hypothesis. Straddling the line that separates the authentic from the commercial can be a challenge. After all, it's hard to maintain the essence of "hoodness" when your products are walking around suburban Minneapolis or being driven to school in Des Moines in Mom's SUV. That kind of mass-market creation, however, is exactly what you need to be successful. We think the shelf life for deviant brands will always be short term and limited, but the market for brands that can function in deviant ways is almost unlimited. This means branders have to do two things: continue to nurture their brand equity while simultaneously finding new arenas to play in, arenas that allow them to revisit the well of authenticity just long enough to keep the brand vital.

There's a great deal of variance in deviant brands, but they do have some things in common. Left to their own devices, brands functioning in deviant ways tend to perform at a consistent level regardless of who owns them—that is, their identity exists separate from the company that created them. Snapple is a case in point. In 1994 Quaker Oats purchased Snapple from Triarc Beverages for an unprecedented $1.7 billion. Quaker dismissed the spokespeople who had built the brand, changed the advertising, and repositioned what had been an "each" business (one in which the product is sold one unit at a time) into one that relied on multipacks. The public, which had enjoyed buying a different variety of Snapple every day, wasn't ready for (very heavy and very fragile) glass twelve-packs of one variety. Three years later Quaker sold the brand back to Triarc for $300 million. Snapple was just too deviant for Quaker to manage. Despite a 20 percent decline under Quaker, the brand has begun to gain back much of the ground it lost. The problem was that Quaker just wouldn't let Snapple be itself.

Some brands can transfer their promise to a wide range of goods and services. This is why Disney sells Imagineering and McDonald's could easily go into the daycare business if it wanted to. Truly deviant brands have legs, perhaps in large part because they tend to be rule makers or rule breakers but never rule followers. This freedom to lead lets them set their own agendas.

These brands have only a nodding tolerance for tradition. Compare Xerox with Nokia. Xerox chose to remain singularly focused on copying. Nokia, on the other hand, moves to where new opportunities arise. The company was founded by Finnish mining engineer Fredrik Idestam, who opened a wood-pulp mill in southern Finland in 1865. The company has by turns been a galosh and raincoat manufacturer and a wire cable maker. Over time, and once its patent protection ran out, Xerox's fortunes declined. Nokia, on the other hand, has prospered and will probably continue to do so, provided it doesn't get too hung up on telephony.

Brands functioning in deviant ways create market opportunities. We think this helps explain the popularity of Spam, the potted meat product, and Dr. Martens shoes with young people. The youth markets grabbed on to these brands because they seemed orphaned by mainstream culture, in the same way that John Lennon once popularized the style of eyeglasses handed out by the British welfare system. These are products that become "hot" precisely because they are so uncool.

Despite their mass consumption of things inauthentic, consumers can always smell a phony. In the summer of 1994 Coca-Cola introduced OK Cola, a sort of twisted Zen, Gen-X beverage designed to appeal to slackers between the ages of twelve and twenty-six. With crude black-and-white package graphics and a so-hip-it-hurts marketing campaign ("What's the point of OK Cola? Well, what's the point of anything?"), Coke was sure it would sell radical ennui right back to its disaffected source. One year, eight test markets, and a disappointing 1 million cases sold later, Coke raised the white flag and pulled the brand.

Deviant brands also appear to retain iconic status through time. It's the only way to explain the ongoing popularity of Betty Boop and Betty Page. Each succeeding generation—no matter how deviant—finds a way to claim them as their own. We think that's because uncompromisingly deviant brands never lose their authenticity, and there's always at least a minority market for authenticity.

And finally, with reprise homage to Arm & Hammer, when a deviant brand's time is done, it reinvents itself.

16

The Deviant's Toolbox

There is no real, there is no imaginary except at a certain distance.
What happens when this distance, including that between the real and
the imaginary, tends to abolish itself, to be reabsorbed on behalf of
the model? Well, from one order of simulacra to another, the tendency
is certainly toward the reabsorption of this distance, of this gap that
leaves room for an ideal or critical projection.

—JEAN BAUDRILLARD

Jean Baudrillard, one of the most influential French thinkers and writers of the late twentieth century, employed the concepts of the simulacrum (a copy without an original) and simulation as tools for describing and understanding the concept of mass reproduction and reproducibility that characterizes the culture of electronic media. Baudrillard's tactic of creating tools to facilitate understanding is one that should not be lost on modern business.

A variety of tools are available that can help you deal with the devox; leverage the consequences of the Abolition of Context; and prosper in what many traditionalists are increasingly coming to see as the No World Order. After all, what's more deviant than using the products of the devox to create new metrics, tools, products, services, offerings (which blend products and services), and markets?

The creation of new tools is a precondition to the creation of new culture. In today's new business environment—where every business problem is really a cultural problem in disguise—we must develop and discover radically new methods and approaches. Think of it as third-millennium corporate anthropology. We're not recommending any capitalistic Rube Goldbergisms, but rather the judicious use of new methods to generate profitable business.

It can begin with something as simple as deviant billing. This could take the form sometimes adopted (when circumstances and cash flow permit) by Cap Gemini Ernst & Young, a valued client and learning partner. In certain cases CGE&Y essentially bets its future revenue, and even its future investment capital, against upticks in the client's business. After all, if you really believe the advice you're giving would work, why wouldn't you want a percentage of future profits instead of a flat fee? Of course, for CGE&Y and others that adopt similar models, this is an approach that works only for some clients and some projects.

The point here is that it's one new tool that allows CGE&Y to build its business along with growing, innovative customers that have good ideas but might be undercapitalized. While innovative fee structures are an interesting tool for selling business, this chapter is more directly concerned with to helping you understand how to build tools that help you think about and do business.

Let's start with really long-term planning. The Kohler Corporation, the plumbing-fixtures company headquartered in Kohler, Wisconsin, may have corporate America's longest extant exercise in formal futuring. Almost a hundred years ago Kohler management wrote two sequential fifty-year plans. We'll discuss part of those plans in a moment, but suffice it to say for now that fifty years ago the plumbing-fixtures company decided it needed to operate America's premier golf resort. Why? The reason may have been lost over time, but in 2001 *Forbes* rated Destination Kohler "the Best Golf Resort" (a judgment echoed by dozens of other magazines). The company's American Club has been honored as the Midwest's only Five Diamond Resort by AAA (September 2000). We're honestly not sure why, half a century ago, a former feed-trough manufacturer saw golf courses as part of its long-term strategy. The point, though, is that the company wasn't afraid to look fifty years ahead and then execute flawlessly against its vision.

Some might argue that it's impossible to create a fifty-year plan, an assertion that makes it hard to explain Kohler's undeniable success. The question every business faces today is if you believe the devox is continually abolishing context, how can you possibly create a realistic strategic plan for fifty years, fifty weeks, or even fifty days? There's an old Chinese military strategy that translates as "send a barbarian to check a barbarian." To understand how the devox is changing your business, arm yourself with deviant tools.

The first of these is *mining a deviant core,* the process of rigorously—and objectively—examining your business, identifying your true core competencies, and finding new, deviantly creative ways of deploying them. Think about it. If we came into your business today and asked what your core competencies were, how would you respond? Would you tell us what brands you make and how strong their franchise is? Would you use some scale or quantifiable measurement, like sales, market share, scope of trading area, or unit movement? Would you describe your infrastructure—number of plants, number of employees, amount of X converted into Y, or amounts of data stored or transmitted? Would you describe yourself through a series of inspirational homilies about the value of the customer, the employee, or the community, or would you instead talk in terms of aspirational statements about the kind of corporation you one day hope to evolve into? Or would you recite a litany of past achievements, from the number of patents you hold to the number of Nobel laureates you employ? We have clients that use all of these approaches (often more than one), but we think that nine times out of ten they serve to constrain the future rather than liberate it.

What would happen if you chose to view your company's core competence through the eyes of a deviant? What hidden skills does your company have that it undervalues or ignores? We're well aware that mining for hidden competence—looking at your own company through the glasses of the devox—is a sure formula for creating instant and certain corporate upheaval. And we're just as sure it's worth all the pain.

Every business pays lip service to the notion of constant reinvention, but most companies are terrified at the idea of deviating one degree away from the formula that earned them past success. It's an approach best known as the "success breeds failure syndrome." To illustrate the potential power of mining the deviant core, let's look at Mattel toys, Hallmark, and Sara Lee.

Mattel believed its core competencies included such skills as negotiating licensing arrangements, Asian sourcing, global supply chain efficiency, and manufacturing, particularly the extrusion of plastics. But after significant effort we convinced Mattel's top management that the company's core competency actually was understanding the nature of play and the role play occupies in people's lives. Convinced that this was true, then CEO Jill Barad and her executive management launched a cultural revolution that—had it not wilted faster than Mao's Thousand Flowers—could have reshaped the organization and, more importantly, significantly improved its future. As it was, there were some modest victories. Mattel set up a theater in the company cafeteria. Executive management no longer just made speeches; they "played" their transfer of knowledge through a series of comedies and tragedies. As a general operating principle, employees were encouraged to dedicate more of their workweek to play.

More often than not businesses suffer from what we call bipolar awareness syndrome. They want their employees informed but hate all the vehicles—reading materials, Internet access, reflective time, and conversation—that could facilitate broadened learning. How many jobs have you had where you were encouraged to read a newspaper, or a trade magazine, or, better yet, a trade magazine from another industry? Not too many, we suspect. Contrast that with an approach used by Feargal Quinn, who runs Superquinn, an Irish company many people believe operates the best supermarkets in the world. One sign that you've "made it" as a Superquinn employee is when you receive your personal subscription to a magazine or newspaper. To the degree possible, each employee receives unique reading materials and is expected to share his newfound knowledge with his peers.

Exceptions like Superquinn aside, most companies discourage "non-productive" activities like reading and learning. When was the last time you had a job that rewarded you for broadening your intellectual horizons on company time? Mattel realized that if middle managers were permitted to play more, they were likely to understand the role of play in life more. As a result, the company encouraged "playtime" during "working hours."

We recommended that Mattel take the concept one step further—really a logical extension—and build a consultancy around the idea of play. The "product" would be a service that helped other management teams to learn how to play together and to understand how play could positively influence their businesses. Play is a profound learning tool. You might not remember how to conjugate those irregular Latin verbs they taught you in seventh grade, but we bet you still remember the rules of tag and hide-and-seek. For every generation play has been a potent learning tool, often more potent than formal educational methods. For the so-called Digital Generation, play in the form of video and computer games not only defines a successful learning model, but it has begun to change young people's basic learning educational model from the anal-compulsive, rote methodology by which we learned things like multiplication tables to a much more intuitive approach. Watch your children or, if you're old enough, your grandchildren as they play. While you're busy reading rules, studying diagrams, or combing the indexes of instruction manuals they're intuitively learning a game or how to manipulate a toy by playing. That's why you never have a prayer of winning any current or future iteration of Tomb Raider or Final Fantasy. It's too late! Now, just wait until those intuitive little monsters start infecting the current organizational models with dangerous ideas like "doing is always better than thinking" and "feeling is safer and faster than formal learning."

People raised on a steady diet of play don't wait to credentialize themselves with higher educational degrees they don't respect, or follow established procedures. On the other hand, they tend to play until a problem is solved rather than watch a clock and keep attacking obstacles until they figure out the "hidden" way around a problem. This helps explain why so many Silicon Valley innovations are led by these young game-slingers. Play could have been an effective bridge not only for fostering innovation but also for providing a bridge allowing Old Economy companies and executives to find their way across to the New Economy.

Unfortunately, Jill Barad's multibillion-dollar acquisition of a learning software company, which ended up forcing a significant write-off, and her subsequent dismissal as Mattel's CEO, dampened the company's enthusiasm for any project too closely associated with her name. The initiative was stopped when a new administration came in—a phenomenon we've come to recognize as "The Queen is dead and so are her ideas. Long live the Queen." Sadly, this was real life, not the set of *Big*. There were no Tom Hanks look-alikes running in, armed with the innocent vision of a twelve-year-old, playing the company back to profitability.

Only a truly deviant leader can embrace the ideas of his or her predecessor. Just look at George W. Bush, the first Republican president in history to find himself placed in the embarrassing position of having to oppose the basically pro-business policies of a Democratic predecessor. If "W" were a deviant he'd say that Big Bill's fiscal positions were sound, even if some of his other positions were questionable, thereby assuring a smoother economic transition. The tradition of adversarial party politics makes this impossible, of course. But imagine what would happen if a real deviant took over at 1600 Pennsylvania Avenue.

Sara Lee partially understood, and even embraced, its deviant core but continually failed to capitalize on it. We were able to help the company recognize its strength as a new product innovator, one of the most deviant of all deviant endeavors. Sara Lee had developed a wide range of new food products, from cheesecake bites and super-extra-large hot dogs to microwavable sausage and breakfast biscuits. In each case, the pattern was the same: develop a breakthrough concept, enjoy excellent test-market results, and, on the eve of the national rollout, watch as the product is co-opted by a less imaginative but more effective competitor. Sara Lee was wonderful at bringing new products to market, but terrible at marketing the new products.

Our recommendation? Become a new products consultancy for the other food companies, including direct competitors. As we saw it, it would be easier, and more profitable, for Sara Lee to concentrate on the development of new products and license it to other manufacturers, taking a permanent percentage in exchange for the innovation. The jury is still out on whether the strategy will be accepted, but the recommendation was taken seriously enough to make it to consideration by Sara Lee's executive committee. Essentially we were suggesting Sara Lee take an important aspect of the devox—its tendency to perpetual innovation—and make that its product.

Hallmark's case doesn't involve the mining of a deviant core competency or the development of the devox into a new product or service offering. What Hallmark offers is a model of successful identification and exploitation of distribution channels by a company that was already somewhat deviant in the way it thought about core competencies. Hallmark understood it had significant core competencies in art direction and copyrighting, not just in the printing and distribution of greeting cards and associated goods. Given these competencies, it might have been natural to explore becoming an advertising agency or even ideation house. What we suggested was that it apply its acknowledged core competencies and traditional commercial activities in truly innovative ways that married all of the company's competencies, including designing and distributing greeting cards.

By looking at the card business (which, outside of holidays like Christmas and Valentine's Day, generally involves the purchases of "eaches" rather than bulk buys) in a deviant way Hallmark created both a new distribution channel and a new service line—both based on using greeting cards as the delivery vehicles for employee communications programs. The idea was simple, elegant, and inspired. It made client companies look employee friendly, kept standard business messages from being instantly thrown away, and transformed Hallmark's "each" business into a mass-communication mechanism. Of course, faced with a new distribution channel, Hallmark needed to develop new marketing programs and a new sales force to call on the senior vice presidents and vice presidents of human resources within Fortune 500 (and smaller) companies.

Hallmark's corporate profile is a study in how to rethink core competencies. The company has taken a skill set (penmanship) needed to produce greeting cards and turned it into a freestanding subsidiary, Irresistible Ink. The company also operates its own cable TV channel and, in a truly inspired piece of deviant thinking, continues to create new "holidays" like Grandparent's Day to open up additional, deviant avenues for the distribution of its traditional products.

Planned Parenthood Federation of America offers yet another example of how easy it is, given a well-conceived and well-executed program, for an organization to develop new core competencies. Planned Parenthood is itself an excellent example of the devox's progress, starting as it did as a Fringe idea that women had a right to control their reproductive destiny and moving through Edgy stages like the Eugenics movement before arriving at its current respectable role. In the case of Planned Parenthood, that program took the form of the development of the twenty-five-year vision project we referenced in Chapter 6. Almost two and a half years into the vision initiative, it began to become obvious that Planned Parenthood had developed a skill set around the construction of vision projects that they could sell to other nonprofit organizations.

The planning regimen for the nonprofit is clearly different from that of the profit or public profit organization. Since there was no established best-of-class model for us to adopt, we were conscious of the importance of cataloging the visioning/planning methodology with an eye on what did and didn't work. We had a clear idea that it was important for all stakeholders in a nonprofit to have as complete an idea as possible about where certain ideas came from and how they evolved.

At the same time we quickly developed a vague, but compelling, feeling that the methodology we were collaboratively engineering might have a life of its own beyond the project. It has been said that there are four dimensions to storytelling: the story finder; the storyteller; the story seller; and—as in this case—the story storer. We wanted to make sure that the story we were finding, telling, and ultimately selling together didn't get lost over time. We believe our Planned Parenthood experience taught us a lesson that is applicable to all corporations—public and private, profit and nonprofit. If companies "stored" the critical activities associated with a major project or initiative, they might find a way to sell not just the fruit of their research and development efforts but the R&D methodology itself.

In the case of Planned Parenthood, we believe that its demonstrated ability to create twenty-five-year vision statements (from ideation to vision creation to communication and ratification) for nonprofit organizations could create an additional revenue stream of somewhere between $10 million and $25 million a year. Here's another way to think about it. How many times in this great Dilbertian universe have you or your management team hired a consultant to help you with a vision or mission statement? How much money have you spent communicating the vision and selling it to the troops? And how often have you done that only to find the results seemed to suffer an uncomfortably short shelf life before the process had to be redone?

Now, think what would happen if that process were an internal product. How much could you save on external consulting or trying to implement plans that had little or no internal support? Understanding the value of inclusive methodologies and effective communications alone is ultimately worth millions of dollars.

Organizations that constantly mine, evaluate, or institutionalize deviant core analysis should develop both tremendous prime-mover advantage over time and an institutional nimbleness or collective ability to roll with the punches. And, given the current environment characterized by a climate of unrelenting discontinuity, and remembering that discontinuity is the mother of innovation, being nimble might prove to be more important in business than being first to market.

The following chart illustrates the potential yields of several deviant core-mining exercises. Imagine how the car industry would be revolutionized if automakers began to think of cars as living spaces rather than just transportation. Or think about what it might mean if Kodak stopped thinking of itself as a film-processing company and began seeing itself as offering personal stability (of memories and the film itself) in unstable times. Ever lose a series of favorite photos in a divorce? It wouldn't be such a problem if you could just easily reorder them from Kodak. And, speaking of divorce, several independent camera stores have already begun offering a unique film-editing service. Have a picture of yourself you really like with an ex-spouse in it? No problem. For a fee, you can have your ex-spouse digitized out and your current love interest digitized in, enabling you to have a visual record of a past life you never experienced. The possibilities are almost endless.

Company	Perceived Core Competency (Competencies)	Potential Competency Emerging out of Deviant Mining
Ford Motor Company	Automotive design, engineering, and production	Using the automobile not just as transportation but as the platform for a third place (in addition to home and work) where people spend significant time and live their lives
Kodak	Film chemistry and processing and camera design	Offering permanent cataloging, storage, and editing of visual images in a world of personal instability where photographs are lost, including the "remastering" of images to add or eliminate other images
Northwest Airlines	Securing routes, gates in airports, reservation systems, and maximizing efficient utilization of aircraft fuel	Invidual and corporate travel planning; full onboard concierge services for destination city; offering targeted new product trials for a range of goods from aromatherapies to books

Company	Perceived Core Competency (Competencies)	Potential Competency Emerging out of Deviant Mining
The Kroger Company	Distribution and resale of consumer package goods, perishables, and non-food products	Leveraging sales data to create new business lines such as wedding or corporate event planning and catering; offering holistic consumer health services (i.e., shopping lists, recipes, etc.), and other forms of consumer lifestyle facilitation, including creation of recipes and shopping lists keyed against the budgets, needs, and preferences of a household
MTV	Television programming, marketing music	Using knowledge of youth buying and style patterns to develop new youth-centric marketing metrics and tools
Industrial Light & Magic	Development of television, movie, and computer graphic special effects	Using multimedia techniques to develop innovative educational tools for students, seniors, and illiterates
Microsoft	Software development and marketing	Leveraging its extensive past legal trouble to offer a service to other large corporations on how to cost-effectively manage legal fees and media relations, and conduct protracted legal campaigns

OPPOSITES ANALYSIS

Think of an opposites analysis as an exercise in corporate "Mirror, Mirrorism." A mirror presents us with a clear, sharp but reversed picture of whatever we hold up to it. Opposites analysis forces you to look at your business and your vision in completely new ways. We've come to see the value of not only articulating a clear goal but examining the apparent (in the most superficial sense of the word) antithesis of that statement. We're not suggesting that the diametrical opposite is always the right answer, just that employing this corporate dialectic helps you examine a much broader range of issues. Asking Planned Parenthood to take a militant born-again Christian "pro-life" position might seem odd, but the exercise would deliver several benefits. It would cause the organization to clearly articulate its own position; clearly articulate its antithesis; and facilitate an analysis of exactly how much or how little it has in common with its perceived opponents or competitors.

The act of searching out an apparent opposite yields any number of possibilities that otherwise might not surface. The automobile industry offers a classic case in point. Traditionally it has worked extremely hard to reduce fixed costs of labor to facilities (diverting more and more of its production work to subassemblers, for example) while continually chasing improved sales and operating results. The best way to grow the enterprise it seems is to develop new and creative ways to reduce infrastructure. If those subassemblers could in turn reduce their fixed costs by standardizing parts among manufacturers, the entire supply chain—right down to the consumer—would benefit. The best way to compete might be to cooperate with the competition.

We assume the very idea of cooperation among auto manufacturers is enough to send poor Henry Ford spinning in his grave. Henry the Elder was so convinced that he had all the answers about how to build and run an empire he barely saw General Motors coming. Ford—like most companies—sees itself as a group of people making a product. One outcome of opposites analysis is that the automaker might see its workforce as a product. How could that product be marketed?

To jump-start its staff's race down the digital highway, Ford bought 136,000 computers for its employees' homes. What would have happened if Ford had established the digital equivalent of a company store in the form of an Internet portal that gave Ford workers access to special discounts on a full range of goods from music to mortgages? Ford could then have created a new revenue stream by selling access to that store to any number of vendors. Ford could also emulate that Internet porn marvel PersianKitty.com and collect a "meter click" on every portal-generated purchase. Assuming that the downturn in e-commerce is a temporary blip that will be corrected as hundreds of thousands of

Mountain Dewed digital children come into their commercial own, we might be bold enough to suggest that within a decade the portal idea might net Ford substantial revenue.

Of course, there's a delicious irony here. The success of the portal scheme would exist in direct proportion to the number of participants: the more participants, the more purchases; the more purchases, the more revenue for Ford. Such a strategy would clearly be hindered in highly outsourced universes, unless of course you extended access to the site to outsourcers' employees. In the real world, opposites analysis generally results not in an either-or model, but rather in two distinct and self-contained sets of tactics and executions, operated simultaneously.

British Airways provides us with another example. As part of a formalized opposites analysis the company decided to focus on the notion of the departure lounge. While it sounds very obvious, it was only through sheer persistence and diligence that a group of deviant BAers concluded that the opposite of a departure lounge didn't imply a different approach to departing and instead surfaced the need for an arrivals lounge.

British Airways went on to pioneer the concept of giving air travelers at least as much attention after they landed as they had received when they took off. For those of you who haven't had the pleasure of experiencing them, BA's arrival lounges offer changing rooms, shower stalls, breakfast, and transportation facilitation. British Airways also used the same concept (that for a passenger a trip really is portal to portal, not just gate to gate) in their first-class "upgrade" when they brought in the sleeper seats and gave first-class and business-class fliers the option of having a white tablecloth dinner in the departure lounge before getting on a plane.

Comfort is the logical opposite of discomfort, but for many commercial air carriers its real opposite is fuel efficiency. Suboptimize the load by doing things like making the seats wider than the average anorexic's waistline or increasing the spacing between seats so you could actually work on your laptop at the same time the person ahead of you is reclining his or her seat and you begin to negatively impact the fuel optimization/profit formula.

Aeronautical engineers aren't in the comfort business; they're in the business of moving the maximum amount of weight through space using the least amount of fuel. That's why if the weather is clear in the city you're leaving and clear in your destination city, your flight can still get canceled because of weather. It simply costs too much (in fuel and dollars) to fly around a storm. Of course, that's not at all how it looks from a customer perspective.

Decreasing seating makes most airline engineers and executives uncomfortable since it means fewer passengers and potentially less profits. However, for most transatlantic passengers, if a completely flat six-foot-six-inch bed doesn't look like comfort, it will be a pretty good placeholder until something better comes along. British Airways was the first carrier to opt in favor of the customer definition of comfort. Naturally, this was a dramatic decision since it involved actually removing seats from its first-class cabin in order to accommodate "cocoons," which allow a passenger to configure his or her seat into a bed and create a space providing an opportunity for a "dinner for two."

One last example from British Airways involves our recommendation to redefine business class as "the bitter class." In this case the opposite of pain wasn't found to be pleasure but rather manageable pain. Business travelers are generally unhappy about the amount of time they're forced to travel, stressed by canceled appointments, lost hotel reservations, and being away from their families.

For professional road warriors, the idea of making air travel into a euphoric experience is about as rational as appointing Bill Clinton, Gary Condit, and Keith Richards to the board of directors of the 700 Club. Since frequent business fliers are by nature a surly tribe almost categorically incapable of feeling joy, our recommendation was to change the philosophy of service from one that tried to make you feel good to one that tried to make sure you didn't feel as bad, a sort of interpersonal damage control. Seats may never be truly comfortable, for example, but they can be made less uncomfortable.

Dorothy Lane Markets of Dayton, Ohio, is another example of the power of an opposites analysis. Almost every grocery chain in America stakes its short-term future on two-page advertising spreads. But one day, in the face of a growing supermarket advertising arms race, Dorothy Lane made the decision to stop advertising. The company realized that advertising was an exercise in unconscious opposite effect, and that rather than building loyalty and interest it was best received by "cherry pickers" who troll Best Food Day sections in search of the best deal. The real opposite of spending money to attract deal junkies is investing in programs that reward loyal customers.

Dorothy Lane didn't decrease its rate of promotional spending, but simply shifted the dollars into activities that rewarded the loyal customer while offering nothing for shoppers who could only be rented week to week. The result is that Dorothy Lane's service satisfaction index, customer retention, and ability to attract new, loyal customers all track well above industry average. And the customers prosper as well as the company. The five highest-volume Dorothy Lane customers actually receive trips on the scale of round-trip, first-class, two-week vacations to Hawaii.

Gateway is one of the most dramatic examples of the successful implementation of an opposites analysis. The company had completely disintermediated its traditional retail channel in favor of selling exclusively on the Internet. The opposite of only selling on the Internet, of course, would be to sell at retail. And the opposite of being a supplier to retailers is to become a retailer yourself, which is exactly what Gateway did, opening its own Gateway Country stores. Ironically, the opposite of a retail store would be a store in which you couldn't make a purchase, and in fact customers can't walk out with a new cow box in hand.

The first store was tested in the Raleigh-Durham area of North Carolina, and a second was opened on the outskirts of New Haven (and Yale University) in Connecticut. The results were astounding. The "average" store would sell $1 million worth of computers in a week out of very limited space and with fixtures made completely out of corncribs. Since each Gateway computer is individually configured, you could pay for one at the store but you couldn't actually take it with you. This gave Gateway millions of dollars of float before any orders were even processed. Gateway is well on its way to having close to three hundred stores, and the program has become one of the strong suits of the company's strategic portfolio. We've now seen Compaq open stores, along with a full host of technology-centric organizations, including Yahoo! and Nortel. There's a dark caveat to the Gateway story. As the company's subsequent performance demonstrates, no business can afford to rest on its deviant laurels. You can't afford to base future success on one rapidly aging idea.

Naturally, the universe of opposites analysis is filled with possibilities, some much more commercially practical than others. For instance, alcohol and tobacco producers continually talk about their concerns with consumers who "abuse" their products. Well, what would happen if Philip Morris sponsored free smoking-cessation clinics, or if Seagram's operated free or low-cost alcohol detoxification and rehabilitation centers? The hue and cry would be tremendous, of course, but wouldn't it be better press than last year's reports that the tobacco industry saw smoking as an effective method of population control in Eastern Europe?

Starbucks offers an example of a company that could profit from a look at some opposite possibilities. Starbucks' Howard Schultz loves to describe Starbucks as the "third place" between work and home. Why not think in terms of a Starbucks that's part of a work environment? Our idea here is that Starbucks secure space in large office buildings and open conference centers that could be rented by the hour, day, or week. The centers would offer all the amenities of a traditional conference center and Starbucks' traditional trappings (coffee, baked goods, ambience) as well as a line of appropriate foodservice offerings. This is really a commercial extension of how Starbucks' customers are already using the company's retail spaces.

Walk the half mile separating FirstMatter's offices from the Starbucks in downtown Westport, Connecticut, and you'll find a variety of businesses using the chain's spartan seating to seal big deals and quietly recruit employees.

Jockey's brand promise is built around the idea of "comfort." Like all great companies that have stood the test of time (Jockey is well over one hundred years old), its product line has migrated fairly far from its origins—in Jockey's case, socks for lumberjacks.

As part of our opposites analysis for Jockey, we recommended the company think about placing its products in environments that were very "uncomfortable." The result was an advertising campaign centered on the idea of making people comfortable in very uncomfortable environments, such as firefighters at work. This approach has migrated into the company's newest advertising effort, captured in the phrase "Jockey . . . the closest thing to being naked." Of course, the campaign is only effective on people who believe they would be really comfortable while being naked.

The following chart illustrates how companies have created markets by looking at opposites.

Product/Service/Category	Model/Practitioner	Opposites Model/Practitioner
Cigarette Lighters	Durability/Zippo	Disposability/BIC
Software	Proprietary monopoly/Microsoft	Anarchistic open sourcing/Linux
Books	Collectibility/Crown	Perishability/e-books
Computing	Pure computational power/Cray	Portability, user's preferences/Dell
Messaging	Distributor-centric guaranteed delivery/U.S. Postal Service	Sender-/Receiver-centric instant delivery/e-mail, fax, pagers, et al.
Personal Digital Assistant	Status/Palm	Flexibility/Handspring
Florist	Delivery of physical flowers/FTD	Delivery of nonphysical flowers and messages/Virtual Florist.com
Newspapers	In-depth community coverage, extensive by-line features/*Detroit Free Press, Chicago Tribune*	National and international headlines/*USA Today*
Consumer Packaged Goods	Unlimited selection/Kroger, Safeway	Limited selection/7-Eleven, Costco
Beef	Consistent taste/McDonald's	Health food/Coleman Organic Beef

BECOMING THE OTHER

Becoming the Other is role-playing with soul. The idea of the exercise is to stop being yourself and start being someone, or maybe even something, else. This isn't as silly as it sounds. Let's say you're in a consumer-facing business—anything from running a gas station to operating a telephone call center. Now, set aside all your motherhood-and-apple-pie mission and vision statements and think about how you really run your business. What metrics do you use? Sales per square foot? Transactions per hour? Number of calls concluded? Volume of units put up on a shelf? And let's not forget corporate America's favorite metric—relation of direct labor cost to sales.

That's why when you go to any potential queuing situation from shopping in a supermarket to clearing Customs to buying a ticket in a movie theater you have the same experience—there aren't enough open lines, so no matter how much you study the situation, the line you pick is always guaranteed to be the wrong line.

Now, when you're running your business—or helping your boss run her or his business—you forget about all the frustration commercial metrics cause. You manage to forget about your personal pain and practice an almost Zen-like state of denial. You're perfectly willing to inflict the same kind of standards that drive you nearly mad on those cute customers you love to say are so important to you. And, deviant that you are, you never understand the bitter irony that's at work. Now become the other—or, in our last example, just be yourself, the one that exists before, after, and between work.

So, how does the world look to you now? Do all those concerns about productivity still make sense? If people could actually become the other for ten minutes, we're pretty sure we'd have a clear shot at world peace, but that's not very practical. But we do believe that learning to think like the other—particularly when the other is a customer—could help you instantly improve your business. The chart on the next page illustrates how this might manifest itself.

Activity	Corporate View	Becoming the Other View
Air Travel	Fleet utilization/fuel efficiency	Comfort
Supermarket Front End	Throughput	Recognition and respect
Insurance Claim	Minimize payout	Salvage a disaster
Personnel Review	Optimize expense	Threaten livelihood
Waiting at the Bar for a Seat in a Restaurant with a Vibrating Pager in Your Hand	An opportunity to sell you drinks you otherwise wouldn't order	Another expensive irritant between you and the dinner you're trying to buy
Car Salesman Talking a Deal over with His Boss	A chance to con you into thinking they're on your side	The same tired con job you're forced to endure every time you buy a car
Surveys that Accompany Video Checkouts in Hotels	Cheap and efficient marketing	A pain since you're trying to escape
Rain Checks	Consumer pacifiers	Reminders of an out-of-stock situation
Consulting Services	High cost but incredibly valuable insights	Parrots who tell the boss what his employees already know

Anyway, you get the idea. The reason Chevrolet was the only American car brand to make significant headway into the Hispanic market in the 1940s and 1950s was that (a) it recognized the market existed and (b) it became the other long enough to understand that if the other spoke Spanish, it had better run ads in Spanish. We wouldn't have all those Paul Rodriguez jokes about "chopped Chevys" if somebody at General Motors hadn't instinctively practiced what we're preaching.

CROSS-FUNCTIONAL 360-DEGREE ANALYSIS

Cross-functional 360-degree analysis involves assembling individuals with disparate skill sets and/or from different industries who are hand selected to talk about a client's problem as they see it. It is the ultimate stakeholder/outsider analysis tool, since it can bring up to a dozen fresh eyes to a problem, and far more importantly up to a dozen brains that haven't been preconditioned to reject an idea because it's "already been done."

This tool shouldn't be confused with the 360 analysis used to evaluate employees. We've noticed that on a one-to-one level most 360 analyses are ultimately self-defeating. They require you to lobby your friends, minimize the impact of your enemies, and generally move superiors and subordinates around with the skill and speed of Boris Spassky simultaneously playing ten Big Blues.

Even assuming you can master manipulate any and all around you, you still have to lose in the end. After all, everyone is only so perfectible. Once you hit the point of personal perfectibility, your 360s are going to yield increasingly diminishing returns.

In our version, you always win because you always capture that most elusive of all ideation butterflies—the outside/in perspective. A team is assembled from inside a company and then put through a facilitated process along with stakeholders, customers, outside experts, and sometimes even competitors. The idea is to break out of the confines of corporate culture. It can be used to solve a very specific problem like rethinking supply chain relationships or to generate new product or business opportunities. There is no downside, unless you're pathologically addicted to the status quo. Developing the ability to understand the value of the outside/in perspective lies at the heart of our business, and we think we can offer some concrete examples of why it should live at the heart of yours.

Think of a Jeep. To Main-Street America, the Jeep is the symbol of the outdoor life: rugged, rough, covered in mud—the ultimate symbol of off-road machismo. But in the urban contemporary world the Jeep is a luxury car, tricked out with a sound system that can run into the thousands and, more likely, tens of thousands of dollars. And it shouldn't come as a big surprise that most people aren't too excited about the idea of rolling a $40,000 or $50,000 stereo through the mud. Marketing Jeeps as tools of the rugged outdoors in ethnic, urban America just doesn't make much sense. We suspect Chrysler would have been significantly ahead of the game years ago if it had a few hip-hop musicians, youth experts, and other thoughtful outside observers sitting down with its design and engineering teams. They might have discovered nontraditional markets for established products as well as understood the potential for high-end dealer or factory customization of sound systems. Any competent social scientist will point out the value of watching behavior rather than poring over the entrails of long-dead consumer data hoping for a favorable augury.

BEGINNER'S MIND

Alvin Toffler, the father of all futurists, once said that the difference between classical education and future education was that the former involved learning and then stopping learning, while the latter involved learning, unlearning, and relearning. That line of thinking is a sterling example of the tool we call beginner's mind, a Zen Buddhist concept.

At its heart is the notion that a mind filled with secular structures and worries isn't properly prepared for contemplation or spirituality. Achieving Zen mind is a form of psychic flagellation that eliminates the ability to retreat to the comfort of conventional thinking.

But rather than trot out some esoteric Eastern thinker to illustrate our point, we offer up Michèle Rigaud-Paccagnin, a deviant in the relatively conservative oil exploration industry. In the 1960s, fourteen-year-old Rigaud-Paccagnin demonstrated her deviant tendency by signing up for industrial arts classes in her native France—an option generally not open to women. After working her way around the chauvinism of the French state school system (which forced her to pursue an advanced degree in a private school since the state school classes she wanted were closed to women) Rigaud-Paccagnin accepted a position with ELF, the French petroleum firm. Eventually she was sent to Emeraude in the Congo to help build an oil-drilling platform. Because she had been effectively barred from learning the "rules" governing platform design, Rigaud-Paccagnin was forced to resort to an "out-of-the-box" six-sided platform design, which became the talk of the industry. Since Rigaud-Paccagnin didn't understand what couldn't be built, she went ahead and created a breakthrough platform design. The hallmark of the Zen mind is that it doesn't wait for permission.

How could Beginner's Mind change the way you see your business? Let's turn briefly to another great deviant—Clarence Saunders, who founded the Piggly Wiggly supermarket chain in Memphis in 1916. At the turn of the century, grocery stores operated as full-service businesses with clerks picking orders for each customer, one item at a time. Saunders looked at the business with Beginner's Mind, reconfiguring the problem of how to best sell food. The result? He patented the idea of self-service supermarkets. Along the way he pioneered the use of shopping baskets; created the world's first shelf tags; built the first checkout stands; created the system of individual item price marking; pioneered the use of refrigerated cases; and became the first store manager to put employees in uniform. In short, he invented the modern supermarket.

We love Saunders because unlike many business deviants, once he became successful, he just kept deviating. He was the last person to actually "corner" the stock market and pioneered two automated stores: the Keedoozle (Key Does It All), which opened in 1937, and Foodelectric (which never opened). And, in true deviant fashion, after he had made several fortunes Saunders managed to die broke.

Now think about what would happen if General Motors had to unlearn its orientation to planned obsolescence. The company would be forced to view its products as either inherently obsolete or create a system of upgrades (similar to those available for software) that would guarantee that the car's design, engineering, and performance were state-of-the-art. Imagine a Corvette 17.0!

There are lots of examples of Beginner's Mind. Sometimes the exercise is forced on you. Think of the shock the British monarchy felt when they were forced to confront the fact that they were less popular than Diana, their estranged daughter-in-law. The order that closed the doors of Westminster Cathedral to the British public during her funeral couldn't silence the devox's impact on how that public saw their queen. By the same token, during the Clinton administration, Republican members of the U.S. Congress were forced to adopt a Beginner's Mind when it came to their understanding of what the American public looked for or would tolerate in a leader. The old rules governing presidential morality simply didn't apply.

Another example of Beginner's Mind comes from our work with the U.S. Navy and involves a principle we call intelligent disobedience. Intelligent disobedience is the method used to train Seeing Eye dogs—an approach characterized by the phrase "Do what I tell you to do . . . unless you have a better idea." Seeing Eye dogs will faithfully obey their master's or mistress's commands—unless, of course, it involves walking the owner in front of an oncoming vehicle.

Our U.S. Navy client is Vern Clark, a four-star admiral and chief of naval operations. The foundation of most navies was the press-gang (as in pressed into service), roving gangs that "drafted" people by knocking them on the head and imprisoning them on board a ship until it had sailed from the harbor. As a result, most navies still tend to think of labor as essentially free and design work assignments accordingly. In a vicious cycle, redundant work is demanded to keep sailors busy, but the redundancy fuels a constant demand for people satisfied with essentially mindless assignments. As a consequence, they develop procedures (like the constant scraping and painting of ships) designed to keep that free labor occupied. It's obviously not a model that works anymore. First of all, you can't just kidnap people into the service; and second, even the dullest third-millennium citizen needs a bit more challenge than endlessly painting, scraping, and repainting the same surface.

Our answer? Why not think of a naval ship a different way—as a piece of high technology operated by a minimum number of people? Every sailor could then have a stateroom and, more importantly, some privacy. Morale would be improved, and the number of people needed to keep the navy at full efficiency would be substantially reduced. All of a sudden, thanks to a little deviant thinking, you find a better way to run a navy.

Although it might seem counterintuitive, if you looked at most businesses it really does take a *left brain and a right brain* to create a whole mind. Given the devox's dervish dance and the resulting Abolition of Context, maintaining the balance between the creative and the analytical is more critical now than ever. We're not talking about some smarmy Big Sur, getting-in-touch-with-your-creative-self stuff here. What we are talking about is first recognizing that there is a difference between the anal retentive and the free spirit; accepting that this difference is not only tolerable but can actually benefit your organization; and then finding ways to harness the anal and the free to your advantage.

There are probably dozens of business examples we could cite that come close to capturing what we're talking about here, but none quite so clearly as the Acorn program established by Tom's of Maine, headquartered in Kennebunk (http://www.toms-of-maine.com). (By the way, when you visit the site note how the company backs up its mission statement with a statement of beliefs—http://208.5.178.253/mission/stmt_blf.htm—an appropriate approach for a company whose cofounder holds an advanced degree in theology.) We remember waiting our turn to speak at a consulting symposium in San Francisco when Tom Chappell, the Tom in Tom's of Maine, took the dais.

We were moved by several parts of Chappell's story, and we suggest that if you don't know about his company you learn a bit more. For example, every tube of Tom's toothpaste has a customer testimonial letter included with it. So one day, a great debate ensued about which department should bear the cost of printing the inserts. Were they part of the packaging, advertising, or a marketing program? After every department had weighed in on why the printing shouldn't appear on its budget, Tom O'Brien, the company's COO, suggested that the cost of printing the notes should be properly assigned to the manufacturing budget—since customer goodwill was actually the most important ingredient in every one of the company's products.

This same innovative style characterizes the company's approach to new-product development. While Tom's has a traditional research department, it also uses what it calls the Acorn Program to develop products. The program pairs a creative type with a great idea and a hard scientist into a team whose mission is to see if an idea has the stuff to grow (as in mighty oaks from little acorns grow) into a full-fledged product. The success of the program is based on using both people's unique skill sets to build a common good—making sure ideas are fresh and innovative as well as practical.

The Kohler Company not only wrote fifty-year business plans, it developed the whole right brain/left brain tool into a program it calls Arts/Industry, which opens the doors of the company's pottery and iron foundries to internationally recognized artists. In a program administered by the John Michael Kohler Arts Center, artists-in-residence labor side by side with Kohler employees during long-term residencies that allow them to work on projects of their selection, provided they utilize industrial technology. Over the years, the aesthetic fruits of the program have been distilled into a series of innovative new products—the perfect commercial marriage of right and left brain activities.

We know it's probably a little retro-Trotskyish, but we favor fomenting permanent revolution within the corporate revolution, or, in the case of the devox, a tool we call *serial deviation.* In a world of constant change, there are no answers and precious few intelligent questions.

Whatever you find on the Fringe tends to become your conventionally accepted reality—that's why you have to keep flogging through the Fringe. The idea that any deviant analysis would surface anything approaching a final answer is almost laughable. Since the devox abolishes context as it goes, there is no high ground offering sanctuary from the rising tide of individual, social, and market chaos.

One day Old Economist capitalists are riding high on the proverbial hog. The next they've been sent to the sidelines and replaced by a bunch of New Economy nerds. On the third day, the Old Economy guys are back and the geeks are being carried off the field, their hip-slick-and-cool T-shirts torn apart by the fangs of the same analysts who, just a day before, had been climbing on each other's backs to pour the Grey Goose in their Red Bull.

But before the wing-tip set gets too comfortable again, we'd like to offer up a fairly serious caveat: The nerds will return, and next time their "Gee whiz, isn't this cool" attitude will be tempered with the bitter wisdom that accompanies watching the value of your options (and therefore your net worth) evaporate before your very eyes. Ecclesiastes (and Bob Dylan) warned that the first one now shall later be last. But we believe that thanks to the Abolition of Context, first and last may actually be the same place.

And in a world like that you have to learn how to tap dance on quicksand.

If this seems hard to understand, do a little research. How long did it take Sam Walton, a deviant Ben Franklin operator, to become the largest retailer on earth? How long did it take for the formerly deviant Bill Gates to establish a virtual monopoly on operating systems? And (we think to Bill's point) how long did it take the decidedly deviant Linux to displace Microsoft in terms of the amount of material transmitted? How long did it take Ray Kroc to parlay a deviant vision of food into the foodservice behemoth McDonald's became? How about an unquestioned deviant like Larry Ellison (who wanted to make sure he could launch a preemptive strike against Bill Gates's house) and Oracle?

We're not Gatesian apologists by any means, but even we're forced to admit the guy was right when he told Congress that a kid in a garage could knock him off tomorrow. So, given that, we assume Microsoft (and every other company hoping to survive) ought to be paying just a tad more attention to the manifestations of the devox.

DISASSEMBLING AND RECONSTRUCTION

Disassembling and reconstruction takes apart a concept, idea, icon, image, or object (we've successfully done it with everything from the blues to Monopoly boards) to discover new nuances of meaning and purpose. Let's look at some examples.

For RTKL, one of the leading global architectural firms in the world, we facilitated a disassembling of the concept of a building—

which involved looking not at how a building appeared or how it was designed and/or built, but rather at how people used the space after it was constructed. Using a hospital as a metaphor, we showed how a clearly signaled grieving space for those who had just lost a loved one was as important as a celebratory space for those whose loved ones had been saved or who had brought a much-loved child into the world. We looked at a hospital not as a collection of functionalities—operating theaters, elevators, lead-shielded rooms, hallways wide enough to accommodate dueling gurneys—but rather for what it really was: a place where lives were ushered into the world, lost, and saved.

Together we discovered that a hospital is not just a physical place, but several emotional places coexisting in time and space. Hospitals are places of highs and lows and lots of boredom in between: places for the sick and the healthy, for those with a mission, and those who arrived at it expecting nothing more than a paycheck. Now, if you were an architect, would you or could you think in those terms? If you couldn't—or didn't—you'd design sterile, efficient, industrially antiseptic structures that conveyed a sense of purpose and institutional might.

But those aren't the kinds of backgrounds against which most of us live out our lives. And it's certainly not the kind of backdrop against which most of us would choose to end our lives. It doesn't really cost more to design a more human-feeling environment. It doesn't compromise health standards, or public safety, or even efficiency. It just doesn't occur to us to do it.

There are a variety of ways to teach people to use this tool. In one case, for example, we conducted an exercise for Textron that required them to disassemble and reconstruct the idea of the City of Chicago. The city was simply employed as a metaphor. What we really wanted to discover was whether it was possible to get at the authentic essence of a concept. The process is far more useful than any specific outcome. To avoid devolving into a session inventorying your corporate or personal baggage, you may initially want to start with a concept fairly well removed from your everyday business. Try it in your company. Disassemble anything from one of your products to your favorite sports team. Take it apart and put the resulting pieces together in new and deviant ways.

This involves more than deciding whether a jail is a place where people are punished or rehabilitated; it's the subtle nuance of painting holding cells pink because you know (for reasons that still aren't overly clear) that pink is a calming color that helps people under great stress to relax and that whatever else you know, or think you know, about jail, it's a place where people are under great stress.

The early modern painters used this approach, formalizing it in schools like Cubism and action painting. But we're suggesting a much more deviant approach. What we're talking about here is approaching a business problem like a one-year-old playing with blocks—building a structure you've never seen only to knock it back down and construct another in its place. Like the notion of serial deviance, this is a process that could be employed over and over again—each time yielding a new result. The game can go on indefinitely, or at least until you arrive at the same answer twice. Remember the first rule of the devox: Nothing's more foolish than conventional wisdom.

17

Making Deviance Work for You

Everybody is somebody else's freak . . .

—HENRY ROLLINS

The devox has touched us all, mostly when we weren't looking. We'll use this last chapter to explore how you can make deviance work in your life. We want to teach you not just how to pick the voice of the devox out of the whirlwind, but, and this is critical, how to let it speak through you.

Let's recap our thesis: Innovation—all innovation, positive and negative—begins as a deviant idea germinating in the mind of a person dwelling on the Fringe of society. Slowly that idea, product, image, impulse—the thing we've labeled the devox—makes its way from the Fringe to the Edge and through a series of measured steps and stages until it is accepted at Social Convention. At each stage it loses authenticity, but gains market potential. Finally, at its moment of maximum market potential, the devox begins an equally inexorable trip, a dislinear journey that will take it toward Cliché, and result in the creation of a new Icon or Archetype or plunge it into Oblivion.

The pace of this change is increasing at the same time that we're witnessing a radical contraction in the distance from the Edge to the center of Social Convention. The result of this acceleration is the Abolition of

Context, the disintegration of the social, cultural, and commercial framework. In commercial terms this means that market opportunities are created and disappear with a frequency that can't be monitored by conventional business thinking. The only way to understand deviance is to become the deviant.

We've looked at individual aspects of the devox—its impact on subjects as diverse as sex and science and human relations and marketing—but we need to spend a little time talking about the cumulative effect of this iterative deviation. Parts of your life and business don't stand still while other selected and discrete aspects change. You don't get to pick which aspects of the devox will wash over you and which won't. It's the aggregate impact of this endless iteration, the absolute inability of context to form and hold in the Post-Information Age, that makes life, and business, so problematic. This cumulative impact magnifies the exponential nature of change. We have no real, permanent sense of place, and the placeholders we cling to are more short-lived than ever.

As a result we're desperate for authenticity—a crumb of the real deal. Authenticity is like a long life, tried and tested and found to have been lived well. It's never been easy to be authentic—as a person, as a society, as a business, as an offering, or as a brand.

Charles Handy tells a story about Richard Harries, the bishop of Oxford, that helps explain what we mean by authenticity. It seems there was once a sad rabbi whose name was Zuzya of Hannipol. Every day of his life Rabbi Hannipol wept because he could not be a second Moses to his people. One day God looked down on Zuzya and, taking pity on him, said, "Cease your crying and your sorrow. In the next world I will not ask you why you were not Moses, only why you were not Zuzya."

In our haste to keep even with the pace of change, we find ourselves running faster and faster. The problem is that we're running in place. The "reality" and context we're responding to has changed by the time we've formulated our position. Eventually, in our headlong rush to keep pace with the devox, we seem to lose ourselves. And when that happens we abandon any hope of remaining authentic. Earlier in this book we wrote about the idea of a simulacrum—the copy without an original. It's an ironically perfect metaphor for an epoch so desperately searching out an original without a copy.

We want to believe things are true. And so we say they're true, and lo and behold, they are true, but only for a moment, and then they're gone. The lily dies before it can be gilded, and when we go to replant we find that the soil has been poisoned and rendered barren forever. No business generation in history has been so unsure of the validity of its own assumptions, and rightly so. New products arrive stillborn to market. We confuse activity with understanding. At the same time, whole new businesses have arisen out of the ashes of the chaos like the "extreme-value retail channel"—retailers who used to be better known as liquidators and closeout merchants. They're offering a much wider variety than they used to. After all, there's a lot more failed product out there to choose from.

The same demons that haunt product development haunt us. We feel ourselves losing our integrity, our personal authenticity, as we move through life. A compromise here, a nip and tuck to the ethics there, and the deviant becomes Babbitt.

With the abolition of traditional markets, consumer products race gracelessly from innovation to commodity in the blink of an eye. That 1970s era, four-function Texas Instruments calculator that cost several hundred dollars has been replaced by solar-powered multifunctional calculators built into disposable pens that retail for under two dollars. There's more computational power in a musical greeting card today than John Glenn had on board his first space flight. We're amassing mountains of high-technology equipment that's hopelessly obsolete. Older products used to work, sometimes as well as newer products. Our old products—like the IBM XT, once the "hottest box" in personal computing—don't work at all. This isn't because they don't function, but rather because the world has moved past them, making function all but impossible. The XT, for example, used disks that really were, in a quite literal sense, "floppy."

Ours is a world in which we want to believe, but somehow know better. We keep hoping the Next Big Thing will buy us some breathing room, knowing it never will. We comb the frontiers of society looking for a few seconds of market advantage, but we compete in a commercial universe where the troops—and the generals—switch sides so fast that there are no secrets. Our commercial wars lack authenticity. We just wage them for the exercise and to give the generals an opportunity to conveniently meet. More often than not, at the height of the commercial struggle, as the troops are busy trying to kill each other for a share point or two the generals are sitting on the sidelines cutting a deal between themselves, figuring out how many condos they can build on the battlefield, or how many of their own troops they can kill in preparation for the next fight, or how they might personally profit from surrender.

It's enough to make a grown capitalist cry, but there is some hope. Deviant wars require you to be armed with deviant weapons. Radically new problems require radically new tools. The world is changing far too fast to be effectively measured by last year's metrics or shored up with last week's tools.

As Charles Handy wrote: "The road we have been on, through this [the twentieth] century, has been the road of management, planning and control.... There should be a rational response to everything we thought; it should be possible to make a better world. It hasn't worked. Management and control are breaking down everywhere. The new world order looks very likely to end in disorder. We can't make things happen the way we want them to at home, at work, or in government, certainly not in the world as a whole."

As context is abolished, it's all about building new culture, and this demands a whole new set of plans and equipment. We need new language to communicate what we're about. We need to get beyond the wisdom of the ages and learn how to embrace the wisdom of the moment. We need to toss out the standards and design new standards. We need to not view employees as dogs that are purchased and lovingly scratched so long as their loyalty is unswerving, only to be dispatched the first time they snap back at their masters. We need to learn to see them as the assets we always claim they are, but deviant assets, modular fixtures in the corporate environment who may—at any time for almost any reason—detach themselves several times from us as they try to find the structure of their own lives.

As businesspeople we need to understand this culture piece not in our heads, but in the pit of our stomachs. We're good at developing products, creating services, and manipulating markets and supply chains, but we're lousy anthropologists, sociologists, and social psychologists, and terrible, terrible trend forecasters. We are creatures of certitude forced to seek our fortunes adrift in a sea of complexity.

To quote Charles Handy again: "The hope lies in the unknown, in that second curve if we can find it. The world is up for re-invention in so many ways. Creativity is born in chaos. What we do, what we belong to, why we do it, when we do it, where we do it—these may all be different and they could be better."

We need new structures of thinking, and we need to understand that the dance of the devox has moved us from the land of linear logic to a Möbius strip reality where there's no difference between internal and external, front and back. Our logical minds "know" that by tracing a straight line across the strip we should be able to get our bearings, but we keep tripping over that little half-twist. The way we think our way into problems is almost never the way we think our way out. The truth is that there are no paradoxes, just an infinite number of planes of resolution. Our struggle is to find the right plane.

Our friend Durk Jager, the former CEO of Procter & Gamble, used to passionately and tirelessly argue for transparency in business. Today's business universe is translucent at best. Transparent seems hopelessly out of reach. We search for clear definition, definition we can almost see and touch, but in the end it eludes us. A change in the lighting and we're not sure what we really see at all. We compete in a commercial marketplace where there are no secrets and no knowledge—where everything is revealed and nothing is known.

There are other lessons we need to learn. In the epoch of the devox decisive actions are rewarded by great success and great failure. Mediocrity is the by-product of consistency. The same mind that produced

E.T. gave us *Howard the Duck.* Those who are not great demand consistent greatness. Those who are great understand it's impossible to deliver. Think of your business. How many times have you seen the mediocre rewarded and promoted when more talented risk takers have been dismissed after one of their projects failed to meet expectations? We wonder why we have a leadership crisis in the world's most advanced economies and yet the answer is obvious—look how we pick our leaders.

Most of us learned to manage from the center, bringing everything into a stable environment where it can be standardized and processed. We hope we've made a case that the real trick is to manage the Edge, not the center. The real deal is out there somewhere—raw, messy, and untamed. By the time the devox reaches the center, it's a mere shadow of its formerly deviant self, stripped of authenticity and power and impact. This requires a constant exposure to ideas and people that are foreign and uncomfortable and, sometimes, downright hostile and threatening.

Building real diversity into your organization is all about ideas, perspectives, and sometimes good old-fashioned weirdness, not race, age, or gender.

The endgame is that there is no endgame. The goal is permanent transformation, not onetime self-definition. This Hero's Quest is the end in itself—no Penelope unraveling her weaving to keep the suitors at bay; no search for a Golden Fleece; no loved ones returned from the Underworld. This is hard slogging for the joy of slogging, and it's clearly not for everyone.

Where do you start? How do you leave the comforts of conformity and embrace the devox? There are at least as many answers as there are people; here are some classic models to think about. The devox has always been with us, and its attendants are some of the best-known archetypes of our culture. So let's examine the public faces of deviance to see if their characteristics might be adoptable in a business environment.

Let's begin with the Trickster. Carl Jung once wrote, "In picaresque tales, in carnivals and revels, in sacred and magical rites, in man's religious fears and exaltations, this phantom of the trickster haunts the mythology of all ages, sometimes in quite unmistakable form, sometimes in strangely modulated guise."

Trickster images appear in almost every known culture, making it one of the world's few truly universal archetypes. The Trickster is the boundary crosser—a creature that moves from spirit to flesh, part god, part criminal. The Trickster's gift is the ability to cross boundaries at will, his tools language and lies and confusion. Eshu, the West African Trickster, gave people the ability to know Heaven. In Greece, Hermes gave the gifts of sacrifice, language, and fire. In the Norse pantheon, Loki eventually tumbled the gods and Heaven itself. In Genesis the Trickster, in the form of the serpent, operated a cosmic produce stand.

As Lewis Hyde noted in his wonderful study *Trickster Makes This World: Mischief, Myth and Art,* "Trickster is the creative idiot, therefore the wise fool, the gray-haired baby, the cross-dresser, the speaker of sacred profanities. When someone's sense of honorable behavior has left him unable to act, trickster will appear to suggest an amoral action, something right/wrong that will get life going again. Trickster is the mythic embodiment of ambiguity and ambivalence, doubleness and duplicity, contradiction and paradox."

The Trickster is also a creature of deep, insatiable appetites, compelled to join humanity but repelled by his or her nature at the idea of belonging. The Trickster longs for the comfort of the fire, but is fated to live in its shadows. We see the Trickster as the seminal incarnation of humanity's earliest recognition of the devox. The Trickster is the only creature from the Edge condemned never to find its way to the center of Social Convention, the perpetual provocateur incapable of finding any form of lasting peace. The lessons of the Trickster are legion. Among them:

- Outsiders bring great gifts, but they're often fated to remain outsiders
- The power developed when boundaries are crossed
- The importance of creating language
- The power of ambivalence

If you don't relish lies and shadows, there's always the Clown. Mythologist Joy Thompson has suggested that Clowns were humanity's first police officers. "It is not so hard," she wrote, "to imagine how a clown might be an effective cultural policeman. The mechanism is shame, that most ignoble of human emotional states, the polar opposite of pride."

Clowns would literally go off, mocking an unwanted behavior (say, pomposity) and causing an assembled crowd to laugh at the person practicing the offending behavior. Clowns (*deikeliktas,* or "those who put on plays") roamed the streets of ancient Greece mocking everyone from soldiers to gods.

If the Trickster's mission was to deceive, it was the Clown's job to keep us honest. We eventually relieved Clowns of their responsibility for keeping public order, asking them only to keep making us laugh. But the best clowns, from Lenny Bruce to George Carlin, stay true to their initial charge. Like the Trickster, the Clown brings many gifts, including:

- First and foremost, the gift of laughter
- The ability to convey a great truth in ways that delight
- The understanding that life, and self, shouldn't always be taken so seriously
- The knowledge that building a common understanding is the first step to building change

Our next deviant archetype is the Wizard or Magician, a figure that haunts the Western canon from Egypt's Imhotep (c. 2800 B.C.) to all of the incarnations of Merlin, to Gandolf in *The Lord of the Rings,* to the Yoda character in *Star Wars.* The Wizard or Magician is in tune with the hidden forces of the universe, at once both their master and servant. Wizards and Magicians are conscious manipulators of these forces, sometimes aligned with God or gods, but more often pantheistic scientists whose skills are rooted in physical reality.

Wizards and Magicians hold the knowledge of "power spots," supposed reservoirs of primal energy. Robert Moore and Douglas Gillette described the Magician this way: "[He] has access to the whole terrain of the human unconscious. He knows the passwords that can take the Ego in and out of these magical realms. He can voyage inside himself without getting lost, or falling under the enchantment of any one place or structure in sacred geography.... He wrestles with demons and power animals, and is on intimate terms with complexes; he used his knowledge of these structures to keep himself free of them." Later in history, by the way, the Wizard morphs into another of our favorite archetypes, the Alchemist. The Wizard and Magician show us:

- That the universe we find ourselves in is ruled by forces beyond our comprehension
- That these forces can be harnessed
- The value of understanding where real power lies hidden
- The benefit of striving for harmony
- That no matter how chaotic life appears there's a way to discover enough order to get the job done

Shamans represent yet another way to connect to the devox. The Shaman is the knower of hidden truth, generally more spiritual than the Magician and less bent on control than the Wizard. The Shaman is a particularly instructive metaphor for business. Shamans are in the vision business. If they had Armani wardrobes, they'd probably be knocking off $500,000 at a crack building mission statements for the Fortune 100. Since visioning is their business, they're also expected to have a broad worldview and varied interests.

If Magicians hoard secrets, Shamans promote universal connectivity. Describing the Shaman, Joseph Campbell once said, "The shaman is the person, male or female, who in his late childhood or early youth has an overpowering psychological experience that turns him totally inward. It's a kind of schizophrenic crack-up. The whole unconscious opens up, and the shaman falls into it. This shaman experience has been described many, many times. It occurs all the way from Siberia right through the Americas down to Tierra del Fuego."

Campbell goes on to note the difference between the Shaman and a priest this way: "A priest is a functionary of a social sort. The society worships certain deities in a certain way, and the priest becomes ordained as a functionary to carry out that ritual. The deity to whom he is devoted is a deity that was there before he came along. But the shaman's powers are symbolized in his own familiars, deities of his own personal experience. His authority comes out of a psychological experience, not a social ordination." The Shaman's gifts include:

- Understanding the power of an authentic vision
- The knowledge that a broad perspective is best, even when addressing narrow issues
- The notion that a personal transformation is necessary to create a sustainable vision
- The knowledge that true authority is the product of individual experience, not arbitrary entitlement

Seers, Mystics, and Visionaries are the kissing kin of Shamans. There's a tight, but significant, distinction between the role of the Seer or Mystic and that of the Visionary. In an earlier work we wrote: "The role of the visionary—the role you will soon assume—we came to understand wasn't to be a seer but to be the provocateur: to present a series of visions of the future against which those who want to prepare for the future can react." But what Seers, Mystics, and Visionaries have in common is the ability to see beyond the fray and into the realm of possibility. Joseph Campbell believed the vision quest existed in pretty much the same form in all known mythologies. "You leave the world that you're in and go into a depth or into a distance or up to a height," he wrote. "There you come to what was missing in your consciousness in the world you formerly inhabited. Then comes the problem either of staying with that, and letting the world drop off, or returning with that boon and trying to hold on to it as you move back into your social world again. That's not an easy thing to do."

Earlier we told you that part of our reason for writing this book was to try to understand why companies appeared to be so willing to pay for advice they clearly weren't prepared to take. Every futurist, trend spotter, cool hunter, corporate anthropologist, scenario planner, long-range strategist, creative consultant, visioning expert, mission statement consultant, and ideational expert we've ever met has had the same experience. People in corporate America—and we suspect corporate World—love to talk about the view from the Edge but are unwilling to step off it into the abyss. The Seer, the Mystic, and the Visionary can give you their view of the world—but it isn't much good if you don't want to act on it. The Visionary's power comes from:

- The power he accumulates on his journey
- Bringing a new consciousness or awareness to a problem
- A willingness to sacrifice everything in exchange for a moment or two of clarity

Powerful as these gifts are, execution often falls to the characters we call the Saboteur or the Provocateur. Saboteurs are really creations of the Industrial Age. The word comes from the French *sabot,* a wooden shoe worn by early industrial workers. When the workers had a complaint, wanted to make a point, or were just tired, they would take their shoes off and throw them into the machines they were working on, jamming gears and causing production to come to a (literally) screeching halt. Saboteurs and Provocateurs both disrupt, but there's a critical difference between the two. A Saboteur's work essentially involves destruction—sometimes for a greater good, often for its own sake or as an act of retribution.

Provocateurs, on the other hand, disrupt for a reason. Like Socrates, the überprovocateur, they force us to ask the questions we're afraid to even whisper. They also raise unholy possibilities, deflate pomposity, and expose hypocrisy and contradiction. The most damning question most Provocateurs ask, of course, is "If all this is true, why don't we ... ?" Where the Saboteur comes to the job with a predetermined set of beliefs and truths, the Provocateur's job is to question whatever the agreed-upon truth is, no matter what it is. The Saboteur is armed with answers. The Provocateur is armed with questions.

So, what can we learn from Provocateurs and Saboteurs?

- There's a real power—for good or bad—in disruption.
- No system is beyond interruption.
- If you don't face your own demons, there's always somebody close by who's more than willing to invite them over to tea.
- Not all attacks on authority are created equal. Some allow you to build, while others only allow you to destroy.

Our penultimate deviant role is that of the Monk, the Hermit, or the Mendicant. These figures generally exist far outside the social mainstream. And while they generally share the qualities of seeking out contemplative existences designed to get them closer to God, they demonstrate some oddly varied ways of supporting their search for the truth. Monks live in a community; Hermits in isolation; and Mendicants on the largesse of society as a whole. They illustrate three separate approaches to the truth: the path in common; the solitary path; and the path of chaos and uncertainty. Monks establish collective order. Hermits establish highly individualized orders. And Mendicants are dependant on someone else's sense of order.

We don't want to spend too much more time on these three other than to note their collective contribution to our search for ways to access the devox:

- Contemplation is a critical element in all three lifestyles.
- A shunning of established order is seen as a prerequisite for achieving that contemplative state.
- There are distinct parallels between these lifestyles and the way we attack business problems. Monks translate into the "team" approach. Hermits are embodied in the lone-wolf style of leadership. And the Mendicants? Why, they're the consultants, of course.

We saved the best deviant for last. Our final entry to this deviant pantheon is the Fool. Known in many guises from the Holy Fool to the Medieval Jester, the Fool combines elements of the Clown, the Provocateur, the Saboteur, the Magician, and the Trickster. In 1 Corinthians 4:10, for example, St. Paul tells the Corinthians, "We are fools for Christ's sake."

Intriguingly, St. Paul used the Greek word *moros,* which generally conveys a sense of being insane or blind to conventional truth, to describe the kind of fool he's talking about. Holy Fools often take on unique physical characteristics, from the Drunken Monkey Zen Master to St. Phillip Neri (1515–1595), who used to wear his clothes inside out, carry a bouquet of whisk brooms instead of processional flowers, and— like a Zen monk—send his followers out to pursue apparently senseless tasks.

The Fool tradition is long and rich. As Gary Eberle noted, "The earliest recorded fool was a Negro dwarf in the retinue of Pharaoh Pepi I, and rulers as diverse as Roman emperors, the eight-century caliph Haroun Al-Rashid and William the Conqueror had paid fools. They were not just comedians. Their deeper purpose is best revealed in the Roman triumphal processions wherein fools walked beside the conquering heroes poking fun at them and reminding them of their mortality."

Like the original Clowns, the Fool is charged with entertaining and speaking the truth, at least as he knows it. The Fool is the original insider/outsider—totally loyal and totally free of ambition and restraint. As Eberle noted, "Fools, as necessary as they are, cannot be put in charge. . . . The fool, to be effective, must remain independent, transcendent, and unattached. His archetypal role is to stand on the border, whispering in our ears that we are mere mortals, flawed creatures. If we stifle our inner fool, we pave the way for tragedy. If we listen, however, we may learn to achieve a happy ending on this stage of fools."

We urge you to get in touch with your inner Fool. He or she is in there and just can't wait to get out. The Fool's contributions to getting in touch with the devox include:

- Understanding that without a constant outside/in perspective leaders tend to fall into immediate denial.
- Sacred values are fine. Sacred cows are not.
- If you can't laugh, especially at yourself, you're in serious trouble.
- It's possible to be totally loyal and lack further ambition.
- If you don't have someone close to you telling you the truth, you're probably listening to a bunch of lies.
- Humor is a powerful weapon.

And, oh yes, never, ever forget: Fortune favors the Fool.

If you don't think you have it in you to adopt any of these deviant personas, we strongly recommend you make sure you employ people who can. Good business is based on the ability not just to latch onto the Next Big Thing but on knowing when to let go of ideas, attitudes, products, metrics, and procedures that are old and tired.

Businesses today are overly fond of quick "magic wand" answers to their problems. But the world—and especially the world of business—is moving too fast for blanket answers.

The strengths of the devox are its innovation and its ability to challenge and smash Social Convention. The strength of a great company rests in the ability to innovate and, when necessary, break old rules in order to set higher standards. We know that some of you may be wondering what pornographic Lego figures, Medieval Jesters, rabbits that glow green under a black light, and all the other weirdness we've trotted out before you have to do with your business.

Well, here's the punch line: We didn't invent any of this stuff. It's part of the installed infrastructure of the world you live in today; you just didn't know it was there. Now, what else do you suppose is standing in those shadows?

NOTES

1. GREETINGS, FELLOW DEVIANTS

3   *Mad* (magazine) has become mainstream   Chris Hedges, "For Mad, a Reason to Worry; Struggling for Relevance in a Sarcastic World," *The New York Times,* March 28, 2001.

10   Neither of us could have anticipated   Ben & Jerry's Homemade, Inc., News Release, April 12, 2000.

10   Unilever believes the super premium segment   Ibid.

10   We are delighted to welcome   Unilever Press Release, April 12, 2000.

13   The Post-it note has a similarly twisted history   For the official history of the Post-It note, see http://www.3m.com/about3M/pioneers/fry.jhtml.

2. FROM FREAK TO CHIC: THE EVOLUTION OF THE DEVOX

16   At one time a young man   Cited in Marshall McLuhan with Wilfred Watson, *From Cliché to Archetype* (New York: Viking Press, 1970), p. 12.

25   NBC Sports president Dick Ebersol   *USA Today,* May 11, 2001, sec. C, p. 10C.

25   "As strange as it may seem"   Ibid., p. 1C.

26   Consider a story from *USA Today*   *USA Today,* May 15, 2001, sec. B, p. 1B.

26   "These guys [targeted trendsetters]"   Ibid., p. 2B.

27   like Procter & Gamble, whose ill-fated Tremor   Fred Crawford and

Ryan Mathews, *The Myth of Excellence: Why Great Companies Never Try to Be the Best at Everything* (New York: Crown Business, 2001), pp. 100–109.

27 entrepreneurs like Nico Golfar   See Niconetwork.com.

27 "I'm referred to as a connector"   Dave Gardetta, "You Mean You Don't Know Nico?" *Los Angeles Magazine,* January 2001.

30 Rowling's U.S. publisher   *Business Standard: The Strategist,* July 18, 2000 (http://www.bsstrategist.com/00jul18/2story.htm).

31 "This audiobook defies category and convention"   Amazon.com review.

32 By 1994 sales of the once popular shoe line   Malcolm Gladwell, *The Tipping Point* (New York: Little, Brown, 2000), p. 4.

32 "How did it happen?" Gladwell asks   Ibid., pp. 4–5.

32 Gladwell's examples   Ibid., pp. 3–8, 169–171.

33 "embraced the romance of technology"   See http://www.focus247.com/detroittechno/the history.

33 The first Detroit Electronic Music Festival   See http://www. electronic musicfest.com/information/index.html.

33 Ford Motor Company announced   See http://www.fordhaven.com/news/news1.html.

33 "We are excited about this integrated sponsorship"   Ibid.

34 "The Ford Focus and Techno music"   Ibid.

34 Less than two weeks before the 2001 festival   Wendy Chase, "Rift Threatens Music Fest," *The Detroit News,* May 16, 2001, p. 1A.

34 "Everyone in the community is upset and angry"   Ibid.

34 "The mythology of this festival"   Ibid., p. 2A.

3. FROM CHIC TO BLEAK:
THE FURTHER ADVENTURES OF THE DEVOX

39 Over a twenty-year period   Kalle Lasn, *Culture Jam: The Uncooling of America* (New York: William Morrow, 1999), p. 63.

40 Twenty years from now   In fact, the court found that the government's case was based on entrapment, and the case was dismissed. But for millions of baby boomers the image of DeLorean holding up a bag of cocaine on the sting tape of his arrest has obscured the actual crime he was accused of.

40 Remember Clifford Irving   In 1972 Irving produced what he claimed to

be the autobiography of Howard Hughes. Both McGraw-Hill and *Life* magazine agreed to publish the book. Eventually, Irving admitted the work was a hoax. He was forced to pay back a publisher's advance of $765,000, was convicted of fraud, and had to serve fourteen months in a federal prison. The Hughes "autobiography" was eventually published on the Internet in June 1999. See http://www.cbsnews.com/now/story/0.1597.154661-412.00.shtml.

41 "He who receives an idea" Andrew Lipscomb and Albert Bergh, eds., *The Writings of Thomas Jefferson,* memorial edition, vol. 13 (Washington, D.C.: Thomas Jefferson Memorial Association, 1903–1905), p. 333.

42 the projected 70 million Napster users Napster audience size (year-end 2000) estimates taken from U.S. District Judge Marilyn Hall Patel's oral ruling granting an injunction against Napster. The entire ruling is available online at http://news.cnet.com/news/0-1005-201-2426706-0.html?tag= bplst.

44 "because people made a big deal about it" "May the Farce Be with You," *USA Today,* January 14, 2002, p. 1D.

45 Detroit's annual Woodward Avenue Dream Cruise For more information, see http://dreamcruise.org.

45 albums guitar god Jimi Hendrix released See www.allmusic.com and www.amazon.com.

46 Quaker's Quisp cereal For more than you might want to know about Quisp, visit http://www.quisp.com.

49 Today there's an official Spam website See http://www.spam.com.

49 "We didn't come up with the idea" Ibid.

53 Had the King's estate not been so vigilant The estate is privately held and does not release public financial data.

53 ubiquitous Elvisness became the subject See http://www.dla-law.co.uk/corp/news34.htm.

53 Shaw maintains a website See http://www.elvisly-yours.com/epe_files1.htm.

54 heirs of the late Rick Nelson See http://www.elvis.com/news/full_story.asp?id=20.

54 We have been approached See http://www.elvis.com/news/rick_nelson.asp.

54 Disney demanded—under threat See http://www.snopes2.com/disney/wdco/daycare.htm.

55 In 1994, the U.S. Supreme Court   Jesse Walker, "Copy Catfight: How Intellectual Property Laws Stifle Popular Culture," *Reason,* March 2000.

55 But in 1996, the U.S. Court of Appeals   Ibid.

55 "If something becomes an essential part"   Ibid.

59 "When consumers buy a Virgin product"   Jesper Kunde, *Corporate Religion: Building a Strong Company Through Personality and Corporate Soul* (London: Financial Times/Prentice-Hall, 2000).

60 Garry Trudeau has kept   See http:www.doonesbury.com/strip/thecast/html/duke.htm.

61 In his autobiography, Ralph "Sonny" Barger   Sonny Barger with Keith Zimmerman and Kent Zimmerman, *Hell's Angel: The Life and Times of Sonny Barger and the Hell's Angels Motorcycle Club* (New York: William Morrow, 2000), p. 53.

61 Microsoft Windows is the Archetype   See Linus Torvalds and David Diamond, *Just for Fun: The Story of an Accidental Revolutionary* (New York: HarperBusiness, 2001).

4. THE ABOLITION OF CONTEXT AND THE POST-INFORMATION AGE

64 The past, present, and future   R. U. Sirius, St. Jude, *How to Mutate and Take Over the World* (New York: Ballantine, 1996), p. 8.

66 "capitalism could only emerge"   Fernand Braudel, *The Wheels of Commerce: Civilization and Capitalism, 15th–18th Century,* vol. 2 (New York: Harper & Row, 1982), p. 600.

68 Even Theodore Kaczynski's "Unabomber Manifesto"   "The Unabomber Manifesto" is available at any number of places, including http://www.ed.brocku.ca/~rahul/Misc/unibomber.html.

70 "Today we definitely see"   "The Merchants of Cool" transcript is available at http://www.pbs.org/wgbh/pages/frontline/shows/cool/interviews/cunningham.html.

70 "in Cyberia at least"   Douglas Rushkoff, *Cyberia: Life in the Trenches of Hyperspace* (New York: HarperSanFrancisco, 1994), pp. 48–49.

70 Nothing interesting ever happens   Richard Kadrey, *Covert Culture Sourcebook* (New York: St. Martin's Press, 1993), p. 1.

72 "We're analogous to the single-celled organisms"   Cited in John Brockman, *The Third Culture: Beyond the Scientific Revolution* (New York: Simon & Schuster, 1995), p. 385.

5. SCHWINNS TO CYBERSPACE: SEX AND THE PATH OF THE DEVOX

79 We have conquered otherness   Jean Baudrillard, *The Illusion of the End* (Stanford, Calif.: Stanford University Press, 1994), p. 109.

79 "In every era"   Marty Klein, "The History and Future of Sex," *Electronic Journal of Human Sexuality,* vol. 2, August 10, 1999 (available at http://www.ejhs.org/volume2/history.htm).

80 "Before the bicycle was invented"   Ibid.

80 Just look at the popularity of books   Elizabeth Abbott, *A History of Celibacy* (Cambridge, Mass.: Da Capo Press, 2001).

81 Anne Fausto-Sterling advanced a model   Anne Fausto-Sterling, "The Five Sexes," *Sciences,* New York Academy of Sciences, March–April 1993.

81 "I had intended to be provocative"   Ibid.

81 "But to each their own"   Chris Hables Gray, *Cyborg Citizen: Politics in the Posthuman Age* (New York: Routledge, 2001).

81 extropian   Extropians are believers in extropy, a system of beliefs built around the principle that human intelligence and technology will allow life to expand indefinitely and in an orderly, progressive way throughout the entire universe.

81 We may become as excited   Natasha Vita More, "Future of Sexuality," presented at EXTRO 3 Conference (1997), available at http://www. natasha.cc/sex.htm.

83 The first issue of *Playboy*   Circulation numbers, Spring 2001 MRI data available at http://www.playboyenterprises.com.

84 TV sexuality is a campaign of disinformation   Kalle Lasn, *Culture Jam: The Uncooling of America* (New York: William Morrow, 1999), p. 18.

85 "like Picasso's gray period"   Farhad Manjoo, "Porn in the Palm of Your Hand," *Wired News,* available at http://www.wired.com/news/business/ 0,1367,41336,00.html.

86 Eruptor Entertainment's PortaPam   Elisa Batista, "Look, It's 'Palm'-ela Anderson," *Wired News,* available at http://www.wired.com/news/ technology/0,1282,41095,00.html.

87 Pfizer has sold   Pfizer 2000 Annual Report, available online at http://www.pfizer.com/pfizerinc/investing.annual/2000/pfizer2000ar26. html.

6. WORDS WITHOUT MEANING

90 Where would we be without language? Georges Bataille, *Erotism: Death and Sensuality* (San Francisco: City Lights Books, 1986), p. 276.

91 will at least say Cited, with a fascinating commentary, in Mark C. Taylor, *Hiding* (Chicago: University of Chicago Press, 1997), p. 52.

92 "It is the role of the association" Mary Kathleen Flynn, "Nations Fear English Language Dominance on Net," CNN.com, January 12, 2000.

92 McDonald's, for example, "owns" 131 words and phrases Kate Silver, "Serving Up the McDictionary," *Las Vegas Weekly,* April 26, 2001.

93 "The more natural corporations seem" Mark Greif, "The Corporate ABCs," *American Prospect,* vol. 2, no. 7, February 14, 2000, available at http://www.prospect.org.

104 The typical Filofax entry Tom Wolfe, *Hooking Up* (New York: Farrar, Straus & Giroux, 2000), p. 7.

105 The efficient replenishment maturity index Kurt Salmon Associates and Joint Industry ECR Operating Committee, *1997 ECR Industry Benchmarking Survey,* 1998.

110 There is no clearer proof point See http://www.thewordcompany.

110 Although protonyms such as "smorp" "Busch-Reisinger Exhibit, the Word Company, Displays Words Invented by Artist Adib Fricke," *Harvard University Gazette,* May 25, 1999, available at http://www.news.harvard.edu/gazette/1999/03.25/word.html.

111 "The Word Company" Ibid.

7. ART—A TRAP WITH NO EXIT

112 Doesn't the paint say it all? Dorothea Tanning, *Between Lives: An Artist and Her World* (New York: W. W. Norton, 2001), pp. 326–327.

113 "the immediate interface" "Playboy Interview: Marshall McLuhan—a Candid Conversation with the High Priest of Popcult and Metaphysician of Media," *Playboy,* March 1969.

113 "The paintings of mental patients" J. G. Ballard, *The Atrocity Exhibition* (San Francisco: Re/Search Publications, 1990), p. 40.

114 Art, like gesture, is a form Alvin Toffler, *Future Shock* (New York: Bantam Books, 1971), p. 173.

114 "In art, as in language" Ibid., p. 177.

115 "there is no doubt"   Herbert Read, *A Concise History of Modern Painting* (New York: Praeger Publishers, 1975), p. 13.

115 "L'exactitude n'est pas la vérité"   Ibid., p. 44.

117 Kevorkian's CD   Kevorkian's ominously titled 1997 release, *Kevorkian Suite: Very Still Life,* featuring Kevorkian and the Morpheus Quintet.

118 "It seems to me that the modern painter"   Cited in Jason-Spingam-Koff, "Medium Isn't the Message; Art Is," *Wired News,* available at http://www.wired.com/news/culture/0,1284,42106,00.html.

119 "Behind much art"   Jack Burnham, *Beyond Modern Sculpture: The Effects of Science and Technology on the Sculpture of This Century* (New York: George Braziller, 1968), p. 312.

119 artist Amy M. Youngs argued   Amy M. Youngs, "The Fine Art of Creating Life," *Leonardo Electronic Almanac,* vol. 33, no. 5, 2000, pp. 377–380.

120 article titled "Transgenic Art"   Eduardo Kac, "Transgenic Art," *Leonardo Electronic Almanac,* vol. 6, no. 11, December 1998, available at http://mitpress.mit.edu/LEA/.

120 "More than make visible the invisible"   This quote was taken from p. 1 of the article cited above but was sourced from Kac's website, http://www.ekac.org/transgenic.html.

120 "a new art form"   Ibid.

120 Kac hoped to extract   For the scientifically inclined, Kac was after GFPuv, a variant of GFP, a protein some 238 amino acids long that the Pacific Northwest jellyfish—*Aequorea victoria*—emits when exposed to ultraviolet or blue light. He proposed GFP K-P could be created by microinjecting the GFPuv DNA construct into a pronuclear embryo that in turn would be used for the implantation and production of a founder GFP transgenic dog.

120 "Chimeras, however, are no longer imaginary"   Kac, "Transgenic Art," p. 5.

120 "As a transgenic artist"   These quotes were taken from a reprint of Eduardo Kac, "GFP Bunny," p. 4, found at http://www.ekac.org/gfpbunny.html; Peter T. Dobrila and Aleksandra Kostic, eds., *Eduardo Kac: Telepresence, Biotelematics, and Transgenic Art* (Maribor, Slovenia: Kilba, 2000), pp. 101–131.

120 The boundary between science and art   Ibid., p. 2.

121 While some artists have never questioned   Darryl Van Rhey, "The Art

of Burning Man," available at http://www.burningman.com/art_of_ burningman/art_ofbm.html.

122 "Burning Man is a quintessentially freaky West Coast event" Brian Doherty, "Burning Man Grows Up," *Reason,* February 2000.

122 "Burning Man is an art gig" Bruce Sterling, "Greetings from Burning Man," available at http://www.wired.com/wired/archive/4.11. burningman.html.

123 "a member of a renegade class" Van Rhey, "The Art of Burning Man."

123 "The avant-garde" Ibid.

123 "immediate and involving" Burning Man and the Art of the Nineties: A Conversation with Larry Harvey and Darryl Van Rhey," 1997, available at http://www.burningman.com/art_of_burningman/90s_art.html.

123 "Our technique is to appropriate elements of mass culture" Ibid.

124 Jaron Lanier has a vision of the future For more on Lanier, visit his website at http://www.well.com/user/jaron.

124 "If kids are growing up" "Jaron Lanier: A Cyberspace Renaissance Man Reveals His Current Thoughts on the World Wide Web, Virtual Reality, and Other Silicon Dreams," available at http://www.sciam.com/ interview/lanier.html.

8. SCIENCE AND THE DEATH OF OBJECTIVE REALITY

127 If we ask, for instance J. R. Oppenheimer, *Science and the Human Understanding* (New York: Simon & Schuster, 1966), p. 69.

128 "Reality? We don't got to show you" Robert Anton Wilson, *Quantum Psychology* (Phoenix: New Falcon Publications, 1990), p. 69.

129 "old science" and "new science" Ian Marshall and Danah Zohar, *Who's Afraid of Schrödinger's Cat? All the New Science Ideas You Need to Keep Up with the New Thinking* (New York: William Morrow, 1997), pp. xvii–xxx.

129 "the world was thought to consist" Ibid., p. xix.

129 "Where the old science stressed continuity" Ibid., pp. xxvi–xxvii.

131 "Science began with the Promethean affirmation" Ilya Prigogine, *The End of Certainty: Time, Chaos, and the New Laws of Nature* (New York: Free Press, 1997).

131 "In the last 500 years" Freeman Dyson, *Imagined Worlds* (Cambridge, Mass.: Harvard University Press, 1997), p. 50.

131 "quantum-mechanical revolution that Kuhn took as his model" Dyson

is referring to a model contained in Thomas Kuhn's *The Structure of Scientific Revolutions* (Chicago: University of Chicago Press, 1996).

131 The effect of a concept-driven revolution   Ibid., pp. 50–52.

131 "The dominant science of the twenty-first century"   Ibid., p. 86.

132 "The 'new' biology"   Quoted in John Brockman, *The Third Culture: Beyond the Scientific Revolution* (New York: Simon & Schuster, 1995).

132 "Unfortunately, the study of business communities lags"   James F. Moore, *The Death of Competition: Leadership and Strategy in the Age of Business Ecosystems* (New York: HarperBusiness, 1996), p. 10.

132 Richard T. Pascale, Mark Millemann, and Linda Gioja   Richard T. Pascale, Mark Millemann, and Linda Gioja, *Surfing the Edge of Chaos: The Laws of Nature and the New Laws of Business* (New York: Crown Business, 2000), p. 5.

132 "Old companies faded away"   Gary Hamel, *Leading the Revolution* (Boston: Harvard Business School Press, 2000), p. 5.

133 "We often see somewhat mystical interpretations"   Susanne Kelly and Mary Ann Allison, *The Complexity Advantage: How the Science of Complexity Can Help Your Business Achieve Peak Performance* (New York: Business Week Books/McGraw-Hill, 1999), p. xvii.

133 "Science, the principal avenue to knowledge"   Joël de Rosnay, *The Symbiotic Man (SIC)* (New York: McGraw-Hill, 2000), p. 275.

133 MIT's Ray Kurzweil has suggested   Ray Kurzweil, *The Age of Spiritual Machines: When Computers Exceed Human Intelligence* (New York: Viking Press, 1999).

133 "we have created a digital wilderness"   George B. Dyson, *Darwin Among the Machines: The Evolution of Global Intelligence* (Reading, Mass.: Helix Books/Addison-Wesley, 1997).

134 "Things we denote as 'living'"   Cited in Richard Morris, *Artificial Worlds* (New York: Plenum Trade, 1999), p. 1.

135 "The laws of science are demonstrable"   Kary Mullis, *Dancing Naked in the Mind Field* (New York: Pantheon Books, 1998), p. 112.

135 *The Archaic Revival*   San Francisco: HarperSanFrancisco, 1991.

135 *Food of the Gods*   New York: Bantam Books, 1992.

135 *The Invisible Landscape*   San Francisco: HarperSanFrancisco, 1993.

135 "The purpose of science"   Ralph Abraham, Terence McKenna, and Rupert Sheldrake, *Trialogues at the Edge of the West* (Santa Fe, N.Mex.: Bear & Company, 1992), p. 120.

135　Biologist Rupert Sheldrake　Author of works including *A New Science of Life* (Los Angeles: Jeremy P. Tarcher, 1981) and *The Presence of the Past* (New York: Times Books, 1988).

136　"By the end of the twentieth century"　Michio Kaku, *Visions* (Oxford, U.K.: Oxford University Press, 1998), p. 4.

136　an interesting mini case study　Jeremy Rifkin, *The Biotech Century* (New York: Jeremy P. Tarcher/Putnam, 1998), pp. 41–42.

9. SEEING AND BELIEVING, WAR AND MORE

141　The vehicle for the arrival of the Kingdom of God　Mark C. Taylor, *Nots* (Chicago: University of Chicago Press, 1993), p. 186.

143　twelve classical world religions　Baha'i, Buddhism, Christianity, Confucianism, Hinduism, Islam, Jainism, Judaism, Shinto, Sikhism, Taoism, and Zoroastrianism.

143　twice that many serious faith systems　See Adherents Home Page, http://www.adherents.com/Religions_By_Adherents.html.

144　Escuela de Yoga de Buenos Aires　Viviana Gorbato, "School of Yoga of Buenos Aires: Sex, Yoga & Rock & Roll," available at http://www.websitemaker.com/gorbato/magazine/notao0312.htm.

144　Uganda's doomsday cults　See http:///www.gospelcom.net/apologetics index/m08.html.

145　*The Life of the Cosmos*　New York: Oxford University Press, 1997.

145　Stuart Kauffman's *Investigations*　New York: Oxford University Press, 2000.

147　"How Important Would You Say Religion Is"　Gallup Organization, available online at http://www.gallup.com/poll/indicators/indreligion. asp: copyright © 2001 Gallup Poll—all rights reserved, reprint with permission of Gallup Organization.

147　"Did You Happen to Attend Church"　Ibid.

148　It's easy to offend the devout　Take the example of Soka Gakkai, one of the subsects of Nichiren Shoshu, a Japanese sect that follows the teachings of a thirteenth-century Buddhist monk named Nichiren. In 1992 the parent sect excommunicated the estimated 8 million international members of Soka Gakkai. The dispute between Nichiren Shoshu and Soka Gakkai is the stuff of heated theological arguments and even lawsuits. Doctrinal disputes between Japanese Buddhists may seem a tad removed from your business until you remember that there are millions of people involved and Soka Gakkai International actively promotes itself to Americans (http://www.sgi-usa.org). In August 2001 Soka University of America opened for business in Aliso Viejo, California (http://www.soka.edu/homeav.html).

150 "Technology in the service of virtue" James Der Derian, *Virtuous War: Mapping the Military-Industrial-Media-Entertainment Network* (New York: Westview Press, 2001), p. xi.

150 "the technical capability and ethical imperative" Ibid., p. xv.

150 "On the surface" Ibid., pp. xv, xvi.

10. THE DEVIANT ECONOMY

157 Life, death, preservation, loss Chuang Tzu, *Basic Writings,* trans. Burton Watson (New York: Columbia University Press, 1969), p. 70.

158 "This new economy" Kevin Kelly, *New Rules for the New Economy: Ten Radical Strategies for a Connected World* (New York: Viking Press, 1998), p. 2.

158 "Since the Web is a fast-growing world" Evan I. Schwartz, "*Webonomics: Nine Essential Principles for Growing Your Business on the World Wide Web* (New York: Broadway Books, 1997), p. 2.

162 Today the trade in illicit drugs Bruce Zagaris and Scott Ehlers, "Drug Trafficking and Money Laundering," *Columbia International Affairs Online,* vol. 6, no. 18, May 2001 (http://www.ciaonet.org/srchfrm.html).

166 released a study McKinsey & Company, "U.S. Productivity Growth, 1995–2000," available online at www.mckinsey.com/knowledge/mgi/feature/index.asp.

166 "Surprisingly, the primary source of the productivity gains" Virginia Postrel, "Economic Scene: Lessons in Keeping Business Humming, Courtesy of Wal-Mart U," *The New York Times,* February 28, 2002, p. C2.

11. CORPORATE CULTURES—DEVIANT AND OTHERWISE

169 It just shows the flexibility of the human organism   Quoted in *Mondo 2000: A User's Guide to the New Edge* (New York: HarperPerennial, 1992), p. 201.

173 notes in the site's history section   See http://www.fhs.ch/english/Ehistory.htm.

174 Every time you click a mouse   Michael Hiltzik, *Dealers of Lightning: XEROX PARC and the Dawn of the Computer Age* (New York: Harper-Business, 1999), p. xxv.

174 "The best-publicized aspect"   Ibid., p. xxvi.

178 *The Nissan Report*   Steve Barnett, *The Nissan Report* (New York: Doubleday Currency, 1992).

180 Davis traced the history of the corporation   Davis's model was radically recast in Art Kleiner's *The Age of Heretics: Heroes, Outlaws, and the Forerunners of Corporate Change* (New York: Doubleday Currency, 1996), one of the best initial studies of what happens when deviants square off against the corporation.

183 "immortality . . . individuality . . . [and] properties"   Jack Beatty, ed., *Colossus: How the Corporation Changed America* (New York: Broadway Books, 2001), pp. 84–85.

184 reinvent yourself as General Electric did   The transformation of the GE business model is skillfully dealt with in detail in Adrian J. Slywotzky and David J. Morrison, *The Profit Zone: How Strategic Business Design Will Lead You to Tomorrow's Profits* (New York: Times Books, 1988).

190 Perhaps the classic illustration   Robert I. Sutton, *Weird Ideas That Work: 11½ Practices for Promoting, Managing, and Sustaining Innovation* (New York: The Free Press, 2002), pp. 177–179.

192 Communities of practice   Mary E. Boone, *Managing Interactively, Executing Business Strategy, Improving Communication, and Creating a Knowledge-Sharing Culture* (New York: McGraw-Hill, 2001), p. 27.

192 Communities of purpose   Ibid., p. 28.

192 "Communities of purpose have goals"   Ibid.

192 "Leader presumes follower"   Ibid., p. 67.

12. THE UNDERSTANDING AND CARE OF THE DEVIANT CONSUMER

197 You can talk about Cited in *Mondo 2000: A User's Guide to the New Edge* (New York: HarperPerennial, 1992), p. 170.

204 Their sense of personal context Fred Crawford and Ryan Mathews, *The Myth of Excellence: Why Great Companies Never Try to Be the Best at Everything* (New York: Crown Business, 2001).

205 The breakdown in the traditional sense of community For an exhaustive treatment of this issue, we recommend reading Robert D. Putnam, *Bowling Alone: The Collapse and Revival of American Community* (New York: Simon & Schuster, 2000).

205 access, experience, price, product, and service Crawford and Mathews, *Myth,* Chapters 1–3.

13. DEVIANT MARKETING FOR DEVIANT MARKETS

210 Gone will be so-called quantitative marketing studies Janine Lopiano-Misdom and Joanne De Luca, *Street Trends: How Today's Alternative Youth Cultures Are Creating Tomorrow's Mainstream Markets* (New York: HarperBusiness, 1997), p. 163.

210 "It is perfectly normal for women" Larry Tye, *The Father of Spin: Edward Bernays and the Birth of Public Relations* (New York: Crown Publishing, 1998), p. 28.

211 "Age-old customs" Ibid., p. 31.

213 *The Tipping Point* Malcolm Gladwell, *The Tipping Point* (New York: Little, Brown, 2000), pp. 15–29.

213 *Permission Marketing* Seth Godin, *Permission Marketing* (New York: Simon & Schuster, 1999).

213 *Unleashing the Ideavirus* Seth Godin and Malcolm Gladwell, *Unleashing the Ideavirus* (New York: Do You Zoom, 2000).

213 "The spread of buzz" Emanuel Rosen, *The Anatomy of Buzz: How to Create Word-of-Mouth Marketing* (New York: Doubleday Currency, 2000), p. 99.

14. THE DEVIANT PRODUCT

218 Normality is the route to nowhere   Jonas Ridderstråle and Kjell Nordström, *Funky Business: Talent Makes Capital Dance* (London: Pearson Education Limited, 2000), pp. 221–222.

218 Torvalds has been described   These observations come from journalist David Diamond, with Torvalds the coauthor of *Just for Fun: The Story of an Accidental Revolutionary* (New York: HarperBusiness, 2001). Diamond's remarks were made in a speech to an executive audience at a Discoveries program hosted by Georgia-Pacific Corporation's North American Consumer Products Division in Paris, 2001.

220 Microsoft spends a good deal of time   Byron Acohido, "Microsoft Memo to Staff: Clobber LINUX," *USA Today,* January 3, 2002.

222 The word *hacker*   If you're really interested in this new breed of cat, we recommend you start by reading David and Linus's *Just for Fun* and Pekka Himanen, *The Hacker Ethic* (New York: Random House, 2001), which has a prologue by Linus; see also Eric S. Raymond, *The Cathedral and the Bazaar: Musings on Linux and Open Source by an Accidental Revolutionary* (Cambridge, Mass.: O'Reilly & Associates, 2001).

224 "In a world where technology can transform nature"   John Naisbitt with Nana Naisbitt and Douglas Philips, *High Tech High Touch: Technology and Our Search for Meaning* (New York: Broadway Books, 1999), p. 11.

224 Naisbitt's rather utopian take   Ibid., p. 14.

225 Lara Croft—the "real" one   For more than you ever wanted to know about the Croft character and *Tomb Raider,* visit http://tarchive.ctimes.net.

15. THE DEVIANT BRAND

230 Research has shown   Fred Crawford and Ryan Mathews, *The Myth of Excellence: Why Great Companies Never Try to Be the Best at Everything* (New York: Crown Business, 2001), pp. 25, 135–157.

231 Take Eddie Bauer, for example   A description of the full line of licensed Eddie Bauer products is available at http://www.eddie-bauer.net.

231 Harley-Davidson goes Eddie Bauer several better   Harley-Davidson, Inc., 2000 Annual Report.

233 "Hello Kitty is an icon"   "ICHIBAN: Ten Reasons Why the Sun Still Rises in the East," *Wired,* September 2001, p. 121.

236 Coke raised the white flag   OK fans, take heart. You can sign a petition to bring your favorite soft drink back at www.home.pacifier.com~ntierrney/oksoda2.htm.

16. THE DEVIANT'S TOOLBOX

237 There is no real   Jean Baudrillard, *Simulacra and Simulation* (Ann Arbor: University of Michigan Press, 1994), pp. 121–122.

241 Play is a profound learning tool   This idea has been explored in great detail by several other authors. If you're interested in learning more, we'd suggest starting with Douglas Rushkoff, *Playing the Future: How Kid's Culture Can Teach Us to Thrive in an Age of Chaos* (New York: Harper-Collins, 1996).

244 a freestanding subsidiary, Irresistible Ink   See http://www.irresistibleink. com/pmp2.html.

248 Henry the Elder   See Jack Beatty, ed., *Colossus: How the Corporation Changed America* (New York: Broadway Books, 2001), pp. 223–255.

257 Michèle Rigaud-Paccagnin   See http://www.elf.fr/odyssee/us/mag/mag 04/index.htm.

261 The Kohler Company   See http://www.kohler.com/corp/ai/artsindustry. html.

17. MAKING DEVIANCE WORK FOR YOU

265 Everybody is somebody else's freak . . .   Henry Rollins, *BANG!* (Los Angeles: 2.13.61 Publications, 1990), p. 29.

266 Charles Handy tells a story   Charles Handy, *The Age of Paradox* (Boston: Harvard Business School Press, 1994).

268 "The road we have been on"   Ibid., p. 11.

269 "The hope lies in the unknown"   Ibid., p. 286.

270 "In picaresque tales"   C. G. Jung, "On the Psychology of the Trickster Figure," which appears as pt. 5 of Paul Radin, *The Trickster: A Study in American Indian Mythology* (New York: Schocken Books, 1972), p. 200.

271 "Trickster is the creative idiot"   Lewis Hyde, *Trickster Makes The World: Mischief, Myth and Art* (New York: Farrar, Straus & Giroux, 1998), p. 7.

272 Clowns were humanity's first police officers   Joy Thompson, "A Fool's History of Civilization," *Parabola*, vol. 26, no. 3, August 2001, p. 8.

273 "[He] has access to the whole terrain"   Robert Moore and Douglas Gillette, *The Magician Within: Accessing the Shaman in the Male Psyche* (New York: William Morrow, 1993).

273 "The shaman is the person"   Joseph Campbell with Bill Moyers, *The Power of Myth* (New York: Doubleday, 1988), p. 85.

274 "A priest is a functionary"   Ibid., p. 100.

274 "The role of the visionary"   Watts Wacker and Jim Taylor, *The Visionary's Handbook: Nine Paradoxes That Will Shape the Future of Your Business* (New York: HarperBusiness, 2000), p. 177.

274 "You leave the world that you're in"   Campbell and Moyers, *The Power of Myth,* p. 129.

277 St. Phillip Neri   Philip Zaleski, "Holy Folly," *Parabola,* vol. 26, no. 3, August 2001, p. 33.

277 "The earliest recorded fool"   Gary Eberle, "A Child of Providence," *Parabola,* vol. 26, no. 3, August 2001, p. 68.

277 "Fools, as necessary as they are"   Ibid., p. 71.

INDEX

ABOUT THE AUTHORS

RYAN MATHEWS is a futurist and principal of FirstMatter, a trend-watching consulting firm. Hailed as one of the few true philosophers in modern business, Mathews has been profiled in publications from *Fast Company* to *Wired*. He is a coauthor of the bestselling *The Myth of Excellence* and lives in Detroit, Michigan.

WATTS WACKER, also a futurist and principal of FirstMatter, has been profiled in such publications as *Fast Company* and *Forbes* and was called one of the 50 smartest people in the business world by the *Financial Times*. He is a coauthor of *The 500-Year Delta* and *The Visionary's Handbook*. He lives in Westport, Connecticut.